Reporting of Social Science in the National Media

Carol H. Weiss
Eleanor Singer

with the assistance of Phyllis Endreny

Russell Sage Foundation / New York

The Russell Sage Foundation

The Russell Sage Foundation, one of the oldest of America's general purpose foundations, was established in 1907 by Mrs. Margaret Olivia Sage for "the improvement of social and living conditions in the United States." The Foundation seeks to fulfill this mandate by fostering the development and dissemination of knowledge about the political, social, and economic problems of America. It conducts research in the social sciences and public policy, and publishes books and pamphlets that derive from this research.

The Board of Trustees is responsible for oversight and the general policies of the Foundation, while administrative direction of the program and staff is vested in the President, assisted by the officers and staff. The President bears final responsibility for the decision to publish a manuscript as a Russell Sage Foundation book. In reaching a judgment on the competence, accuracy, and objectivity of each study, the President is advised by the staff and selected expert readers. The conclusions and interpretations in Russell Sage Foundation publications are those of the authors and not of the Foundation, its Trustees, or its staff. Publication by the Foundation, therefore, does not imply endorsement of the contents of the study.

Library of Congress Cataloging-in-Publication Data

Weiss, Carol H.
  Reporting of social science in the national media.

  Bibliography: p.
  Includes index.
    1. Mass media—Social aspects—United States.
  2. Social sciences—United States.   3. Journalism—
  United States.   4. Communication in the social
  sciences—United States.   I. Singer, Eleanor.
  II. Title.
  HN90.M3W43   1987   302.2'34   87-43099
  ISBN 0-87154-802-X

Text design: Huguette Franco

The paper used in this publication meets the minimum requirements of American National Standard for Information Sciences—Permanence of Paper for Printed Library Materials, ANSI Z39.48-1984.

10 9 8 7 6 5 4 3 2 1

Acknowledgments

THIS STUDY WAS FUNDED BY THE RUSSELL SAGE FOUNDATION, WHICH HAS HAD A long-standing interest in the relationship of social science and journalism. We would like to thank the Foundation and particularly our project officer, Peter de Janosi, and the Director of Publications, Priscilla Lewis, for their support. We would also like to thank the members of the advisory committee to the project: Allen H. Barton, Jonathan Cole, Christopher Corey, Philip Meyer, Judith A. Serrin, and Harold Watts.

The study could not have been done without a group of wonderful staff and students. On the interview study, key participants were Lisa Lightman, Sharon Lobel, Elihu Davison, Rebecca Dulit, and Nomi Stolzenberg. Erin Phelps and Robert Brennan did the computing. Lynne Sussman and Renee Hobbs conducted case studies of the reporting of two stories, each of which enriched our understanding of the journalistic process. Lynne Sussman also did the fieldwork for the incoming communications study reported in Chapter 6, and Lawrence Rothstein did the coding and follow-up. Richard Schmertzing did the survey of journal editors and authors of journal articles. Norma Diala, Joan Bahamonde, and Wendy Angus typed successive drafts of the manuscript with good cheer and high professional standards. On the content analysis, we appreciate the yeoman work of coders Kathleen Allen, Kathy Cole, Anna DiLellio, Diane Elebe, Doris Newman, and Thuy Tranthi; the research assistance of Anastasios Kalomiris; and the fine typing assistance of Kristin Antelman, Alan Flippen, and Sally Otos. Marc Glassman handled the data analysis with his usual acumen. We both want to thank Phyllis Endreny for her friendship and dedication to the project.

A number of colleagues read early drafts of the manuscript and gave us stimulating feedback. We particularly thank Herbert Gans, Robert Merton, Stephen Hess, and Janet Weiss. Conversations with David Altheide, Sandra Ball-Rokeach, Jonathan Cole, Sharon Dunwoody, Albert Gollin, Irving Louis Horowitz, Ronald Milavsky, and the 1983–84 Fellows of the Nieman Foundation probed and challenged. Above all, we would like to thank the many people who gave of their time and knowledge—reporters and social scientists whom we interviewed, journal editors, staffs of professional associations and media information services, public affairs officers, and everyone else whom we waylaid in search of information. It has been an education.

Carol H. Weiss
Eleanor Singer

Contents

The Nature of the Study

Carol H. Weiss

THIS BOOK TAKES A SYSTEMATIC LOOK AT THE REPORTING OF THE SOCIAL SCIENCES IN major media in the United States: what the media choose to report and how well they report it. The original idea for the inquiry came from a series of studies I have been doing on the influence of social science on public policy (Weiss 1974, 1977; Weiss with Bucuvalas 1980; Weiss 1983, 1987). In the course of those studies it became clear that an important way in which policymakers hear about social science, even in their own areas of specialization, is through the mass media. Although they may have their own research and analysis staffs, and sit at the nodes of specialized communication networks, often it is not until the media carry a story about social science that they become aware of it. A report from their own aides may lie unnoticed on their desk, but a story in the *Washington Post* or on CBS television news demands—and receives—immediate notice. The visibility that the media provide means that other policymakers will have read or heard the story, too, and they will have to be ready to answer questions, parry attacks, or capitalize on advantages. The media are a potent channel for conveying social science not only because they carry information but also because they create incentives for attending to the information.

Others have noted that the media function as interoffice memos in government and industry. Louis Heren, a former deputy editor at *The Times* of London, wrote: "The *New York Times* and the *Washington Post* were the 'house magazines' for the powerful. The government could not function effectively without them. Official channels existed, but not for the nods, winks, leaks, and kite-flying of politicians and officials anxious to promote their programmes" (Heren 1985:142). Gallagher and Sanders (1981:22) noted that "those in decision-making positions—in industry and in the executive, judicial, and legislative branches of government—learn about the work in the professional fields through the media. The busy legislator will read the newspapers or watch the 11 o'clock news; he or she will not, in all likelihood, read technical reports by professors. What the media relay about these technical reports is often all the decision-makers receive."

It was the realization of the media's importance that provoked the inquiry reported here. If the mass media have the capacity to capture attention for social science, it becomes important to find out which social science the media report. There are enormous quantities of social science available. Out of it all, which do journalists hear about and how do they hear about it? How much of what they hear about winds up in print or on the air, and what determines the selection? When they do report, how accurate are the stories? In sum, how useful are the media as a conduit from the social sciences to policymakers? To what extent does the media's selection of social science coincide with what social scientists think is important, and to what extent do the media use different standards of selection and introduce their own interpretation and misinterpretation of what social science means? We recognize that serving as a channel for social science messages is not the function of the media, but we are concerned with knowing whether policymakers, if they heed what they read there about social science, will become better informed.

Of course, the media are only incidentally house organs for policy-makers. Their primary responsibility is to the public. They are, after all, *mass* media. We are also interested in understanding how well they serve as transmitters of social science to the public audience.

These, then, are two purposes for our inquiry—to understand what social science the media select to report and how accurately they report it for both policymaking and public audiences. Upon media performance hinges people's knowledge of what social science has to offer. Third, we want to understand why reporting happens as it does. We want to understand how social science changes as it moves out of the domain of the academy and research laboratory and into the world of news. It is obvious that a story about sociology or economics in the *New York Times* or on CBS network news is not just a shortened and simplified version of an academic paper. It is a different creation, crafted by different professionals according to different norms to serve a different purpose. We want to understand the two key processes that lie behind the transformation—the process by which journalists *select* the social science they will report and the process by which they *convert* social science into a news story.

Two metaphors characterize this aspect of our inquiry. The first is the media as filter. We visualize the social sciences as producing a great deal of information on issues that have potential interest for both general and specialized publics; they provide data, generalizations, theories, and ideas on subjects ranging from personality to taxation. The media can report only a tiny fraction of what the social sciences offer. They filter most social science out. We want to learn the selection criteria that they use and how they apply them, and what special features distinguish the social science that manages to pass through the filter and reach a mass audience.

The second metaphor is transformation. When reporters move social science from the domain of the disciplines into the domain of news, they strip it of certain features, such as complex statistics, and recast it in terms compatible with the norms and procedures of journalism. They provide a "news peg," a handle to hang the story on, and they cast it in a narrative form that corresponds with the modes in which news is written. Journalistic rules replace social science rules, and the material takes on the simpler, livelier countenance of a news story. To what extent transformation involves sacrifice of the hallmarks of social science is an important issue. Are certain attributes of news organizations or certain characteristics of newswork practice incompatible with accurate reporting of social science? Are oversimplifications, biases, or distortions inevitable? Or does the organization of newswork allow skillful journalists to retain the essential elements of social science?

These themes have roots in the sociology of knowledge. Scholars of the sociology of knowledge analyze the relationship between ideas and the social structures in which the ideas arise (for example, Mannheim 1936; Merton 1968 [1957]; Barber 1975). As Merton has noted (1968:495), the European variety of the sociology of knowledge tended to focus on grand systems of ideas and ideologies; American scholars have been more concerned with the influence of specific subsectors and institutional environments on the shape of information. In keeping with the American variant, our interest is in the relationship between the practices of newswork and the characteristics of the social science that becomes available on the newsstand.

The fourth and final purpose of the investigation is a practical one: to see whether we can recommend steps for the improvement of social science reporting. The sponsor of our study, the Russell Sage Foundation, has had a longstanding interest in improving communication from the social sciences to the media and through the media to the public. In the late 1960s the Foundation funded a conference on the subject (Yu 1968) and an analysis of the feasibility of establishing a Social Science Information Center to "collect, organize, and evaluate, with respect to their scientific validity, the latest findings in the social sciences, and to assist journalists and others in interpreting these findings in a meaningful way" (Russell Sage Foundation 1968–69). After a year of intensive consultation with many people active in both journalism and the social sciences, the study team concluded that the time was not yet ripe for a large-scale effort to increase the flow of behavioral science reporting in the mass media:

> *It would be premature and unwise at this time to initiate a program designed to induce a large number of reporters to try to cover the behavioral sciences on a regular basis. Given the present norms existing in much of journalism, this would produce, at best, a flow of hastily prepared, unsophisticated, and vastly oversimplified stories. It would also be likely to lead to widespread frustration on the part of journalists (because of the difficulties in covering this field) and on the part of behavioral scientists (because more poor coverage is likely to be generally viewed as a setback). . . .*
> *[Communications Institute 1970]*

We want to learn whether the conditions that lay behind this statement still obtain. Or is the time ripe for intervention? As a result of our study we hope to identify ways for improving exchanges between the two domains.

Images of Journalist–Social Scientist Interaction

The kind of social science that appears in the media depends on the interaction of two professional fields, journalism and social science. The interaction takes place on the home court of the journalist, and it is journalistic rules that prevail. Still, it seems reasonable to expect that actions that social scientists take or fail to take can affect the nature of the outcome.

In some ways the professions have a great deal in common. They are both engaged in chronicling human experience. They both do "fieldwork," using empirical methods to gather their data. While social scientists use more systematic and structured methods of data collection (in fact, for many of them "journalistic" is a term of opprobrium) and work more consciously within organized conceptual frameworks (which sound like "jargon" to reporters), both professional groups set high store by accuracy and work hard to ensure that they represent facts fairly. They are both engaged in understanding and interpreting the data they collect. Both social scientists and journalists usually aim to prevent their personal values from intruding on their analysis, and there has been considerable discussion in both professions about the meaning of "objectivity." While social scientists are probably more aware of the existence of multiple realities and the difficulties of achieving anything approximating objectivity, both groups have to contend with similar dilemmas in their work. In the end they both produce reports to illuminate the nature of the social world for an audience.

Tunstall (1971:227) points out another interesting similarity:

> *Both occupations [journalism and sociology] are interested in the seamy side of life; both occupational ideologies stress that reality is shielded by facades, things are not what they seem, and that many social appearances have been deliberately contrived. Both sociologists and journalists often anticipate deceit, self-seeking and corruption in public life.*

Or as Heren (1985:132) wrote, "As a young reporter I had been advised to ask myself 'Why are these lying bastards lying to me?', advice that had stood me in good stead in many capital cities of the world." Both groups often have idealistic motives, although they (perhaps journalists particularly) may tend to conceal them behind a facade of cynicism (Janowitz 1960:223–24).

Yet the differences are striking, too. Audience, organization, and tempo stand in marked contrast. Journalists report events for a mass audience, rather than for a relatively small circle of colleagues. They work in large, bureaucratically structured organizations, where schedules are geared inexorably to a daily (or at newsmagazines, weekly) deadline. Although experienced reporters are given considerable autonomy, their work remains subject to editorial review. The emphasis is on the new and unexpected, controversy, and reader appeal. The job retains an aura of excitement and glamor, but it also requires its daily quota of routine, not least because of the unpredictability of the news. Max Weber (1948 [1919]) wrote:

> *Not everybody realizes that a really good journalistic accomplishment requires at least as much 'genius' as any scholarly accomplishment, especially because of the necessity of producing at once and 'on order' and because of the necessity of being effective, to be sure, under quite different conditions of production.*

By contrast, the pace of the social sciences is much more leisurely and the page space available more expansive. The emphasis is not on daily events but on building a body of cumulative knowledge. The search is for enduring generalizations, not discrete and engaging stories. Central to the enterprise is the task of explanation, and the development of theory has special repute in the disciplines. The academic organizations in which most social scientists work allow them almost total control over their own research, although social scientists in research firms and government agencies have their goals set by others and are subject to bureaucratic supervision. The primary audience for social scientists is usually colleagues in the same area of specialization.

What kinds of relationships can we expect between members of these different professional groups? One possibility is that reporters ignore social science and social scientists and leave them out of reported news. As we know, that is not the case today, although no doubt it was the common situation until a generation or so ago. At the other extreme, reporters might view social scientists with such respect that they try to adopt their priorities and worldview and to report social science with conscientious attention to matters that matter to social scientists. Properly, this is not the case either: News and social science are different undertakings, and vive la différence.

There are other possible accommodations between the two spheres. Drawing on reports of colleagues, anecdotes, journal articles about the reporting of social science, and sociological research on media practices in general, we set out five hypotheses about the reporting of social science in the media. The hypotheses are not mutually exclusive, but they emphasize different aspects of the journalist–social scientist relationship. In the following chapters we will see to what extent each of them is supported by the data we have collected.

1. Journalists appreciate social science and find some of its doings newsworthy. However, they are the arbiters of what is news, and they treat social science as they treat any other subject. They select those elements that interest them, cut and shape the content to fit the conventions of their craft, and on occasion even subtly distort the material to make a better story.

2. Social science has acquired so much prestige that journalists seek to use it to enhance their own credibility. They make use of research data and they particularly seek out commentary from social scientists to increase the repute of their work. One version of this premise would be that journalists know the story that they want to write ahead of time and draw upon social science to support their own analyses and legitimate their interpretation of events. A sunnier version would be that they are willing to learn from social science and use it to extend and elaborate, as well as confirm, their reporting.

3. Because there is no institutionalized system to transmit social science to the media, the social science that comes to journalists' attention may be a ragtag, hit-or-miss assortment. Visibility of social science depends on the promotional activities of individuals and organizations which allot vastly differing degrees of effort to the task. Some social scientists, particularly those who believe that any kind of social science promotion is unseemly, suspect that the body of work that journalists hear about is peculiarly shaped by those relatively few social scientists who actively court coverage. *Which* social science is reported may be determined less by the importance of social science in terms of either the disciplines or the media than by the aggressiveness of entrepreneurial social scientists.

4. Journalists are not well trained in social science concepts and methods. Their educational shortcomings, according to this hypothesis, have three types of consequences. First, reporters make mistakes in reporting, emphasize inappropriate aspects, omit key elements, or fail to provide context. Second, they are unable to distinguish good studies from poor ones or qualified from unqualified "authorities," and thus wind up giving room to shoddy research and inexpert "experts." Third, they may be unduly trusting of social scientists and accept too much of what they write and say on faith, without adequate investigation or scrutiny. The obverse of this hypothesis is that journalists have developed effective techniques for critically reviewing social science and reporting it accurately and well.

5. Journalistic practices regarding social science arise not only from the type of people attracted to newswork and the values of the profession, but also from the structure and operating procedures of news organizations. Conditions of media operation impose restraints designed to reduce the uncertainties of news and to increase the efficiency of its production. These structural constraints lead to rules and policies that set the framework within which journalists operate and thus their treatment of social science.

Obviously there is considerable overlap among these hypotheses. The first hypothesis focuses on journalists and the discretion that they have for determining what is news and how to present it. It suggests that news criteria determine the way in which social science will be treated, even to the point of occasional misrepresentation. The second hypothesis stresses the societal repute of the social sciences. Recent research has shown that social science is circulated and cited in decision-making chambers in executive agencies, legislatures, and courts, and in the private sector as well (for example, Kingdon 1984; Derthick and Quick 1985; Weiss with Bucuvalas 1980; Deshpande and Zaltman 1983). While social science does not drive the decision-making machinery, it is widely used to provide evidence for debate and to give credence to decisions that are made. This hypothesis suggests that journalists share the tendency to cite social science sources to validate, as well as to inform, their work.

The third hypothesis concentrates on the supply side. It assumes that social scientists and social science organizations vary in the effort they put into disseminating their work. Some social scientists shun all contact with the media, while others seek publicity. Certain social science organizations, such as think tanks and research institutes, may have special interest in making their contributions visible, since visibility enhances their reputations and their ability to attract funding. A consequence of differential promotion may be that the body of social science that journalists have available and from which they make their selection is unrepresentative of the work in the disciplines. Another implication is that more responsible action by social scientists in bringing their work to the notice of journalists would improve the caliber of reporting.

The fourth hypothesis, about journalists' limited knowledge of social science, stresses the difficulties that journalists have in finding their way through the technicalities and rarefied constructs of the several disciplines. Without specialized training, they are called upon to choose from a large body of complex research studies of varying quality and to write clear news stories about them. To exercise critical judgment about new and pioneering research and to translate its complexities accurately for a lay audience are demanding requirements. Without sufficient training, they can easily fall prey to error, either through accepting the flawed work of social scientists or by introducing flaws of their own.

The final hypothesis is that much of reporting practice is determined not so much by the proclivities of reporters and social scientists as by the basic conditions of news organizations. For example, to cope with the endemic uncertainty of news, reporters are assigned to regular "beats," and the topic of the beat largely determines which stories they are exposed to. Another example: Television news puts a high premium on action footage. Therefore, the location of camera crews in particular locations has a heavy influence on which places will and will not generate news. A further example is the media's need for circulation and audience, which requires that stories capture attention and appeal to popular tastes. Stuff that is too "highbrow" or abstruse will have a hard time getting past the barriers. In sum, this hypothesis suggests that because news practices have their roots in structural conditions, journalists have limited latitude to alter their ways of work and thus the manner in which social science is reported.

Workings of the Mass Media

That the mass media are a significant institution in the United States today needs little emphasis. They provide us all with a common basis of experience. Through their daily chronicle, we make sense of the onrushing stream of events and come to understand the social order. People's commonsense notions of how the world works develop out of their shared experiences of everyday life, and the media are a major contributor to the sharing of experience. The media signal what to think about and how to think about it, and in so doing they provide common mental patterns for what is important in government and politics and in many social realms as well. To the extent that the social sciences are incorporated into the media's view of the world, they have a chance to become part of the mental apparatus with which people make sense of the world.

The media that we studied in this inquiry are the major national news organs: the three weekly newsmagazines, *Time, Newsweek,* and *U.S. News & World Report;* the three network nightly newscasts, ABC, CBS, and NBC; and four newspapers, the *New York Times, Wall Street Journal, Washington Post,* and (as an instance of a major regional newspaper) the *Boston Globe.*

Perhaps a brief sketch of the workings of the media will be helpful as prelude. The daily newspapers in our study are large organizations with extensive reporting staffs. The *Times, Post,* and *Globe* publish seven days a week, with extra sections on Sunday: travel, sports, entertainment, book reviews, magazines, business, and analytic and interpretive accounts of the news. The *Wall Street Journal* publishes five days a week. Its front page and to some extent its "second front" (the first page of the second section) present an eclectic range of news and features; the back page has political articles; the inside pages are confined mostly to business news.

Many newspaper reporters are assigned to a "beat," which can be either an organization, such as the White House, State House, or the city police department, or a function, such as education or business. Beat reporters specialize in the news in their area and keep in touch with the key news sources. They are usually expected to be generalists on call as well, since it is assumed that a good reporter can be an instant expert on just about anything. General assignment reporters, who have no specialty, are assigned by editors to cover the events of the day. Each newspaper keeps a calendar of upcoming happenings, and the wire services also transmit "daybooks" that list the day's events. Editors dispatch reporters to those events that promise the most newsworthy stories.

Most news reporting deals in events. Hess (1981) found that about 80 percent of Washington reporting has to do with "breaking news" (actions, legislative hearings, speeches, statements by public figures, press conferences). Some reporters, particularly beat reporters, also have the opportunity to develop their own interpretive pieces. Often called "enterprise journalism," these accounts are not tied to daily events but are undertaken at the reporter's initiative to investigate or analyze developments that need deeper or more reflective reporting.

Each day the top editors, subeditors, and reporters have to fill the day's "news hole," the amount of space in the paper that is not taken up by advertising or such other regular commitments as syndicated columns and stock market quotations. Much of newswork is done on the phone, as reporters locate sources, get statements, check facts, and follow leads. On morning papers reporters spend the morning and early afternoon collecting information—checking periodically with editors about the shape of the emerging story. By late afternoon the story is written and edited, and top editors meet to decide which stories will make it into the day's paper.

Television news requires more structure, and producers exercise greater control. Because of all the technological apparatus—cameras, lights, and sound recording—news teams represent a considerable investment. The networks station camera crews in cities that are most likely to generate news. Each day news executives and producers select a limited number of topics, usually no more than 20 or 30, as possible items for the evening newscast. Their selection is influenced by reporters who have enough advance information about potential stories to decide on their feasibility (Gans 1979). Camera crews are dispatched and film the story on their own or under the direction of a producer or correspondent. Before air time, producers select the stories to be shown, correspondents or producers sketch a narrative story line, and editors shape the film into a story of the prescribed length (Epstein 1973). A lead-in is written for the anchorperson who will introduce the story.

The half-hour nightly network newscasts actually contain about 22 minutes of news. They usually consist of five or six stories with film (usually taped) about the day's events, one or two features, and perhaps a dozen stories in which the anchorperson reads the story accompanied by still pictures or charts in the background (sometimes called "tell" stories). Tell stories tend to be short, 30 seconds or less. The average story on network news is about 100 seconds, but important events or events with dramatic action footage can run 6 or 8 minutes or longer. The structure of television stories differs from newspaper stories. In a newspaper, the first paragraph gives the most important facts (who, what, when, where), and subsequent paragraphs present less and less vital information. A television story, on the other hand, has the structure of drama. According to Reuven Frank, then executive producer of the NBC Evening News, every news story "should have structure and conflict, problem and denouement, rising action and falling action, a beginning, a middle and an end. These are not only the essentials of drama; they are the essentials of narrative" (quoted in Epstein 1973:4–5).

The implacable shortage of time and the emphasis on action film make television the medium least receptive to stories about social science. A further limiting factor is that television news attempts to appeal to everyone in the audience. To quote Reuven Frank again:

A newspaper . . . can easily afford to print an item of conceivable interest to only a small percentage of its readers. A television news program must be put together with the assumption that each item will be of some interest to everyone that watches. Every time a newspaper introduces a feature which will attract a specialized group, it can assume it is adding at least a little bit to its circulation. To the degree a television news program includes an item of this sort . . . it must assume its audience will diminish. [Epstein 1973:40]

Newsmagazines publish once a week and have the time and space to put the week's news in perspective. They generally present about fifty pages of news and pictures. *Time* and *Newsweek* classify the news into a series of titled sections; the "front of the book" consists of national news, international news, and business, and the "back of the book" includes such sections as law, education, religion, art, and medicine, plus reviews of books and films. Back-of-the-book sections usually appear only once or twice a month, sometimes less often. What social science appears is usually in sections entitled "behavior" or "life/style," but it can also appear under whatever subject matter it deals with, from national news to religion.

Time and *Newsweek* maintain bureaus in cities around the world, but headquarters is in New York. The week's schedule starts with the collection of story suggestions from the bureaus. New York tentatively selects stories, sets a word limit on them, and assigns them to reporters. During the week some stories are cut and others are added as new developments occur. By Thursday and Friday, reporters send their memos and their answers to queries to New York or write stories to space. Writers in New York usually write the final copy based on the files that have come in. Reporters get a chance to check copy and argue for changes, but as a *Time* executive said, "The key thing is that New York decides and shapes what 'the story' is—the reporter doesn't" (Hess 1981:44). *U.S. News & World Report,* which has its headquarters in Washington, concentrates on foreign, domestic, and business news. Using a variety of formats and type faces, it provides signed news reports, analyses, and interviews, plus "insider-letter"-type advice on managing money and investments. It prides itself on concise reports of important news without "fun, fudge, foam, and fizz," "gossip from New York and Hollywood . . . [or] book and film reviews" and without "'back-of-the-book' editors fighting for space, lobbying to have vital reports . . . bumped . . ." (*U.S. News,* March 8, 1982, p. 28).

Previous Research

Relatively little research has been done on the reporting of social science in the mass media. A number of social scientists have written case studies about media coverage of a particular social science report, such as the Coleman report on equal educational opportunity (for example, Grant and Murray 1985) and Coleman's "white flight" study (Weigel and Pappas 1981), about their personal experiences with media reporting (for example, Walum 1975; Rubin 1980), or about the reporting of a particular form of social science, such as opinion polls (for example, Paletz et al. 1980; Gollin 1980; Broh 1980; Atkin and Gaudino 1984). Several first-rate discussions of the relationship between social science and journalism have appeared (for example, McCall and Stocking 1982; Stocking and Dunwoody 1982; McCall 1985; Rubinstein and Brown 1985), but empirical work has been of limited scope. Much more extensive study has been done of media reporting of the natural sciences. Researchers have studied the amount of science content in the media, readership of science stories, science writers, and the accuracy of science reporting (for example, Krieghbaum 1967; Tichenor et al. 1970; Wade and Schramm 1969; Dubas and Martel 1975; Friedman et al. 1986; Nunn 1979). But science reporting differs in important ways from the reporting of social science, not the least of which is that news organizations recognize the need for specialized reporters to cover science but see no parallel need for specialists in the social sciences.

The more general literature on the media is also provocative. Of particular relevance are the studies that explicitly or implicitly examine media reporting in terms of fairness or bias. Following Golding and Elliott (1979), we can see three main traditions in these sociological studies. Early studies focused on "gatekeepers," such as wire editors who chose stories for the paper from the wire service (for example, White 1950; Donohue et al. 1972). Researchers watched and talked to the journalists who selected stories, and tried to identify the personal, political, and professional criteria that influenced their choices. Published news was seen to be biased by gatekeepers' predilections.

A second stream of research was less concerned with deliberate manipulation than with unwitting bias. Thus, Lang and Lang (1953, 1970) stationed observers along General MacArthur's parade route and compared their observations with accounts of the parade that appeared in the media. Halloran et al. (reported in Golding and Elliott 1979) compared events at a London anti–Vietnam war rally with press and television coverage. In both cases the media sought out pockets of excitement and thus gave misleading impressions of events.

More recent studies have moved away from studying conditions that foster conscious or unconscious bias in short-term reportage and have concentrated instead on the processes of news production that determine the nature of news in the long term (Epstein 1973; Sigal 1973; Roshco

1975; Gans 1979; Tuchman 1978; Golding and Elliott 1979; Schlesinger 1978; Fishman 1980). The titles of most of these books stress the social construction of the news; they do not refer to news gathering but to "newsmaking," "deciding what's news," "making news," "news from nowhere," "manufacturing the news"; and they point to the organization and structure of news production as the overriding determinant. It is the imperatives of the organizations within which journalists work, their professional practices and routines, that create the social product called news.

Along with this recognition has come a more basic critique of imbalance in the news. Scholars have noted that by focusing on individuals, rather than social and economic forces, and by its fascination with drama and conflict, rather than long-term conditions, news gives a superficial and fragmented picture of reality. It highlights the doings and values of certain groups, most notably government officials, and largely ignores less powerful segments of society. It clings to status quo values that are broadly accepted and formulas of storytelling with which the public is familiar. News takes the perspective of the prevailing consensus, which tends to bolster the position of those in positions of control.

Scholars who have studied the media in this tradition are exquisitely sensitive to the impossibility of providing an "objective" picture of the world and the inapplicability of any notions of "holding a mirror to events." They know that their own reality is only one of a countless number of versions. Much recent writing in the social sciences has discussed the extent to which all depictions of the world depend on consensual agreements and definitions. Yet, if they do not have the key to "truth," they can recognize gross deviations when they see them. They know that their reality is closer to real than is today's news, if only because they are not blinkered by the organizational imperatives of turning out a daily issue of news under conditions of high uncertainty and within the bounds of economic profitability.

These three streams of analysis have become increasingly sophisticated in their study of the procedures of news production and the effect of those procedures on the contours of the news. Each of them is concerned with bias, conscious and unconscious, short-term and long. Our inquiry partakes of some of the same characteristics. Like the gatekeeper studies, we want to see the types of social science that journalists select for the news and the basis for their decisions. Like the observers of parades and rallies, we want to compare what journalists report about the social sciences with what social scientists have actually said and written. We ask social scientists who have been reported in the media to draw these comparisons for us. In the third tradition, we want not only to look at the social science news that is published and analyze the way it is reported but also to talk to journalists about their practice. Our concern is both with judging how well the news reflects the world of social science in its native state and with seeing which particular accounts and people from the social sciences become part of the daily news, and how and why and how accurately they are presented.

The Research Study

Our investigation of the reporting of social science consisted of two major parts: a content analysis of all social science stories that appeared in ten major media over a five-month period in 1982 and an interview study with journalists and social scientists, based on a subset of the stories. The media we studied were the *New York Times, Washington Post, Wall Street Journal, Boston Globe, Newsweek, Time, U.S. News & World Report,* and the ABC, NBC, and CBS nightly network newscasts.

The first step of the study was a definition of what we meant by social science. We built up the definition on two dimensions—the fields that qualified as social sciences and the journalistic content that should count. The fields we included were sociology, political science, economics, psychology, anthropology, criminology, demography, epidemiology, and behavioral medicine. If research results were cited, we included education, policy analysis, public administration, and market research. If research results had a distinctively social scientific orientation, we included area studies, history, urban planning, and psychiatry.

The fields constituted the warp. To enter our study, the story also had to satisfy the requirements of the woof. The types of content we specified for inclusion were results of studies; quotations from or stories about social scientists; social science data from a list of specific indicator series; discussion of social science methods; social science theories; news of social science organizations; and institutional aspects, such as government funding of the social sciences or enrollments in social science departments.

In the content analysis, all these kinds of references were counted, whether they appeared in news, features, business, sports, obituaries, book reviews, editorials, columns, letters to the editor, graphs, even comics and cartoons (of which a few dealt with social science!). We included items not only when social science was the focus of the story, but also when social science constituted a paragraph, one or two sentences, or even part of a sentence. This was an essential procedure if we were to collect those brief but telling instances where social science amplified the reporting of regular news. (See the Methodological Appendix for further details.)

The content analysis identified and coded all stories that met these criteria in seven weeks (every third week of the five-month period). The number of stories with social science content came to over 2000. For purposes of comparison, we analyzed six of the same print media for a similar but shorter period in 1970. This enables us to see whether the frequency of social science reporting has increased and whether it has changed in style. Part II reports on the content analysis.

Out of all the social science that appeared, we drew a subset of stories for interviewing. We limited eligible stories to two categories: results of social science research and quotations from social scientists. We selected stories only from the mainline social science disciplines; namely, sociology, political science, economics, psychology, and anthropology, and then only if social science was a substantial element in the story. The stories about which we interviewed were the "big" social science stories of each week.

Interviewing began within a day or a few days of the appearance of each story. We conducted standardized telephone interviews with the reporter who wrote the story and with the social scientist whose research was reported or whose comments were quoted. We completed both reporter and social scientist interviews on 127 stories of the 130 we attempted. One reporter and one social scientist refused the interviews, and for one story we were unable to identify the reporter who wrote the copy. We have complete interview data on 80 stories that report social science studies and 47 stories that quote a social scientist. Ten journalists and two social scientists were interviewed in connection with two different stories. From our interviews comes a description of the reporters and social scientists involved, the nature of the reporting process, and social scientists' judgments about the adequacy of the story. After these phases of the study were complete, Phyllis Endreny conducted interviews with editors and television producers at the same media we studied, in order to investigate the role that editors play in the reporting of social science, and we report some of her findings here.

Another component of the investigation consisted of three explorations of the kind of social science that the media fail to report. By definition, it is easy to read, count, and classify the social science that appears in the news. But to find out which social science is neglected requires some known universe of social science for comparison. One inquiry takes as a base all the social science symposia presented at three meetings of the American Association for the Advancement of Science (AAAS) and looks at which topics made their way into print. A second involved collecting all press releases, periodicals, and other communications received by five news bureaus and watching to see which items were and were not reported. Still a third looked at lead articles in the leading social science journals to see which of them were reported in the mass media. We also talked to the executive officers of the major social science associations, editors of major social science journals, and staff in public affairs offices. The interview study and these investigations are reported in Part I.

Our study concludes with the appearance of social science in the news. We make no attempt to look at the public's reception of it. We can say nothing about readership, public interest, or understanding. Those are subjects for another day and another study.

PART I
Interview Study

Carol H. Weiss

for Daniel E. Weiss, novelist

2

Processes of Reporting

THE *NEW YORK TIMES* FOR APRIL 9, 1985, CARRIED A STORY IN THE SCIENCE TIMES section headlined, "Study Stresses Pre-School Benefits." Written by Larry Rohter, it gave the results of a follow-up study of poor black children in Harlem who at the age of 4 had entered early education programs in the New York City public schools. The researchers—Martin Deutsch, Theresa J. Jordan, and Cynthia P. Deutsch of New York University's School of Education—found that the youth, aged 19 to 21 at the time of the follow-up interviews, were twice as likely to be holding jobs as a comparison group of youth from the same area and background who had not participated in the programs. The story described additional findings, including differences by gender (boys benefited more than girls, partly because males received positive reinforcement from teachers in regular classrooms after the enrichment program, whereas girls were penalized for assertiveness and nontraditional role expectations). According to the *Times* story, the study "will be published this fall," and the findings come from a preliminary report.

The lead article in *Time* for July 21, 1986, dealt with the report of Attorney General Edwin Meese's Commission on Pornography. Entitled "Sex Busters," and written by Richard Stengel, it quoted about a dozen reactions to the report. One was from Edward Donnerstein, "a University of Wisconsin psychologist who has studied the effects of sexually violent

TABLE 2.1

Location of Stories and Journalists

	Number of Stories	
	Appearing in	Reported by
New York Times	42	39
Washington Post	26	20
Wall Street Journal	18	18
Boston Globe	13	7
U.S. News & World Report	9	9
Newsweek	6	6
Time	4	4
NBC	4	3
CBS	3	3
ABC	1	1
Parade (with Sunday Globe)	1	1
AP	—	6
UPI	—	4
Knight Ridder	—	3
Los Angeles Times	—	1
Chicago Sun Times	—	1
Jack Anderson	—	1
TOTAL	127	127

material." He reportedly said that the crucial variable in promoting violence against women is not explicit sex but graphic violence.[1]

We are interested in finding out how stories like this come to be written. We want to know how reporters hear about studies, and we want to know what motivates them to seek out social scientists for quotable statements. Out of all the social science and social scientists, how do they light on the particular ones they write about? This chapter pursues the processes of reporting, from the initial connection with social science, reporters' criteria for selecting some social science in and the rest out, the degree of contact between reporters and social scientists while the story is being written, to the ways in which reporters check the accuracy of the stories they write.

Data come from 254 interviews with reporters and social scientists. For each of 127 big social science stories, we interviewed the reporter who wrote the story and the social scientist whose work or comments were reported. Table 2.1 shows the media in which stories appeared and, since some stories came from wire services and syndicates, it also shows the

---

[1] Neither of these stories was included in our inquiry. We describe them as illustrations of a "study story" and a "quote story."

23

news organizations for which reporters worked. Only eight of the stories appeared on the television networks, even though our selection process gave priority to television stories. Conditions of network news production, as noted in chapter 1, limit television's responsiveness to social science. Our analysis, therefore, is based primarily on the print media.

Distinguishing Between Study Stories and Quote Stories

The process of reporting differs between stories that report the results of a study and those that quote the remarks of a social scientist. In study stories the study generally comes to a reporter's attention from outside—for example, through a press release. In quote stories the reporter takes the initiative in locating and contacting the social scientists. Because of the different origins of the two categories of stories, the social scientists who appear in them vary along several dimensions.

	Study Story	Quote Story
In university department	35%	64%
Tenured professor	30	55
Hold Ph.D.	61	85
Economist	29	45
Psychologist	24	15 (n.s.)*
Male	75	87 (n.s.)*

*The difference is not statistically significant.

When reporters seek out a social scientist, they are significantly more likely to go to a university department, to a person holding a Ph.D., to a tenured professor, to an economist. There is also a discernible, although less significant, trend to go more frequently to men. Social scientists who are reported because of a study they have conducted are less likely to fall into these categories and are somewhat more likely to be psychologists.

The characteristics of the 127 social scientists who appeared in "big stories" in the media during our study, are:

- 80% are men[2]
- 70% have Ph.D.s, 6% M.D.s, and 2% Ed.D.s

---

[2] A brief note on the twenty-six women: Twenty were in the media because of research they had conducted. Ten held the Ph.D. and one had an Ed.D. (that is, 42 percent had doctorates compared with 87 percent of the men who had Ph.D.s, Ed.D.s, or M.D.s). Forty-six percent worked in government compared with 18 percent of the men. Twenty-seven percent worked in universities compared with 63 percent of the men. Twenty-seven percent held research positions compared with 19 percent of the men.

- 33% are economists
- 23% are psychologists
- 18% are sociologists/anthropologists/demographers
- 12% are political scientists/policy analysts
- 4% are epidemiologists or in behavioral medicine
- 10% are other
- 45% are in university departments; 10% are in university research institutes
- 21% are in unaffiliated research organizations (10% nonprofit and 11% profit)
- 19% are in government, 5% other

That economists should constitute the largest segment of social scientists in our inquiry, and an even larger fraction of those who are quoted, is not surprising. This was a time when issues of inflation, government budget cutting, unemployment, and productivity were high on the media agenda. All the newspapers and newsmagazines have a business section, and the *Wall Street Journal* is largely devoted to business. Moreover, it has long been a tradition in business reporting to seek the opinions of economists, particularly their forecasts of future conditions.

Another difference between study and quote stories is the way that social science is used. In 80 percent of the study stories in our inquiry the study and its findings are the focus of the story. The reporter is recounting the results of research. In only 20 percent of the study stories are study findings introduced as ancillary material. On the other hand, in quote stories, the quote is never (in our pool of stories) the reason for the story. The reporter is pursuing a topic, and the social scientist gives information or opinion to elaborate or explain. As a consequence of this difference, the frequency of contact between reporter and social scientist differs, as does the nature of their interaction.

Accordingly, we discuss study and quote stories separately in the remainder of the chapter.

Study Stories

Research doesn't happen in places routinely covered by the press. Reporters don't regularly patrol the social science beat. Even those who specialize in a subject on which social science research is frequently done rarely have such a narrowly defined beat that they can routinely scout the social science part of the territory. In the interviews, some reporters told us that their beats were as broad as "China, the western United States, and environmental issues," "economics and Soviet affairs," "retail, energy, and agriculture," "space, nuclear issues, drugs, and the National Archives," "the U.S. Departments of Health and Human Services and Education." With all that ground to cover, they don't have the time, even if they had the inclination, to root out and discover all relevant research. Most beat reporters say that they take the initiative in developing stories, but they are usually dependent on outsiders to alert them to relevant research information, including research results.

Only a few reporters cover beats that bring them into regular contact with social science. Some of the reporters covering personal relationships, crime, and economic forecasting are alert to social science, especially if they have been on the same beat for a number of years. As one reporter said, "I've been covering the Justice Department and crime statistics for four years. I've written up FBI statistics and prison populations eight times. Over the years, I've talked to a whole host of people. I'm familiar with the major explanations offered by researchers." But this receptivity to social science wasn't true for all reporters with such beats. Personal predilections as well as structure and opportunity seem to matter.

Finding Out About the Study

However receptive they are, reporters need a mechanism for learning about social science. In our study, 60 percent of the social scientists said that they or their organization had sent out a press release about the research. The type of organization in which they worked made some difference. Those associated with profit and not-for-profit research organizations were most likely to report a press release (73 percent), followed by those in government agencies (69 percent). This compared with 49 percent of those from universities. The differences are not statistically significant, but they are suggestive.

Of course, sending a press release is no guarantee of media attention. In our analysis of incoming mail to five media offices, we found that most press releases about social science research, like releases about everything else, never make their way into print. (See chapter 6.) The media are besieged with seekers of publicity, from corporations to symphony orchestras. Yet it would appear that without a press release—or its functional equivalent—the odds are lower that reporters hear about a study.

Social scientists talked about other ways that reporters could have heard about their research: they talked at a press conference or at a meeting covered by the press (38 percent); a report appeared in an organizational newsletter (24 percent); the social scientist contacted members of the press (19 percent) although not always the journalist who wrote this particular story; a paper was published in a professional journal (7 percent). Over half also reported that stories had appeared earlier in other mass media. Social scientists tended to believe that the key attention-getter was the initiative of the sponsoring agency or their own organization in making the research visible.

When we talked to reporters about the origin of the story, they tended to emphasize the routines of the newsroom. Almost three in ten said that they were assigned to the story by their editor. Six in ten said the story was their own idea, and the remainder said that it was a joint decision, a group decision, or routine. The source of the idea for the story, in their reports, was similar enough to social scientists' accounts to sound familiar. They, too, talked about press releases, press conferences, and contacts by researchers. But they stressed the demand side as well as the supply side: We do a regular feature in this area (21 percent), I or my editor has a personal interest in the subject (8 percent).

They also indicated reliance on stories that had appeared about the research in other mass media. Editors and reporters are voracious consumers of other media; they read newspapers, magazines, the wires; they listen to radio news; some read a host of specialized journals. They look up past events and personalities in what used to be called the "morgue," and is now the library, the paper's file of old clippings. Many of them maintain personal files of material on story ideas that they are planning to develop some day, and they constantly add clippings to the file. When an event or a new study activates the file, they can draw on all the clips that they have tucked away over the months. An article about a research study that appeared in another newspaper or magazine months earlier can now see the light of day.

By piecing together the accounts of both the social scientist and the journalist, we can see the course by which stories developed. Table 2.2 shows the primary channels through which information about research studies traveled. The organization that sponsored (or, less often, conducted) the research was the primary purveyor of information in 50 percent of the cases, primarily through press releases and press conferences, informal contacts with reporters, and regular organizational bulletins. Reporters took the lead on about a quarter of the stories. Previous stories in other mass media were the route to journalists' attention for 10 percent of the stories. Individual social science investigators were the prime movers in 6 percent of the stories, and a variety of other sources accounted for the rest.

TABLE 2.2

Original Source of Information on Research Studies

Source		(N = 80)
Sponsoring Organization		50%
Press conference/press release	27	
Contact at organization	14	
Organizational publications	9	
Journalist		26
Reporter sought information on own initiative	15	
Reporter attended conference	6	
Other journalist	4	
Editor suggested	1	
Other Mass Media		10
Third Party		8
Social Scientist		6
		100%

Developing the Story

We can organize the same data somewhat differently, in terms of who took the main initiative for translating the study into a story. In a sense it is always the journalists' initiative, since they choose which sources to attend to. Still, in almost half the cases social science sponsors and performers promoted the stories, either through press releases and press conferences or through personal contact with reporters by members of the sponsoring organization or by the researchers themselves. In the other half of the cases, journalists had to *notice* items in organizational publications and stories in other media, and they had to attend to information conveyed by third-party sources, before a story could be crafted. Table 2.3 presents this breakdown of the data.

Over a quarter of the study stories were obviously triggered by a press release or press conference and nothing else. Usually it was the sponsoring organization that contacted the press. Organizations included the Educational Testing Service, the U.S. Bureau of the Census, the Heritage Foundation, the Community Service Society, the Labor Department, the National Academy of Sciences, the Justice Department, the Small Business Administration, the Federation of Jewish Philanthropies, the National Association of Business Economists, the Brookings Institution, and the University of Illinois. In these and similar cases a press release or notice of a press conference went out, often directed to the editor or to the editor of the appropriate section of the paper/magazine. A release was sometimes

TABLE 2.3

Initiative for Translating Study Into Story

	(N = 80)	
Journalist		53%
Sought information	15	
Attended conference	6	
Other journalist brought to attention	4	
Editor suggested	1	
Noticed item in other mass media	10	
Noticed item in research sponsor's publication	9	
Paid attention to third party	8	
Sponsoring Organization		47
Press conference/press release	27	
Contact at organization	14	
Social scientist	6	
		100%

addressed specifically to the reporter who was most likely to be interested. As one social scientist told us, "The public affairs director, having been a journalist herself, personalized letters to those journalists she knew."

If a press conference looks important, the information will be entered in the daybook, the calendar of upcoming events in the city. An editor may assign a reporter to cover it, or an interested reporter who notices the entry may volunteer to go. If the topic falls within the reporter's beat, s/he generally decides whether or not to cover it.

Some organizations, including government agencies and voluntary associations as well as public relations firms, do more than hold a press conference. For example, after a press conference attended by three hundred media people, one government agency "contacted a 'flash list' of about fifty people to explain the finer details of the study." After a press release an organization may follow up by phone to emphasize the importance of the study and answer questions.

Reporters who attend a press conference usually receive a release or a copy of the research summary (and sometimes the full report). They have the opportunity to ask questions, and many of them talk further to the organization spokesperson and to the researchers after the conference. If they have time and interest, they will call the researcher later and get more information.

Closely related to the press conference and press release is the "personal contact" at the organization. Again, the organization takes the initiative in reaching the press, but the contact is less formal and ritualized.

Examples: One journalist had a friend in the public relations office at Washington University who told him about a press release they were working on. Another reporter said that "we have contacts in the federal government who call us or we find out about their reports." In this case it was the U.S. Commission on Civil Rights. Another reporter said, "I heard about the study from a contact at the Police Foundation who called five days before the press release, as he usually does. His effort meant it was possible to read the full report ahead of the press release from the Justice Department, and so do a more comprehensive news story." A columnist had a friend who does publicity for the National Academy of Sciences, who alerted him to a study reported in an in-house publication. About one study story in seven came to notice through these relatively informal channels.

Somewhat more indirect were leads from "sources" not connected with the organization that did the research or that sponsored it. One reporter heard about a study through a public relations person at the American Psychological Association, who had interviewed the social scientist about a new book he had written on child-rearing. A book publisher sent notice to the media about a forthcoming book on fatherhood in transition. Former Secretary of Health, Education, and Welfare Joseph Califano held a news conference on publication of his own book which included data from a study by the Rand Corporation. A columnist's staff person heard about a Justice Department study from a Congressman. Such links accounted for one story in twelve.

Another one story in ten came to journalists' attention primarily through organizational publications and specialized journals. One reporter received the *Population Bulletin,* along with a press release from the Population Reference Bureau. Another saw an article in the *New England Journal of Medicine.* "We regularly go through it. If it's important, we do a review of it." Other journals that stimulated stories were *Vital Statistics* from the National Center for Health Statistics, *Morbidity and Mortality Weekly Report* from the Center for Disease Control, and the Senior Citizen Law Center Newsletter which mentioned a forthcoming study on medical care for minorities.

Other mass media were the primary channel for about one story in ten. A writer at *Newsweek* saw a story in the *New York Times* and thought that it would make a good article for their life/style section. He read the book on which the *Times* article was based and discovered a story more complicated than he had anticipated. Another reporter had seen an article in the *New York Times* about six months earlier that "piqued my curiosity. Since then I've been gathering material." A reporter at NBC saw a *Washington Post* story and "we were all interested. Even though one paper had it already, we thought there was enough general interest that we should have it also."

Reporters took the major initiative in about a quarter of the study stories. One reporter saw a newspaper story about the formation of a group of local women who were not receiving child support payments. She wondered if this was "part of a trend" and looked for data. She called the Census Bureau and found study results on the nonpayment of support. Another reporter, who was thinking about quitting smoking, wanted to know the success rate of alternative stop-smoking programs. The Department of Public Health gave him the name of a social scientist who had done relevant research. Another reporter who was active in the peace movement heard from friends that their children were frightened of nuclear war. She started interviewing and was referred to the social scientist's article. Another reporter had been assigned a year before to write a story on the effects of Reagan's budget cuts on cities. He decided to do a follow-up a year later, and he went back to the social scientist who had supplied research data for the earlier story.

Some reporters attended academic or quasi-academic meetings. One reporter said that he regularly attends the Midwest Political Science Association meeting. "They're a knowledgeable bunch of people. It's good for me to hear what the smarter academics are thinking about." During our study he went to a panel on the consequences of the 1978 civil service reform and wrote a story based on the papers presented. Another reporter was invited to a Bush Institute workshop on children and families and received a copy of a study that was being discussed there. Another reporter had gone to the American Criminological Society annual meeting. Later when he was doing a story on gun control, he got in touch with a criminologist who had been on the program and asked him to send copies of his papers. Meeting attendance accounted for 6 percent of the stories.

In a few cases another journalist was the link between reporter and researcher. One social scientist, who had given a copy of his study to the university news bureau, was interviewed by a local reporter. The local reporter called the AP, which sent a science reporter to cover the study. In another case a reporter had gotten wind of the study over a year before, while the study was still in progress. The social scientist could not provide data then, but when he completed the study, he called the metropolitan desk, only to find that the original reporter had left the paper. The desk assigned a new reporter. In another instance a CBS reporter heard about a study of the employment of ex-prisoners through a CBS news researcher. Fellow journalists gave rise to 4 percent of the stories.

The social scientist was the prime mover in 6 percent of the cases. One social scientist dropped off a press release at the *Post,* and the desk assigned a reporter to write the story. The social scientist said, "I put out releases to control what I want said." Another social scientist sent copies of his research report to newspapers and the wire service. One social scientist credited his co-author, "who wants attention," with calling the study to the attention of the *Times*. He complained about an inaccuracy in the story which he thought might have been his colleague's "entrepreneurial hype to get the story in the *Times*," but concluded that "I'm happy that he was so entrepreneurial because it generated interest." Another social scientist gave the *Globe* an advance copy of the report a week before the press release and briefed them on "how we wanted them to handle the story."

Selecting the Study

Once editors and reporters hear about a study, they have to decide whether there is a story in it. We asked reporters what made the study newsworthy. Overwhelmingly, the answer was the topic. The newness of the findings, the quality or comprehensiveness of the findings, and the prestige of the source were also mentioned, but much less often. (See Table 2.4.)

What was it that made the topic newsworthy? According to reporters, almost half the time the topic was related to matters in the news. Just under a third of the time the topic was interesting or trendy. One mention in seven indicated that the topic was important, and a scattering of responses mentioned controversy.

Here's how reporters talked about topics:

> *The budget debate is right now. It's coming to a head. Whither goest the economy is newsworthy. Many people are interested.*

> *The problem it studied, lack of work for youth in New York City, is current now.*

> *Everybody is talking about the defense build-up and Reagan's defense budget—the increase in defense spending and the reduction in social services. Then there was this report about how we're falling behind the Russians [in high school achievement in science]. This is newsworthy.*

> *I cover utility competition. Electric utilities are probably going to be decontrolled with natural gas and oil. Reagan will probably deregulate everything. So [a study on utility costs, rates, and profits under monopoly conditions] is newsworthy.*

TABLE 2.4

Journalists' and Social Scientists' Views
on Why the Study Was Newsworthy (Multiple Responses)

Reason	Journalists (N = 80)		Social Scientists (N = 80)	
Topic		90%		95%
Hard news	36		53	
Interesting	30		35	
Important	14		15	
Controversial	10		20	
Newness, Novelty		30		21
Good Findings		19		19
Source		9		5
Not Newsworthy		6		4

The second category of response was the novelty and newness of information. The fact of newness and first-ness touches a responsive chord.

It's the first study of the effects [of unemployment] on children of unemployed workers.

This was the first study showing problem drinking among women going up nationally.

Research quality was not often mentioned as a criterion for selecting a study to report. Although this is not surprising, it is a sober reminder of the different values in journalism and social science. Only four reporters mentioned good findings as their first explanation for why a study was worth reporting, and an additional eleven gave good findings as a secondary reason for the newsworthiness of the study.

What did journalists mean by good findings? Their answers touch on several characteristics—the ability to quantify a phenomenon, the comprehensiveness of the study, the integration of data on different subjects or from different sources. Only one response talks about good findings in terms that resonate with social science definitions—the study's methodological rigor.

On quantification:

He actually states a number. He doesn't just make a forecast based on an educated guess. He has done a study.

> *. . . their study of California inmates and the comparison of addicts to non-addicts was interesting and gave hard numbers.*

Comprehensiveness was mentioned several times. For example:

> *There had never before been such a thorough survey of New York City's Jewish population.*

> *Personally, I was interested because I felt it pulled together statistics on divorce, demographics, and health.*

The one answer to the question about newsworthiness that spoke about the study in strictly methodological terms was this: "It is one of the few [studies] with a large data base and reliable statistics."

Social scientists' responses were very much in agreement on the matter of newsworthiness. They were even more likely to judge that reporters were attracted by the topic, and they assessed the appeal of the topic in remarkably similar ways.

Covering the Story

When reporters (or their editors) decide that a study is newsworthy, they take the initiative in pursuing the story. They often read the research report. In 10 percent of the cases journalists told us that no report had yet been written, but where a report was available, 80 percent said that they read it. Not necessarily all of it, of course. Although the large majority said they read it all, another quarter said they skimmed through it all, some said they read the summary, some concentrated on particular sections, and one candid person said he didn't read much.

Three journalists in five said that they also read other articles or books on the subject of the research. Half of them used information from these sources in the story they wrote, and an additional one in five said s/he used such information as general background.

Over half (57 percent) also got in touch with the researcher who had done the study. Another 5 percent heard the social scientist at a press conference and made no further efforts at contact, and 8 percent spoke to someone else at the social scientist's organization. When they did contact the researcher, it was almost always on the phone, and the number of conversations ranged from one to six. Having one conversation was most common, but in about half the cases the reporter called again.

Mostly what they talked about was clarification and further details of study results. Almost all reporters and social scientists indicated that they had discussed the conclusions, and often the import, of the research. In well over half the contacts the reporter and/or the social scientist said that the methods of the research were discussed. Twenty-one reporters gave an example of the methodological issue that they talked about. One reporter said, "I asked how they got the figures and how they computed them." Another reporter said, "I asked her the size of the sample and who the people were." A social scientist reported that the journalist had asked "how I found people to interview and what the basis of choosing them was."

Some of the journalists' questions were fairly sophisticated. One reporter remarked, "It's very unusual that the *New England Journal of Medicine* would use a mental health piece, but this one had a comparison group. I discussed the comparison group with him." The social scientist to whom this reporter spoke added that she had also asked "about measures. I explained in layman's terms how we measured family emotions. She asked about the duration of the study and what happened to people at the end of it." Another journalist who was writing about a review of existing studies said, "This really wasn't primary work that they had done themselves. . . . So when I asked about the methodology, he said this was a review of what everybody else did that they made critical judgments about. So I asked him on what basis they made their judgments."

Several social scientists commented on reporters' serious pursuit of methodological issues. One social scientist said, "He called two or three times for clarification on the stratified sample. He was very, very thorough." Another said, "He asked very precisely about treatment conditions, the sample, and measurement indices."

Where research methods didn't come up in conversation, a number of reporters explained that such a discussion wasn't necessary inasmuch as they'd read the report and understood it. One reporter said, "No [I didn't ask]. There was a whole chapter explaining methods. The book was very self-explanatory."

Several reporters indicated that they were not particularly interested in the methods of research. Said one, "[I asked] only enough to let the reader know that the study had merit." Said another, "His work is based on records and work at the ——— Institute. It's not necessary to check the validity of his studies."

Sometimes reporters called to check their understanding of the findings. One published story says that "only 63 percent of jobholders who responded said their jobs are safe in the coming year." According to the social scientist, the journalist wanted to say that 37 percent of respondents didn't think they would keep their jobs, and he called back to check the figure. "I said that was going too far. . . . We sat and thought about it.

He asked me: Why don't you say 37 percent? I said it's better to say it this way. . . . I didn't tell him what to say. We discussed it. We spent ten minutes on that one point. I said, 'Don't make people more insecure than they already are.'" The journalist finally agreed.

Checking Information

We asked both social scientists and reporters if the social scientist asked for the opportunity to check information in the story. Most reporters don't like to give sources any opportunity to modify or censor what they write (Dunwoody 1982:198), and, in fact, about a third of the reporters we interviewed said that it is a policy not to give people the chance to review a story. In some of these cases the reporter implied that it was organizational policy not to clear stories with sources; in others it seemed to be the reporter's own policy. Reasons for objecting to checking included unwillingness to take the extra time and not wanting to allow a source the opportunity to dictate content. Reporters said that if they were unsure of facts, they would call back on their own. Another objection to checking came up a couple of times, particularly in quote stories: If you allow sources to reread what they actually said, they'll want to change it—usually by making the statement longer and more complicated. Said one journalist, "I don't check because they don't usually want to say what they said." Another said, "My experience has been that if I reread their quote to them, when they hear their quote, they want to add to it. That makes it more boring."

Only five social scientists—three study authors and two people who had been quoted—said that they had asked for the chance to check the story prior to publication. Several people explained why they didn't make such a request: "He called back so many times to check facts, and I sent him documents. I trusted his journalistic integrity. [He] is a scientist in his journalism." "I never do. It's a quirk of mine. I accept being misquoted as a fact of life." "I didn't ask, but she checked back with me to check for accuracy. I made one correction, and she made the change." "I have infinite faith." "It was too minor a quote. We often do [ask to check] if it's a significant quote, but . . . you can find anyone to say something like that. If it had been about the impact [of the new federalism] on business, then I would have asked to check the quote." "I was interviewed at 3 P.M. It was aired at 7 P.M."

Of the three people who asked to review study stories, two were given the chance. In both cases the reporter spoke to them on the phone. One person found that this worked well, but the other said, "I did review the introductory paragraph over the phone. It's very difficult to review on the phone. I wish I could have done it in person." Nevertheless, with this check and the considerable effort he had spent preparing the reporter in advance, he thought the story was "terrific." The third social scientist who had asked to check was told OK by the reporter, "but he didn't deliver . . . I guess I should be more insistent." He rated the story "fair to poor."

Of the two quoted social scientists who had asked to check, one said, "He quoted back what I had said, so I withdrew my request to see the copy." In the other case the journalist said that he would call the social scientist back but never did. Both of these social scientists were satisfied with the story.

A number of reporters offered the social scientist a chance to review the facts in the story, even when s/he didn't ask. Two reporters noted that they are particularly careful with academics, not so much because their academic status or expertise warrants special treatment as because they complain a lot. Said one reporter of a study story: "I read the story to her, because other academics have complained to me. As a group, academics are finicky."

In all cases in which social scientists said that they requested changes in the story, the reporter made the changes. Whether the social scientist asked to review or the reporter volunteered, there was no example of a reporter failing to accommodate the social scientist's suggestion for change.

For all the study stories we asked the reporter how helpful the social scientist had been in the discussions. Two thirds said extremely helpful, almost a quarter said good, okay; just over one in ten was not very satisfied with the social scientist's cooperation.

Seeking Alternative Perspectives on the Study

One of our original hypotheses was that reporters are sometimes too trusting of social scientists and their research. Weigel and Pappas (1981) and Grant and Murray (1985) have criticized the reporting of two of James Coleman's studies on this ground. We asked reporters if they had checked the research with another social scientist before writing the story.

Most of them said no. They took the press release, the study report, and/or the social scientist's explanation as the basis for the story and proceeded to write. One reporter in five said that s/he had contacted another social scientist about the study before proceeding. Many explained that this particular story was not big or important enough to warrant the effort of talking to other social scientists. Typical of many is this newsmagazine writer's explanation: "I proceeded on my own understanding. If it had been a more substantial article, I would do that [contact other social scientists]. I did a cover story on Freud last year. I spent months on it. I talked to lots of people and read far more than I could assimilate. I steeped myself in that, but not this—a three-column story. That would have been pretentious and burdensome."

Most reporters accepted the expertise of their sources on faith. Several reporters voiced general skepticism about the social sciences, but when it came to reporting a particular story, they assumed that the research was valid and that quoted experts were basing their comments on social science knowledge. They took for granted that people in these university, research institute, or government positions were qualified by virtue of their positions and their credentials, and did not inquire far into the nature of the evidence, the methods used to collect the data, or the cogency of alternative interpretations. As Fishman (1980:93) has said, "The assumed competence of the news source is the matter of concern for reporters and not necessarily the process by which the news source . . . arrives at the assertion."

Reporters usually accepted their social science sources as qualified. Said one, "One doesn't go into a Congressional hearing or write for the Rockefeller Foundation on the basis of whims. He represented a huge body of forceful opinion." Another said, "The [research organization] has been around a long time. I assume they're not trying to lead you astray. I don't check everything. I take it on faith. . . . It has credibility." Even more trusting was this remark: "I don't ask how social scientists went about their research. The public doesn't care. I assume that social scientists know what they're talking about."

Another reason for not seeking outside reviews was the newness of the material. Several reporters said that it was difficult to get social scientists to comment on a new study which they hadn't read yet. As one journalist said, "It would be hard to get reactions until it goes into the public domain or is given at an academic conference. Otherwise you're getting reactions from people who don't know about it, reactions to my description of the study. . . . That gets chancy." Several reporters said that they didn't feel a need to talk to other social scientists because they fully understood the study. "The survey was clear enough and was adequately explained." A few emphasized that they had done considerable reading on the topic and had gained a good sense of what other social scientists were writing.

One fifth of the journalists (16) did contact other social scientists in the course of developing the story. One reporter said he did so "to get more information and other perspectives." Another said, "I never write a column based on findings from just one source." Since the study she was writing about had not yet been released, what she received was not critique or interpretation of that study, but social scientists' reports of their own work on the subject. Another reporter said that she talked to other social scientists because "I didn't want to be led down a garden path. Very often you get Rashomon—separate realities. What we try to do is present as close to the objective truth as possible."

Perhaps the most intensive round robin of cross-checking was evident in this response:

> *The way I work is that I get a foundation of information and I check it with other sources. In this case, I would repeat the conversation that I had with [the social scientist] to the twelve or so experts I spoke to. If I keep hearing the same thing, then I know I have information that can't be challenged. If it is challenged, then I try to find confirmation of the disagreement. For example, for hypnosis . . . there was much controversy and disagreement and I would try to get as much information on both sides as possible. For this article, I didn't have room to get into it. That would make another story. The controversy made me not want to go into it as much.*

Instances such as this were exceptional, and they took place primarily when the story was substantial and the information was patently controversial.

Nine reporters said that the other social scientists they talked to had provided fuller explanation of study results. Two said the social scientists had given further relevant information on the subject, and one said that the social scientist gave a different perspective on the results. Most of the reporters who contacted other social scientists said that they incorporated their remarks into the story.

We coded the stories ourselves and counted the type of additional commentary that appeared in the story and its source. (See Table 2.5.) Each study was counted once, with the most critical material coded. Forty-six stories included no outside comment on the study. Twelve included comments only from non-social scientists. What social scientists provided were critiques of the study (two stories), alternative explanations of the study's results (three stories), and evidence or opinion confirming or elaborating the study's findings (seventeen stories). (Journalists collected some of the evidence in the latter category from reading rather than through personal contact with a social scientist.)

When reporters went to people other than social scientists, they were usually seeking comments about the study's findings. For a story on a crime study, they might talk to a police chief or a district attorney. In one interesting case a television newsman started out looking for a social scientist, but wound up with an official. He was preparing a story on a

TABLE 2.5

Elaboration of Study Findings in the Story

Content	N	%
Criticism of the study by other social scientist(s)	2	2.5
Criticism of the study by non–social scientist(s)	2	2.5
Alternative interpretations of findings by social scientist(s)	3	3.7
Alternative interpretations by non–social scientist(s)	3	3.7
Supporting data/opinion by social scientist(s)	17	21.3
Supporting data/opinion by non–social scientist(s)	7	8.8
No outside comment	46	57.7
TOTAL	80	100.0%

Note: Each story was coded only once. If more than one kind of material appeared, the most critical code (that is, the one that appears highest on this list) was assigned.

report which suggested a causal link between violence on television and children's aggressive behavior. Since the story had negative implications for the television industry, he said, "We want to show we are honest in coverage by covering it." He also wanted to present an opposing viewpoint. His first thought was to go to the researchers who were mentioned in the report as being among the few who had found no link between television and aggression. They worked in the research department at his own network.

> *Since they were mentioned prominently, I considered going to them. I wrestled with the problem of was it going to look bad, because it was an NBC study. Then I figured, "Aw, screw it." At NBC there was some guy in the research department who did the study. I called and asked to have him interviewed in New York. We at NBC have this holier-than-thou attitude when the government refuses interviews. So it really broke me up when NBC wouldn't let him be interviewed. They had put out a wishy-washy statement which I didn't want to use and I was still scrambling for an opposing viewpoint which would take up twenty seconds or less. So at 5:30 with a 6 P.M. hit time, we went chasing downtown to get the VP of the National Association of Broadcasters.*

The vice president of the National Association of Broadcasters appeared on the air that night saying that programming had immeasurably improved in screening out violence.

Editing

Before the story sees the light of day, it goes through an editorial selection and editing process. We do not know how many stories were weeded out by editors and failed to appear. However, given the "any old time" character of many stories, it is possible that even if they were pushed out by more compelling news on one day or week, they had opportunities to resurface. In fact, we may have picked them up in a subsequent incarnation.

Whether a story ever appears will depend on a potluck assortment of factors, such as competition from other news, whether the reporter maintains an interest in the subject, whether unfolding events provide a news peg, or whether information from other sources reinforces the interest or the urgency of the research. The importance of a social science study on whatever metric importance is measured plays only a modest part in its presentation. (See Table 2.4, which shows that 14 percent of journalists mention the importance of the topic of a study as a reason for reporting it.)

Half the reporters told us that editors had made changes in their story after they wrote it. Of these, over half said the changes were minor, and another small number said that the editor had *suggested* a change which they accepted. Very rarely did the editorial change represent a shift in emphasis. Much of the time it was a change in length, with cuts nine times more frequent than expansion. In other cases the editorial intervention was a change in wording. A typical example: "In the preliminary I filed early in the day, the lead was data on the eight-county metropolitan area. That was complicated because it was not the metropolitan area as we usually understand it. It didn't include adjacent cities in New Jersey or Connecticut. The editor suggested leading with figures from the city itself. I agreed as I reread the tortured first paragraph. The first summary I filed didn't make a lot of sense."

Asked whether they were satisfied with the final story, well over half said that they were, and over two fifths gave a "yes, but" answer. Most of the "buts" were yearnings for restoration of the uncut version. Only two reporters were unhappy with the story as it appeared.

Time Lapse Before the Story Appears

The old image of the newsreporter was someone banging out a story to meet a deadline for tomorrow's paper. Newsmagazine people may have a week, but since story ideas aren't settled for a while and new developments keep breaking, they, too, are envisioned as fighting a looming deadline. At least where social science is concerned, and undoubtedly in features more generally, the old image is out of date. First of all, there is not much banging of typewriters anymore. The newsroom has converted to word processors, which are remarkably quiet. Only a fraction of the stories on which journalists work each day are hard news, scheduled for the next edition. Journalists' answers about the length of time that elapsed between their original idea for the story and the time it appeared in print (or on the air) varied from less than a day to over two months. The median was six days. Over a third of the stories gestated for more than two weeks.

Social scientists confirmed the lag. Asked how much time there had been between the press release and publication of the story, they said two days to over two months, with one in five saying over two months. The median was about a week. The time between their conversation with the reporter and publication was somewhat shorter. Almost one in five said that they talked to the reporter the same day the story appeared, and another third said within four days. At the other extreme, one in eight said that they had talked to the reporter over a month before the story came out.

Stories that appeared immediately—the same or next day—constituted 18 percent of our sample of study stories. The headlines give the flavor: underrepresentation of women and minorities in union leadership, high birthrate for Hispanics, increase in cocaine-related deaths, training programs for disadvantaged work best on federal level, mom and pop firms threatened. Nothing about the topics obviously distinguishes these stories from those that waited days, weeks, or even months.

The Role of the Editor

Editors in the print media and news producers in television play an important part in the news process. Phyllis Endreny collected data from thirty-three editors and producers in the same ten media that we followed about a year after our interviews (Endreny 1985). She found that the tasks that almost all of them reported as "very important" in their work day were suggesting and shaping story ideas, choosing stories for publication/broadcast, ensuring reporters' detachment and fairness, and editing copy. Tasks rated as "very" or "somewhat" important by at least two thirds of them included assigning reporters, clarifying news conventions and taste standards, and attending to balance and diversity in story selection.

Like the reporters whom we interviewed, most editors in Endreny's study described themselves as positively disposed toward the social sciences. She talked to them about a specific social science story that had recently appeared in their medium. As in our study, she found that reporters, not editors, had initiated most of the stories. When the editor assigned a reporter to a story, the assignment was made not on the basis of any social science knowledge, but because of general skills and availability: "He's a wonderful writer, perceptive, open-minded," "He is a good fast reporter, but [he was assigned] partly because he was available." Nineteen editors indicated that they had given pointers to the reporter, but the advice was very general: ". . . try and translate it into human experience, go beyond the statistics," ". . . write it well and be interesting."

Endreny asked the editors and television news producers how they assessed the validity of social science studies and the competence of social scientist sources. They said that if study findings "made sense" and were "uncontroversial," they didn't think it was necessary to worry about validity. About a third of the editors said that they relied primarily on the position and institutional affiliation of the social scientist or on his/her reputation. These are assumed to be reasonable proxies for expertise. A few said that they would want to know what other experts thought. Far more often they said that they trusted the reporter's judgment. They relied on the reporter to have determined that the study was respectable and the social scientist qualified. Several people alluded to the quality of the study, but almost every reference was either oblique or cursory. Only one editor, who had an advanced degree in a social science, spoke about reviewing a study's methodology: "Since I'm familiar with experimental design and statistics, I would look at the sample design, size, and statistical applications of the study." He was a rarity. (See Part II for further detail on the interviews with editors.)

Quote Stories

In stories that incorporate quotes from social scientists, the inclusion of the quotation was always the result of the reporter's initiative. S/he found a person or a document to quote in the story.

The use of quotes is part of the standard journalistic repertoire. Quotes serve valuable purposes. First, they give credence to the journalist's account. A statement from a certified authority legitimates the point the reporter is making. Reporters may use experts' quotes in lieu of searching out relevant evidence. It takes time, and some knowledge of a field, to locate authoritative data, but with a few well-placed phone calls, a reporter can usually find a credible source to cite. Shepherd (1981:134) has written, "it appears that the press tends to print the views and interpretations of individual authorities rather than report the results of actual studies." Our inquiry suggests that they do both.

Second, quotes provide balance. When a story is controversial, reporters can use quotes to present the several sides of the argument. When they are skeptical about the official version of events, they are especially likely to seek a qualified source to voice that skepticism and/or present a different explanation. On a variety of stories, quotes provide balance and an image of fairness.

Third, quotes provide elaboration, color, and interest. A source with a novel perspective can amplify a conventional story with unexpected insights; a choice turn of phrase or a colorful metaphor can brighten up an otherwise routine story. If a source makes key points in language more apt and succinct than the journalist's own, the quote improves the story. Fresh ideas and fresh language are important contributions. Occasionally, a quote serves a fourth purpose—to acknowledge the time and effort that a source devoted to helping the reporter.

Reporters may call many people in the course of developing a story to get information, check facts, learn the complexities of the subject. Sometimes they know in advance the point that they want to make and call a person whom they expect to take that position. Often, they call a number of knowledgeable people, and they quote those statements that add credibility, balance, savor, or novelty to the story.

Deciding to Quote

We wanted to know what it was about certain stories that stimulated reporters to seek comments specifically from social scientists. To some reporters the question did not make sense. They talk to dozens of people every day on the subjects they are following. Social scientists are no special breed. If they are credible as authoritative sources and if they say something relevant to the story, then they may make it into print. But these reporters do not consciously define a particular story as requiring social science input, nor do they necessarily look for a social scientist to quote. If they are looking for information or ideas on a story about China, they can just as easily quote an assistant secretary in the State Department as a political scientist specializing in Chinese politics. In fact, it is easier for them to talk to the assistant secretary, since the State Department displays its specialists on an organizational chart, and by virtue of employing them, grants them credibility.

On the other hand, a few reporters intentionally turn to social science and consciously seek out a social scientific point of view. Among the reasons they gave were:

> We interview sociologists to find out the why of it. They're one of the few people who are willing to say why and be quoted on it.

They're invaluable for tough subjects like crime and break-up of families.

I wanted independent and disinterested people. . . . Politicians would be too biased to comment. Professors sit back. They can speak dispassionately.

Whenever I write a story, I try to touch base with the academic community and those who do research and consulting. I try to get a broad perspective.

When I thought of it [the story] as a piece for the science pages, that was a prerequisite for sources. And the major repository of information is with social scientists.

[Social science] was the whole idea of the story. Psychologists' perspective [on the arms race] has never been taken seriously or regarded as newsworthy. . . . All I was trying to do was to suggest . . . a psychological perspective on the arms race.

Journalists don't carry the weight of authority that social scientists do even when they cover a story in depth.

Choosing Social Scientists to Quote

The social scientists who appeared in quote stories were all veterans of the press. Over half of them (57 percent) had been mentioned in the media more than twenty times before. All but one had previously appeared in one or more of the national media that we were following. Quoted social scientists were much more experienced with the media than were the social scientists whose research study was reported, only 15 percent of whom had had similar (more than twenty times) exposure and a quarter of whom had never been covered by any mass media before.

The visibility of a relatively small number of social scientists worries some of their colleagues: Are they talking about subjects in their area of expertise, or are they wandering far afield and becoming what Herzog (1973:36–37) has called "anything authorities." Goodell (1977) has written about "visible scientists," the science celebrities who are willing to make pronouncements on a wide range of scientific, science-policy, and even political issues. By virtue of their eminence in science and their color and style, they are called upon by journalists to "give a scientific point of view" on almost any subject under the sun.

We found almost nobody with such free-wheeling proclivities among the social scientists whom we interviewed. When asked to describe the subjects of earlier news stories in which they had appeared, most of them reported sticking fairly close to their last. Well over four in five said that all their earlier stories had dealt with the same general field as the current story; 14 percent had been mentioned only in connection with the identical topic. When they had been quoted on more than one subject, several people noted that they had done research on each of them. One psychologist had seen his work reported on obedience to authority, quality of life in different cities, and violation of rules of queue behavior. In another case a social scientist quoted on the social effects of recession had been quoted earlier about legal services; he formerly ran a legal services program.

Only one or two people in our sample seemed ready to comment on a wide array of subjects on which they did not describe the source of their special expertise—and even they may have known more than they told us. One was an economist who has appeared in the media on a broad range of economic subjects, and the other was a psychologist who has discussed subjects as diverse as airline safety, Santa Claus, and children's swearing.

How do journalists choose them as sources? Almost a third of the time the journalist had talked to them previously and, in fact, had quoted them in previous stories. (Our data hint that the second social scientist quoted in a story is more likely to have been used as a source by the same reporter before.) In over a quarter of the cases, the reporter learned about them through the reading that s/he had been doing for the story. Said one reporter, "I saw him cited in a clipping file story"; and another, "I've studied their work for a long time, and I knew they were writing a book. I got one chapter of the galleys of the book. . . . It's written in a highly academic way, but it was helpful for making my questions apposite." Other paths to notice: the reporter's colleagues recommended the social scientist, another social scientist suggested his name, the reporter called around and a source in an earlier conversation made the suggestion, the reporter met the social scientist at a conference, the reporter called a university press office which provided the name. Not atypical:

I called around, and I got names of experts from people at the Department of Agriculture and the FHA.

Our Detroit bureau chief called the University of Michigan Institute [of Social Research].

I attended a conference on social security . . . and I heard a variety of experts. . . . One person who spoke seemed to be certain of future birth patterns . . . I got in touch with American Demographics, *which the* Wall Street Journal *recently bought, and people on the staff there recommended [the social scientist].*

There is evidence that reporters go back to the same authorities for a variety of reasons. Some have to do with efficient newsroom procedures. Once having found a person who is reliable and knowledgeable, and whose telephone number you have, it makes sense to return to him/her rather than embark on a quest for someone new. Furthermore, some sources—and these are the valued ones—are willing to cooperate on a spectrum of issues; they speak concisely; they have a flair for the dramatic; as Goodell has noted, they speak in quotes. If they don't feel qualified to talk on a subject, they say so and give you the name of someone who is. At best, they add an original angle to what otherwise might be a routine story. As one *Wall Street Journal* reporter said, "We use him so much, it's getting to be somewhat of an embarrassment."

An article in *Washington Monthly* (Waldman 1986:33–40) describes the press's "addiction" to quoting political scientist Norman Ornstein. Major news organizations quoted him over 140 times in both 1985 and 1986. According to his journalist-followers, his attraction is partly that he is "the master of the pithy quote" (p. 35), who makes "a straightforward, bold, declarative" unconditional statement (p. 34). Part of his appeal is that he is readily available, "one of the fastest phone call-returners" in Washington (p. 35) and rarely refuses to talk on a subject. He is also well informed, perceptive, carefully nonpartisan, and mainstream in his opinions. Waldman suggests, too, that quoting Ornstein is sometimes a "prop" for reporters, giving them a way of making the point they want to make without having to state an opinion of their own. He notes that the *Washington Monthly* itself quoted Ornstein three times in one story just the month before. Arguably more serious is his contention that reporters use Ornstein when they want to reach a conclusion but "they haven't found enough evidence to prove it" (p. 38). He notes that reporters believe that Ornstein quotes "give the story more credibility." The reasons are much like those we heard from our journalist respondents.

Yet after a time sources "wear out." They are overused and editors want new names. So reporters engage in a certain rotation, dropping some old favorites and adding new ones. This doesn't necessarily mean that old sources fade from view; reporters from other media may pick them up and renew their circulation in other outlets.

We asked the social scientists how they had come to be quoted. The reason that they gave most often was the work they had been doing on the topic. Some mentioned books or papers they had published, testimony they had given, conferences they had addressed, or stories featuring them in other media. Another set of answers referred to the channels that linked them to the press. Foremost among these was the recommendation of their name by another social scientist, followed by their own visibility, previous acquaintance with the journalist, recommendation from other journalists, and the fact that the organization they work for is a regular source of information for the press (for example, Brookings). All but one person had a good idea of how they had captured media attention.

Of the forty-seven quote stories on which we interviewed, the reporter and social scientist talked to each other on forty-one. In the other six cases the reporter took the quotation from a book, an article, hearing testimony, or a story in another mass media. All six of these social scientists acknowledged the authorship and accuracy of the quotation.

We asked the social scientists if they felt qualified to comment on the subject that they had been asked to address. Well over 90 percent said yes, some with exclamation points. Nobody said no, but a few people suggested that they were not particularly expert on the subject.

In very few cases did they have time to prepare their remarks. Only four people said that they had advance notice of the conversation and had time to organize their thoughts or information. Three people said that they had their materials in front of them during the conversation. Everyone else responded to reporters' questions on the spur of the moment.

With all the people whom journalists talk to in the course of a day, the quotes they select to include in a story usually have to be special (although in two cases, what was special was only that they came shortly before the deadline). Asked what was special or newsworthy about the quotes they used from social scientists, the leading answers were:

interesting	46%
original, novel, a different perspective	45
clear, succinct, apt	33
provided balance	22
said what I wanted to say	15
social scientist was expert, provided credibility	11

Some of the responses about a different perspective:

He had an unusual way of looking at it.

It struck me, this is a different thing than policy-makers say. Policy-makers' statements were nitty gritty. He said lots of things . . . gave the larger picture.

On aptness of the quote:

> *Generally quotes are used when someone says it better than you can. ——— is quotable, he speaks in simple terms. He basically said who is getting hurt and who is not getting hurt by the recession. It's much better if he says it and not I. It has more credibility. It livens the story up, gives it news value and style.*

On balance:

> *When constructing a story, that paragraph tried to show one extreme of economic opinion.*

A journalist who used quotes to say what he wanted to say:

> *My job in this story was to lay out the situation, to trace roots, to give some idea about what was happening. Basically, it was an analytical piece. . . . Once the situation is tied down, then you contact them [social scientists] and pick out the most illuminating quote.*

On expertness:

> *He is an expert on military manpower problems as they relate to education and demographic trends.*

Talking to social scientists can provide more than a quotable quote. Three quarters of the reporters said that the conversation had influenced the story. Some said that social scientists had expanded their understanding of the subject and broadened the scope of the story they wrote. One journalist said: "He gave a different perspective about what IRAs [individual retirement accounts] would do to the economy, that it's important where the money comes from and not where it goes." Some indicated that social scientists had provided a counterweight to the ordinary point of view. According to a reporter writing on Federal Reserve monetary policy, "I contacted [the first social scientist] because he is the left-most mainline economist. We wanted his perspective. . . . And [the second social scientist] is a well-known name representing a particular policy viewpoint." One third of the journalists said that the social scientists had confirmed, elaborated, and given supporting illustrations for the theme they were developing. Only a quarter of the reporters said that the discussion with the social scientist, other than use of the quote, had failed to influence the development of the story.

Social scientists had similar impressions after reading the story. Over

half believed they had influenced the treatment of the subject. One sociologist said, "He called all my references [people I had recommended] and
used my ideas." Some thought that they may have elaborated or illustrated
the story that the reporter was writing but hadn't altered it. Somewhat over
a quarter believed that they had no influence on the story. As one political
scientist said, "He had a particular story in mind when he called. He called
to fill out the information. He even said, 'This is my thesis and what do you
think of it?'"

So far, the use of social scientists as expert sources sounds much like
the use of any other expert group. Is there anything special about social
scientists? One distinctive characteristic is the degree to which their expertise is grounded in research. Over two thirds of the journalists said they
went to the social scientist in the first place because of the research s/he
had done on the subject. Just under two thirds of them said that the quote
they used in the story was based on social science research. This empirical
foundation, or the supposition that it exists, represents a major element
that distinguished social science quotes from others.

A further distinction, as is apparent in some of the earlier quotes
from journalists, is that social scientists are sometimes assumed to be
dispassionate. They have no particular axe to grind and thus can afford to
be fair and objective in their remarks. Not every reporter is convinced of
this, and as we will see in chapter 3, some reporters distrust the political
bias of social science. Others believe that whatever disinterestedness social scientists may have is outweighed by their bad habits—preeminently
an addiction to jargon. But the lack of a stake in the situation—and a
reflective stance—are widely regarded as special assets.

Of course, some social scientists are newsworthy for exactly the opposite reason. They are widely known as advocates for certain positions—on
economic policy, environmental protection, political party reform. Reporters call upon them when they want their positions represented. But in
most cases social scientists become news sources because of the research
base that underlies their statements and gives them authoritativeness, the
credibility that comes from their credentials and affiliations, and on some
occasions an assumption of unbiased fairness.

Conclusions

One hypothesis presented in chapter 1 was that reporters treat social
science much as they treat any other topic. They select stories by the usual
journalistic criteria and shape them to fit the template of news. The data in
this chapter lend support to that hypothesis. What makes a study news-

worthy is its topic. Reporters were apt to select social science studies for reporting if their subject was related to topics already in the news, if they were interesting and new. The quality of findings in research terms had little to do with newsworthiness.

There appears to be a certain haphazardness in the transition of social science studies into news. Some research organizations and sponsoring agencies put considerable effort into reaching the media, through press releases, press conferences, and direct contact, while others are relatively inactive. When I talked to the chief press officer at my own university, he said that his office rarely releases news about faculty research: "Our faculty are knowledgeable enough so that if they want to publicize their work, they know which media people to take it to themselves." Other universities and research organizations take a more aggressive stance. Since 60 percent of the studies that became stories had held press conferences and/or issued press releases, and over a quarter of the stories were directly traceable to those efforts, the degree of initiative that organizations take would seem to make a difference in which research comes to media notice.

The influence of government sponsors in promoting research is notable. That so many of the stories in our inquiry derived from government public relations is perhaps attributable in part to the sheer volume of research that government funds. Coverage is also likely to owe something to the activity of government press offices and the presence of large numbers of reporters in Washington. Government agencies, unlike universities or research institutes, *are* a beat. Press conferences under their aegis are routinely covered.

One of our original hypotheses presented in chapter 1 was that the pattern of reported social science reflects the entrepreneurial activities of aggressive social scientists. This hypothesis requires modification. To the extent that reporters are responding to entrepreneurialism, it is less the individual social scientist who is responsible for coverage (only 6 percent of study stories could be traced to a social scientist's initiating contact) and more the research or sponsoring organization. Organizational press releases and press conferences were the most common routes to notice. But the data in this chapter refer only to studies that made it into print (or onto the air). We cannot yet say whether they differ in entrepreneurial activity from studies that fell by the wayside. In chapter 5 we will look at press conferences and in chapter 6 we will look at press releases that did *and did not* yield stories.

If there is an erratic quality on the "sending" side, there is also an element of fitful attentiveness on the "receiving" end. From a quarter to a half of the stories, depending on how we count (see Tables 2.2 and 2.3), originated with the journalist; in 15 percent of the cases, the journalist went out looking for a social science study on a particular subject in which s/he was interested. But other reporters are much less interested even in social science that comes in over the transom.

The hypothesis about reporters' lack of social science knowledge is not directly addressed in this chapter. We present data in chapter 3 on their educational background, as well as on social scientists' ratings of the stories they wrote. What we see in this chapter is that reporters and editors paid only passing attention to research quality. They looked to the positions, institutional affiliations, and reputations of social scientists as a way to judge the competence of their research; editors often left the determination to the reporter. While reporters read research reports and even additional articles about the research subject when they believed that a study needed checking, the common procedures were to talk to the researcher (over half of the reporters did so) or to another social scientist (one case in five). They checked with other social scientists primarily when the story was big and the findings controversial.

When reporters quoted a social scientist, it was they who took the initiative in making contact. Quoting authorities is part of standard journalistic practice, and they usually went to social scientists in the same way they go to any source who has relevant information or opinions. Almost a third of the reporters knew the social scientist they quoted from previous contacts, but when they were looking for someone new, their procedures were: find their names through reading on the subject; get recommendations from colleagues in the newsroom, another social scientist, or a non–social science source; make contact at a conference or meeting; get a referral from a university press office. Many reporters were looking for a qualified source, whether or not the source was a social scientist, but some reporters purposely chose a social scientist, usually because they believed that s/he had special research-based knowledge. A few believed that social scientists had a broader perspective and were less constrained or had less of a personal stake. Reporters selected the quote that they used in the story because it was interesting, offered a different perspective, was succinct and apt, provided balance, or (for 15 percent of the stories) because it said what the reporter wanted to say. Most reporters and social scientists believed that their conversation had influenced the development of the story.

These data give only mild support to the hypothesis that reporters use social science to legitimate their work. Only occasionally does a quote serve the function of validating a reporter's a priori position. Still, legitimation may be a not undesirable side effect of the practice of quoting experts. In the next chapter we examine reporters' attitudes toward social science to see if they view it with such respect as to be worth pursuing for legitimation purposes.

Which studies and which social scientists make it into the media appears to be a function of two relatively unsystematic processes. But despite erratic promotion among social science organizations and fitful attention on the journalists' side, the media succeed in reporting a variety of good social science studies. For quotes, they contact established people who say that they are qualified to talk on the subject. An impressive measure of how well they do on both study and quote stories is the recognition that media-reported social scientists receive within their disciplines. According to a review of the Social Science Citation Index, which lists all references to each social scientist's books and papers in the scientific periodical literature, 80 percent of those who appeared in these stories had their articles or books cited by peers in the preceding year. This compares with fewer than half of all social scientists who are cited. The mean number of citations for the media-reported social scientists during the year was 25.5 compared with 4.3 for all social scientists cited (see Part II). Through unsystematic and seemingly hit-or-miss procedures, journalists usually managed to report respectable research and reputable social scientists.

3

How Journalists and Social Scientists View the Reporting of Social Science

We want to know what accounts for the pattern of reporting of social science that appears in the pages of newspapers and newsmagazines and on television news. Part of the answer must lie in the attitudes and values of journalists and what they think about the social sciences. The degree of training and understanding that they have of the social sciences must also have an effect. Social scientists' attitudes probably play a part, too—how they feel about current reporting, their willingness to cooperate with reporters, and their judgment of stories in which they have appeared. These are the topics to which we turn in this chapter.

The View from the Newsroom

Social Science Not a Journalistic Category

In the course of pretesting our interviews, we talked to a number of reporters who had just written a story which we classified as social science, and we asked them if this was the first time that they had written stories about social science. Uniformly they were taken aback; some seemed to think that we were talking gibberish. In their minds the current story was not about social science at all. They were writing about crime or business or politics or education. That they were reporting the results of *research* on the topic or citing the remarks of a *social scientist* was of little consequence. It was the *topic* of the story that provided the frame of reference for their work.

Newspeople do not think about social science as a category and they do not treat it as a category. Sociology seems to be a particularly fuzzy construct. Political science has a more clear-cut image, but one that they do not necessarily include under social science on first encounter. Much of the reporting of political science has to do with elections, and most of it is based on polls and surveys. On other political topics reporters tend to see themselves and their fellows as experts. As Gans (1979:132) has noted, journalists are "expected to have one universal specialty: politics." Economics is the social science whose definition reporters seem to understand best (although they don't always think of it as a social science), and they also have a regular home for it—the business section. Business writers have a closer connection with economists than any other part of the newspaper or newsmagazine has with social scientists of other disciplines. Business was one of the early substantive beats in the press, and reporters in the business sections may come to work with a graduate degree in economics or specialize in economics in the course of their work.

Social science is not a beat. In our study we interviewed only one reporter who said his beat was social science. The specialized assignments that have emerged in the press over the past fifty years slice the world up into different segments. Beats developed in response to events. Labor, science, and agriculture became beats in the late 1920s (Schudson 1978:145, citing Emery 1972). Business and the economy became important after the Great Depression and in the New Deal years. As government grew, reporters were assigned to agency beats, to cover the White House, the Departments of Justice and Defense, the Supreme Court. Agency beats do not call for the same degree of content specialty, since the reporter is expected to write about everything that happens at the agency from fraud to politics.

Science reporting came of age in the 1950s with the space program (Goodfield 1981). Recent years have witnessed specialties in education, health and medicine, law, and the environment. In the newsmagazines writers assigned to such back-of-the-book sections as religion and justice may be or become specialists, although competition for space is so keen that such sections do not make it into the magazine every week.

Television has considerably less specialization on staff than have the large newspapers and newsmagazines, with beats largely restricted to science, health, the economy, and ecology (Gans 1979:132). Smaller newspapers, too, are limited in the extent to which they can afford to deploy specialists. Even among the major print media we were interviewing, beats were often defined in very broad terms, and reporters frequently covered stories that seemed remote from their reported specialty.

What is most significant about the growth of specialization in the media for purposes of the current discussion is its lack of fit with the social science disciplines. Except for economics, the media don't divide up the world along the same lines as does the academy. The result of this discrepancy has profound consequences for the reporting of the social sciences: stories about social science are not covered by a coterie of specialist reporters but by hundreds of different reporters who have little special knowledge about the methods, substance, or theory of the disciplines.

Since there is no social science "beat," it is sometimes supposed that science writers are the logical people to write about the social sciences. However, in our study, only 7 percent of the social science stories were written by science writers. One reason is the emphasis on topic to which we have already alluded. If the social science story has to do with reform of the welfare system, neither editor nor reporter would consider a science reporter suitable; the story would fall more readily to someone who covers welfare or politics. Another reason is science writers' lack of expertise and interest in the "soft" sciences. Some of them seem to have assimilated the norms of the physicists and astronomers with whom they consort and disdain the sponginess of the social sciences. Or else they recognize their lack of knowledge. Dunwoody (1980:19–20) found that none of the seventeen members of the "inner club" of science journalists whom she interviewed professed to have any social science expertise: "Few feel they know enough about social science research techniques to evaluate studies and make news decisions. The typical response is to avoid social science. . . . So what's news to the inner club is *not* likely to be social science."

Writing about the social sciences is dispersed over many different reporters on papers and newsmagazines. The journalists whom we interviewed told us that their regular assignment was:

General assignment	22%
Business/economy	20
Political news	16
Social issues (e.g., crime, welfare)	16
Features (e.g., living, behavior, family)	8
Science	7
Education	5

Social science	1
Column	1
Other	2
Unclear	2 (N = 127)

Educational Preparation

In general, reporters were remarkably well educated. Ninety-seven percent were college graduates, and most had attended high quality schools.
Over a third had graduated from Ivy League colleges, with Harvard the
leading alma mater (eleven graduates) followed by Yale (six). Forty-six
percent had done graduate work, and 32 percent held a graduate degree.
For 27 percent this was a master's degree, about half of which were in
journalism, and for 5 percent a Ph.D. or professional degree. The leading
graduate school by far was Columbia, which awarded eight master's degrees in journalism, five master's degrees in other subjects, and two doctorates. Well over half the journalists had majored in journalism or English
literature, and almost a quarter in another of the humanities. Four of them
had majored in a natural or biological science; fourteen in one of the
social sciences.[1]

We asked if they had taken courses in any of the social sciences in
college or graduate school. Almost three quarters indicated that they had.
Or to put this statement in more newsworthy style, one quarter of the
reporters who are writing about the social sciences in the major media say
they have never taken a social science course. Over half of them took
courses in several social sciences, with political science the most popular,
followed by economics, sociology, and, much less often mentioned, psychology. In addition, over a quarter reported that they have close friends
or relatives who are social scientists.

For most reporters their formal preparation in social science is modest at best. Yet journalists tend to be quick studies. Because they are
expected to master a wide variety of fields in quick succession, they learn
how to find appropriate sources for information, ask questions, and probe
answers. The journalists on these elite media are a particularly knowledgeable group. Without demonstrated success in local or regional media,
most of them would not have arrived in these positions.

---

[1] The reporters in this inquiry had considerably more education than national samples of
journalists that have been studied. In 1971 Johnstone et al. (1976:200) found that 50 percent
were college graduates and an additional 8 percent held graduate degrees. In 1982–83, just
about the same time as our interviews, Weaver and Wilhoit (1986:47) found that 59 percent
of journalists were college graduates and an additional 11 percent held graduate degrees.

Nor are they novices. Their median length of experience in journalism is sixteen years. Four of them (3 percent) have racked up forty years or more. Only 9 percent report fewer than seven years as journalists. In a later chapter we will see that there is little relationship between a reporter's formal training in the social sciences and the relevant social scientist's evaluation of the story s/he had written.

Disposition Toward Social Science

We asked journalists their views about social science. Granted that these were journalists who had just written a story that contained social science elements. Granted that we were social scientists who were doing the asking. Still, the general tenor of response was favorable. Responses to the question about whether their disposition toward the social sciences was positive or negative were:

Unqualifiedly positive	48%
Fairly positive or positive with some qualification	12
Mixed, fairly evenly split between pro and con	17
Neutral	15
Never gave the subject a thought	1
More negative than positive, or mostly negative	5
Other (nonevaluative)	2 (N = 122)

Compared with the responses of such other groups as high government officials (Weiss 1980; Caplan 1977), their enthusiasm for the social sciences is tempered. Yet three in five responded positively compared with one in twenty who responded negatively. Editors at these same media say that their attitudes are even more favorable (Endreny 1985).

When journalists reported their attitude toward the social sciences as positive, most of them did not elaborate. Only a few went further and said such things as these: "Terribly important. . . . Social science can contribute to the public good"; "I have great respect for them"; "They are the most interesting field of study for me"; "They have a lot of expertise that I hope they continue to share with people who don't have the opportunity to meet them first hand"; "As a journalist and as a human being, I'm glad for their tradition of inquiry." The comments were general and very polite.

It was when they had mixed feelings that reporters became eloquent. Among the comments they gave were these:

Mixed. A lot of social science research is rather limited and stupid. But some is very fine. I am biased against a lot of statistical research because you can make statistics lie. I am impressed with research that talks to people. I get angry at many social science research papers that are full of jargon and badly written.

I can't categorize it. Some of it is useful. I have to rely on the validity of scientists and eventually learn by experience who and what seems to be responsible.

Positive. But sometimes social scientists waste time studying obscure issues. There's a huge gap now between what social scientists are doing and governmental and national concerns.

Social scientists like David Riesman are brilliant, original, perceptive thinkers. But I'm not favorably disposed to the idea that you can measure absolutely anything you set out to measure . . . I think it's useful and has a lot to say about our society.

I'm a friendly critic.

Several people mentioned their concern about the politicized nature of social science. There is an undercurrent in many of the interviews that somewhere out there an objective truth exists, and the journalists' task is to find it. They are wary of all sources—bureaucratic, political, or social scientific—that they believe try to lead them away from this image of pure and unalloyed truth. One person said about social science, "I'm skeptical. Certain people and certain research is of consequence. Some is politicized." Another, who reported herself "both positive and negative," said, "I value the information but I'm wary of its political use." Another concluded, "Social science information has to be checked to be respected."

If there is one response that captures the range of positive and negative elements in journalists' views, it may be this one:

Positive. Well, let me amend that. . . . Positive, but keeping my hands on my wallet. Social science research is essential to understanding why, what, and how we do things. . . . But there are more people in social science more interested in empire building than an honest quest for the truth. So you have to evaluate the information while looking at it. I view social science as essential. But you have

*to evaluate the information carefully and present it in such a way
that it is free of polemic and is fair. Researchers are in a position to
ride a variety of hobbyhorses. Just as scientists need to evaluate the
information that's produced and received, journalists do also. But I
wouldn't be writing about social scientists if I didn't feel positive
about them.*

Several scholars have become concerned about the absence of this
kind of healthy skepticism in reporting about the natural and biological
sciences. According to Nelkin (1984) and Goodfield (1981), science writers accept too much scientific research on faith and fail to subject it to
appropriate scrutiny. They tend to portray scientists as impartial arbiters
and solvers of the nation's problems, rather than as fallible human beings
who differ among themselves and create problems as well as solve them.
About the social sciences, Philip Meyer warned journalists almost two
decades ago that "newspapers must learn to recognize" social science that
is "a few data and a lot of 'interpretation' . . . , the absence of true connection between the data and the interpretation . . . hidden by academic
jargon" and distinguish that from "the new breed which digs for facts and
produces solid information which does deserve to be the basis of public
policy. This task, separating the scientific from the spurious, is not being
done today" (Meyer 1967:5). Among today's reporters of social science, at
least an articulate minority present themselves as skeptical enough to want
to check social science evidence with concern and care. In chapter 2, we
looked at the extent to which they follow through on this task in practice.

Reporters' Reference Groups

The kind of audience that reporters have in mind when they write social
science might be expected to influence reportage. Darnton (1975) suggests that journalists do not have a clear image of their readers but tend to
write on the assumption that whatever interests them and their fellow-
reporters will interest the public. Tunstall's study (1971) of British specialist-reporters found that they were indifferent to market research that revealed the composition of the audience. When asked the proportion of
working class members in the audience, half of them did not know or did
not reply, and nine in ten of the rest underestimated the proportion by an
average of 20 percentage points. He concludes that "the specialist pays
more attention to news sources, executives, and competitor-colleagues
than to the millions of audience members" (Tunstall 1971:252). Playwright
Arnold Wesker, who spent several months at the London *Sunday Times,*
quotes one journalist: "Journalists write for other journalists, the people

they have lunch with rather than the reader" (1977:12). Gans (1979), too, says that they write for their editors and their colleagues.

If their image of the audience is hazy and unimportant, and if they care primarily about the reaction of the editor and fellow-reporters, then we might expect that the dispositions of reporters and editors just noted would set the climate for social science reporting. The mildly favorable context of opinion in the newsroom would mildly encourage reportage.

We asked the journalists in our study about the audience they had in mind when they wrote the recent story with social science content. Our question said that we assumed it was important for the story to satisfy their own criteria and those of their editor. "How important was it for the story to also satisfy the criteria of the following audiences: other journalists? the average reader? the informed reader? the social scientist [whom you quoted] [who did the study]? other social scientists?"

Despite what scholars have said about the dimness of the audience in reporters' minds, our respondents overwhelmingly endorsed the average reader and the informed reader as the audience they set out to satisfy. Almost 90 percent said that serving the average reader was the name of the game. Over 80 percent said that they aimed to appeal to the informed reader, with a number noting that their readers *are* informed readers. This is the prevailing rhetoric.

Overwhelmingly they disavowed any interest in satisfying the criteria of fellow-journalists. Of the five audiences we asked about, this was the one that collected the largest pecentage of categorically "not important" responses. Over 60 percent said that other journalists were not important, and another quarter gave such answers as "If I satisfy myself and my editor, I'm satisfying other journalists," or "I never think about them." One in six said that they accorded some degree of importance to their fellows' opinions.

It is not obvious what accounts for the intensity with which most of them rejected the idea of paying attention to what other reporters think. Perhaps they were objecting to the idea that journalism has no clear professional standards and that criteria have to be negotiated on a person-by-person basis. "Satisfying the criteria of other journalists" might have sounded as though journalism lacks a professional code that its practitioners internalize. Or perhaps the question suggested a guild of narcissistic professionals intent only on pleasing each other and deserting their public purpose. In any event, not even social scientists were viewed as quite so irrelevant.

Satisfying the criteria of the social scientist mentioned in the story was considered important by few reporters (9 percent), although relatively few said outright that it was unimportant. Half of them said that what was important was to be accurate; how the social scientist felt about the story was not relevant. Some gave other responses, such as that they don't know what social scientists' criteria are or they don't think about their criteria. One journalist said, "His criteria probably would be that you couldn't tell the story in less than 5,000 words. I'm sure that I don't satisfy any social scientist at all." A pervasive subtext was that they are not in business to please the social scientist or promote his interests. Their job is to write a clear accurate story.

As for the community of social scientists, reporters rejected them as an audience deserving special consideration, too. Some said again that it was important to be accurate and not misrepresent social science; a few others said that they want other social scientists to understand the story. But by a wide margin they said that they were not concerned with whatever other criteria it would take to satisfy social scientists. Worrying about the niceties that absorb social scientists is not their business.

Obviously most of the people from whom journalists get information are not social scientists but officials, politicians, businessmen, football coaches. "Satisfying the criteria" of such sources of news would usually mean presenting them in the best possible light. Although we had worked very hard on the wording of the question to stress satisfying the *criteria* of the different groups rather than the people, it may have sounded like much the same sort of promotion. Journalists disdain interest in such an endeavor. Only a small minority were willing to entertain the notion that it is important to attend to social science norms other than accuracy (such as, perhaps, placing current results in the context of prior research, reporting qualifications and conflicting evidence, recognizing the researcher's judgment of the most significant results). Their answers seem to place more emphasis on keeping their distance and not becoming co-opted than on maintaining a relationship with the source from whom they gathered information for the story and might want to go back to for future stories.

After they responded to the structured question about the importance of other people's criteria, we asked reporters what they saw as the most important criteria for a story such as the one they had just written. In order of frequency, the answers were: accuracy (64 percent), clarity (51 percent), interest (44 percent), helpfulness to readers (20 percent), and balance (15 percent). Accuracy was important in the rule books of all audiences. Clarity was important so that layman and specialist would be able to understand what the story was about. Help to readers was mentioned only in connection with stories on research results, for example, a study on the success rates of different stop-smoking programs. Balance was valued more in stories that quoted the remarks of social scientists, where quoting a knowledgeable expert gave perspective to the report. These responses capture journalistic priorities in writing stories with (and no doubt without) social science content, counterposed to any concern with the criteria of particular groups of readers.

The View from Social Science

What social scientists think about the media can influence their initiative in bringing research results to media attention, their willingness to talk with reporters and answer questions, the care with which they check stories that are being written, and the word they pass along to colleagues about the effect of being reported on one's reputation and career. Although reporting plays out on the home ground of reporters, the actions of social scientists might well have an effect on the shape of social science in the news.

Views on Accuracy, Emphasis, and Omissions

We asked the social scientists whose research or comments had just appeared in a news story, "Do you think that news reporting of social science is generally accurate or not?" More of them gave answers on the "accurate" side of the ledger (35 percent) than on the "inaccurate" side (23 percent), but many found it difficult to generalize or to answer the question at all. The overall impression is one of skepticism. The responses were:

Accurate	8%	
Mostly accurate	11	
Accurate considering media constraints	16	
A great deal of variation, difficult to general-ize	17	
Mostly inaccurate	23	
Other	6	
Can't say	17	
Unclear	2	(N = 127)

This type of mixed review seems typical of the corridor gossip in places where social scientists gather. It is also in line with many of the anecdotes and analyses that have appeared in social science publications (for example, Walum 1975; Weigel and Pappas 1981; McCall and Stocking 1983).

Many respondents made interesting comments about the state of reporting. Some thought that it was likely to be accurate under certain special conditions. Consider this remark with two "if" clauses:

> *Generally if there's a skilled person doing the reporting, I've been impressed by the intelligent consideration given to the material by the person, if they've done some background preparation.*

Others were dubious about accuracy because of journalists' uncritical trust in their social scientist sources.

> *Not very accurate. Reporters attribute expertise too easily. The solution is to account more modestly with qualifications, because truth is often rather slippery.*

Several people were more concerned about the ways in which journalists selected social science to report than about the accuracy of individual stories.

> *What it [the media] does look at is generally accurate. . . . The issue is what is reported and what isn't, because then you get inadequacies. . . .*

> *My concern is not accuracy, but the selection of which stories they choose to report. That's true of all news, not just social science. They gear stories to their readership. A generally vaguely liberal paper cites generally vaguely liberal studies. Accuracy is a relatively trivial concern of mine compared with a more representative selection of all the important findings available.*

> *What needs work is that the media picks up one side, the controversial side, as* the results *and not a portion of the results.*

A few respondents suggested that problems in reporting might be the fault of social scientists.

> *I tend to trust most reporters, as I think they tend to be accurate. More often than not, I think social scientists are to blame for unclear or bad reportage.*

> *I don't think findings in sociology are terribly important. Over the last twenty years, they've contradicted each other every five years. They are more contradictory than the press.*

We also asked social scientists their judgments of the story in which they

TABLE 3.1

Social Scientists' Opinions of Story in Which They Appeared

	Accuracy (N = 127)	Appropriate Emphasis (N = 123)	Completeness (N = 120)
Satisfactory	60%	70%	42%
Mostly Satisfactory, Considering	26	11	20
A Matter of Judgment	—	8	—
Don't Remember	—	—	10
Left Out Things	6	—	28
Emphasized Minor Point	—	4	—
Distorted, Wrong	8	7	—

had just appeared. Here the responses were considerably different. Asked whether the story in which they figured was accurate, three out of five said yes without qualifications. Another 17 percent mentioned a minor error but were basically satisfied, and 9 percent said the story was generally accurate considering media constraints on story length and focus. On the other end, 6 percent said that the story left out information or put findings in a misleading context, and 8 percent said there was a major error or the story was mostly wrong. (See Table 3.1.)

This is a remarkable—and unexpected—endorsement of media accuracy. Eighty-six percent of social scientists whose work or comments had just appeared said that they were basically satisfied with the reporting. Social scientists who were quoted were more satisfied than those whose study was reported. Seventy percent of the social scientists quoted in a story said unqualifiedly that the article was accurate compared with 54 percent of study authors. Reporting the results of a study is a complex undertaking, and there are more opportunities for error.

We asked social scientists whether the emphasis in the news story was appropriate. They were just about as satisfied on this score. More than 80 percent said that the emphasis was satisfactory, or satisfactory considering media constraints. Eight percent said that it was a matter of judgment, suggesting that they would have preferred a different emphasis although the reporter's choice was OK. Only 11 percent said that the story emphasized minor points, omitted major points, or was distorted. Again, people whose statements were quoted were happier with the news account: 85 percent of them unqualifiedly responded that the emphasis in the story was appropriate, compared with 60 percent of social scientists whose study was reported.

The third question asked whether anything essential had been omitted from the story.[2] Given the brevity of most news articles, this is a particularly stringent indicator of satisfaction. Almost everyone (reporters included) would like more space devoted to their work than the cruel world allows. Although they were not as satisfied with completeness as they were with accuracy and emphasis, even here most social scientists were relatively contented. Among the people *quoted* in a story 40 percent said nothing important had been left out; 27 percent said they didn't remember or couldn't identify anything specific. Many had talked to the reporter for a long time and had discussed many things, but nothing leaped to mind as "omitted." A third (33 percent) of those quoted said that some important things *had* failed to make their way into the story.

Among the *research investigators* 42 percent said that nothing essential had been omitted. Another 23 percent said that the story omitted a good deal, but gave the most important elements of the study. Five percent said that the story left out some things that were important in the study but not relevant to the story that the journalist was writing. Another 5 percent said that the study was not the focus of the story, but was used as an ancillary reference. Twenty-five percent indicated that there were important omissions. The last column in Table 3.1 shows the combined response of quote and study respondents.

The proof of the pudding is the willingness to eat the pudding again. We asked social scientists whether they would be willing to cooperate with the media in the future. Only one person said probably not. Three quarters (76 percent) said yes without any qualifications; 11 percent said yes, it's part of my job (many of these were social scientists in government positions); 7 percent said they'd be willing to cooperate but they would be more careful; 5 percent said they would if they had time (several indicating that when reporters descend, they often come in droves, and answering all the calls can consume days). Clearly experience with the media was satisfactory enough to encourage repetition.

Social scientists who have appeared in the news are considerably more positive about the media's handling of the story than the general public. In a poll conducted by the Gallup Organization for *Newsweek* in October 1984 one question asked, "What has been your experience: in things you have been involved with or know about personally, have the media got the facts straight, or have they been inaccurate?" Responses were: facts straight, 46 percent; inaccurate, 37 percent; don't know, 17 percent (*Newsweek,* October 22, 1984). Asked to put themselves in a

---

[2] The interview on studies asks about the omission of "facts . . . essential for understanding the study"; the interview on quotes asked about the omission of "important things you said to the journalist."

position analogous to that of our social scientists—inside knowledge of the situation—the public gives the media a much narrower margin of confidence. Still the public's global ratings of media accuracy are high. When we look at general judgments of the three categories of media most similar to those in our inquiry—"nationally influential newspapers," "newsmagazines," and "network TV news"—we find that 78 percent of the public say that the newspapers and newsmagazines are accurate and 81 percent say TV is accurate.

Complaints About Coverage

Satisfied as most social scientists were with reportage, they still had complaints. For the social scientists whose *study* received media coverage, we asked whether the reporter had added any interpretation of his/her own. In 29 percent of the cases they said that the reporter had done so. Asked whether the reporter's interpretation of the study was reasonable, just under half of this group thought that it was.

The question of whether reporters should add their own conclusions or implications was raised in a study about science news. Ryan (1979) asked both journalists and scientists whether they agreed with the statement, "A science writer should not interpret a scientist's technical conclusions." Journalists and scientists came down on different sides, with scientists agreeing and journalists disagreeing. Apparently, the social scientists in our study would agree with Ryan's scientists—and the statement.

We asked social scientists what they would have liked to see different in the story. Forty-eight percent said that it was fine as it was. Six percent had a minor quibble—mention of a co-author, proper use of a technical term, or such. Thirty-eight percent wished that the story had been substantively different, including those who wanted more of the study's findings or more of what they said included. Seven percent said they would have liked a very different story. The social scientists who were quoted were much more satisfied here again. Sixty-six percent said they wanted nothing different (compared with 37 percent of study authors), and none of them yearned for a markedly different story (compared with 11 percent of study authors).

During the course of the interview, the social scientists voiced complaints about the story in response to a number of different questions. We aggregated all the dissatisfactions and coded them. The most common complaint was oversimplification: 35 percent of the social scientists, at one time or another in the interview, indicated that the story had oversimplified their meaning. Other complaints were much less common. Five percent complained about a misleading headline, and 4 percent (five people) charged the reporter with playing up sensational aspects of their work.

So there are complaints. Yet overall, it is a remarkably cheerful picture and stands in sharp contrast to the views of reporting of social science in general. The discrepancy presents a puzzle worth examining.

Before we try to figure out what accounts for the differences in level of satisfaction, let us note that this pattern of opinion is by no means unique. Studies of science reporting have found very similar attitudes among natural scientists (Krieghbaum 1967; Tichenor et al. 1970). They have jaundiced views of science reporting in general, but they like the stories about their own work.

Several surveys of public attitudes show similar patterns of response. People tend to be dissatisfied with public schools in general, hospital care in general, and Congress in general, but they report considerable satisfaction with the public school attended by their own child, their own experience with hospital care, and their own congressman. Similarly, most people do not believe that newspapers are generally fair or accurate, but they believe that the paper they read is fine. When they have personal experience or knowledge of an institution, people rate it more highly than they rate the whole institutional system. (On education, see Smith and Gallup 1977; Gallup 1981; on hospital care, Harris and Associates 1978; on Congress, Gallup 1983; on newspapers, American Society of Newspaper Editors 1984).

Reasons for Differences in Level of Satisfaction

Coverage by the National Media.   One possible explanation for the difference in satisfaction between social science reporting in general and the specific story is that we are dealing here with the national media. They are, after all, the elite media of the country, and it is possible that they do a more responsible job than regional and local newspapers, magazines, radio, and television. And that does indeed turn out to be what social scientists suggest—but the influence on opinion seems to be marginal.

We asked the social scientists about their previous experiences with the press, and those who had been covered before reported slightly lower levels of satisfaction for the earlier encounters. Although some of the stories that they were referring to had appeared in the same media that we were following, they had also been covered by regional and local papers and radio. When they explicitly compared the current story with earlier coverage, the current story was judged somewhat better. (About half said that this story was much the same; 37 percent said that this story was better;

14 percent said it was worse.) It appears that the elite media are judged to have a modest edge in responsible reporting of social science.

Modest Expectations. Another possible reason for greater satisfaction with the current story is that social scientists have modest expectations for what the media can and cannot do. In general terms they would like the media to provide a dazzlingly good representation of social science, but in dealing with a particular story about their own work, they may be satisfied with less ideal performance. The interviews show that many of them have a realistic appreciation of the limits of the media as a channel for communicating social science. As noted, about a quarter of them qualified their judgments about the story's accuracy by mentioning their awareness of media constraints on space, time, and focus. Elsewhere in the interview, too, many of them acknowledged that reporters have different performance norms from social scientists and cannot be held accountable to the norms of social science. Thus, they do not necessarily apply stringent standards in assessing the quality of the individual story.

Pluralistic Ignorance. As the survey data on schools, hospital care, and Congress suggest, people tend to have jaundiced views about an institution in general and yet register satisfaction with their own particular experience·with it. It is possible that such answers reflect pluralistic ignorance: each person, contented himself, is unaware that other people are equally contented. Each individual may imagine that his/her own experience is a freak, and that others are being badly served. Social scientists may assume that other people's research is being distorted, *their* findings mangled, and *their* opinions misrepresented. They themselves just happen to be lucky. Since gossip focuses on bad experiences, people come to accept those as typical and discount their own experience. This does appear to be a common pattern, with people more apt to accept public views that institutions are in shambles than to extrapolate from their own happy experience.

Advantages from Coverage. Not to be ignored is the likelihood that social scientists enjoy the publicity that they receive and are willing to overlook a lot of reporting sins. They certainly said that they gained advantages from appearing in the media. In response to an interview question, over 80 percent said that reportage benefited them. This was just as true for university faculty as for people in research institutes, private firms, and government. By far the most frequent advantage cited was career advancement; visibility improved chances of being promoted. Substantial numbers of social scientists also cited as an advantage the opportunity of getting their message to the public, making their findings known, and seeing their work have influence. Social scientists in for-profit firms were particularly likely to say that publicity was good for their organization, but the same answer was also given elsewhere (for example, in university research institutes). A slightly smaller proportion of the sample (one fifth of those citing advantages) said that media coverage was an aid in getting research funding; their names became known to funding agencies. About one fifth of the respondents were candid enough to report that attention was good for their ego.

Many fewer people reported disadvantages accruing from media coverage (and only four people reported disadvantages alone). Of the thirty-two people citing disadvantages, over half talked about the likelihood of being distorted by the media. The only other complaint registered with any frequency was the image that was conveyed of not being a serious scholar.

It seems possible that the rosy glow that coverage brings might color social scientists' satisfaction with the story. However, those who mentioned advantages were not more likely than others to say that the story was good; there is no statistical relationship between the two sets of responses. But even if the advantages that the media bring do not help us solve our puzzle, it is noteworthy that satisfaction with the individual story is complemented by pervasive satisfaction with the effects of coverage on career.

Expertise in Dealing with the Media. The social scientists in the study had had extensive experience with the media, and it is possible that they had developed expertise in dealing with reporters. They may have learned how to write good short summaries of their work or make their points clearly and vividly in conversation. It would seem that knowing the ropes could help to produce an individual story that was better than the general average. However, our analysis found no significant relationship between amount of prior media exposure and satisfaction with the current story. If expertise is a factor, it is not a simple function of the number of times one has been reported before.

Simply having control over the story may lead to greater satisfaction. If you are the one whose work is reported, you may have the chance to write or review the press release and manage contacts with reporters, whereas you have no equivalent control over media reporting "in general." The ability to influence the shaping of a story, to be in control, may yield a dividend of satisfaction.

The Missing Nays.   Let us note that the opinions we report are those of social scientists who have recently been covered in the news. Other social scientists who have had bruising experiences with the press or whose distrust of the media is profound may avoid all contact. They are not here to voice their views. Our data derive from social scientists who are willing to be covered.

Discontent with the Structure of Reporting.   A final explanation for the difference between satisfaction in the general and particular cases is that social scientists were expressing discontent with structural features of the reporting system, rather than the individual components. Nicholas Brady, a former Republican senator, is reported to have remarked about the Congress, "The people here are of a higher caliber than I imagined in my fondest dreams. But the place doesn't work very well" (*New York Times,* June 29, 1984). In the case of media reporting, it may be that each story is fine, but the overall picture that the media present of the social sciences is incomplete or misleading. We discuss this further in chapter 6.

Conclusion

Let us see how our original hypotheses are faring. Data in this chapter lend support to the hypothesis that the organization of journalism has important consequences for the way social science is reported. In particular, the absence of a social science beat reduces the chances for reporters to specialize in social science. It disperses the writing of stories across scores of reporters, few of whom have adequate opportunity to become thoroughly familiar with social science concepts, findings, norms, leading figures, or institutions. Most reporters report their disposition toward the social sciences as favorable, although some of them have reservations about purposes, method, and style.

Another hypothesis was that journalists use social science to legitimate their work. We now have information on reporters' attitudes, which shows that they generally regard social science favorably but not so favorably as to suggest that they would set high value on the imprimatur that social science can provide. This finding reinforces the evidence in chapter 2 that they cover social science for its content and not primarily for social validation.

Reporters claim to write stories to satisfy the criteria of the general public and informed publics. They do not generally recognize any special obligations to satisfy their social scientist sources, other than to be accurate and clear. Nor do they see any obligation to the community of social scientists. They also say that once they have satisfied themselves and their editor, they do not have an interest in satisfying the criteria of their journalist-colleagues. Perhaps they are suggesting that the norms of journalism are clear enough not to need personal confirmation from fellow journalists.

Our hypothesis about the inadequacy of reporters' social science training can also be tested. Reporters on the national media are well educated, with almost all having a bachelor's degree and a third holding an advanced degree. Their preparation is usually in journalism or literature, and although three quarters indicated that they had taken courses in a social science in college or graduate school, their social science preparation seems modest. Whether extent of educational preparation is related to the quality of the social science stories they write is one of the topics that we examine in the next chapter.

Social scientists' opinions about media reporting of the social sciences in general range from mildly favorable (a third), to an unwillingness to generalize because of the variability in reporting, to a view that reporting is mostly inaccurate (a quarter). On the other hand when asked their judgment of the story that had just appeared about their research or their statements, the overwhelming majority believed that it was accurate and that the emphasis was appropriately placed. Evidently journalistic norms and social science norms are sufficiently convergent so that most social scientists were satisfied with the stories.

We puzzled over the reasons for the divergence between social scientists' general skepticism about social science reporting in the media and their endorsement of the particular story. We found some clues in the national status of the media that we were following, in the modest expectations that many social scientists had for media performance, and in the idea of pluralistic ignorance, namely, that each person thinks his/her own satisfaction is the exception and accepts the conventional gossip that the situation is bad. We thought that the advantages that social scientists indicate they receive from media publicity (and they report a splendid array of benefits) may make their judgments of the story less critical. However, we did not find a difference in ratings of the story between those who reported advantages and those who did not. We also considered the possibility that social scientists experienced with the media may have learned some techniques to make the stories more satisfactory, but we did not find any relationship between the amount of previous coverage a social scientist had received and his/her judgment of the story.

$$\left(4 \right)$$

A Search for Factors
That Make a Story Good

SOCIAL SCIENTISTS MADE JUDGMENTS ABOUT THE QUALITY OF THE STORY THAT RE-
ported their research or quoted their statements. This chapter undertakes
a statistical analysis to identify factors that are associated with their satisfaction or dissatisfaction with the story.

Previous research has examined the accuracy of *science* news stories.
(In several of these earlier studies social science made up some fraction of
the science news, but usually not more than one third.) Media researchers
have found relatively few factors that are associated with better ratings of
the story by the scientist-source. Among them are whether the origin of
the story was an assignment by the editor (Tichenor et al. 1970), whether
the scientist believed that science reporting was generally accurate
(Tichenor et al. 1970), and whether the scientist read the story before
publication (Tankard and Ryan 1974). Dozens of other variables have been
tested for association with story ratings, but relationships proved to be
elusive. Undeterred, we set out on a similar quest.

Factors Associated with Good Ratings of a Story

To locate elements that would tend to produce a good news story about social science, we examined four types of factors: (1) characteristics of the reporter who wrote the story, (2) characteristics of the social scientist who was featured or whose research was featured in the story, (3) characteristics of their communication linkage, and (4) attributes of the story itself.

First we had to decide how to define a good story. Like just about everyone else who has studied the accuracy of the media, our decision was to accept the judgment of the person featured in the story. Obviously, to rely on the judgment of the social scientist concerned represents a one-sided perspective. However, given the fact that the research being reported is usually brand new and no one else has had a chance to read it, there seems no feasible way of collecting third-party reviews of the news story. Moreover, in those cases where a social scientist is quoted, only s/he knows how accurately the remarks were conveyed. Therefore, we adhered to usual practice.

We used several measures of the quality of the story. Earlier research on the accuracy of news stories found that accuracy is a multidimensional concept. Scientists, when asked to judge the accuracy of a story, may point out some errors of fact, but they are more likely to cite inaccuracies in interpretation. Tichenor et al. (1970), for example, found that scientists mentioned "overemphasis on the unique" as the greatest problem. Omission of relevant information was the second most frequent criticism. Tankard and Ryan (1974), Pulford (1976), and Borman (1978) found that omission of information was viewed by scientists as the greatest barrier to accurate reporting. Accordingly, we decomposed the concept of accuracy into three components. We asked the social scientists to rate the story which referred to them or their work in terms of (1) factual accuracy, (2) appropriateness of emphasis, and (3) omission of important information. The three resulting measures were modestly intercorrelated.[1] Through principal components analysis (Morrison 1976), we constructed a composite of all three items, called "quality rating of the story."

We are interested in discovering which factors in the reporting process or in the characteristics of the participants are associated with the quality rating.

---

[1] Pearson correlations for accuracy and emphasis, .59; accuracy and omissions, .45; emphasis and omissions, .47.

Characteristics of the Reporter

It seemed reasonable to expect that certain attributes of the reporter would be related to higher social scientist satisfaction. Given the fact that no research had yet been conducted on the reporting of social science, we began with relatively straightforward variables. We anticipated that reporters who knew more about the social sciences would tend to report more accurately. We thought it would be helpful if they had studied one or more of the social sciences during their undergraduate or graduate education. They might be particularly successful if they had majored in a social science at either the undergraduate or graduate level. More generally, we thought that higher levels of education might be associated with better reporting of social science, that (for example) reporters with advanced degrees would write stories judged more favorably. With the usual academic bias, we also considered the possibility that those who had attended higher-ranked universities might do better.

Since a good deal of knowledge comes through informal contacts, we wanted to know whether reporters had relatives or close friends who were social scientists. If so, we expected that such associations might be related to more satisfactory reporting. We also asked them about their disposition toward the social sciences, and we expected that those who reported themselves more favorably disposed would write stories that received higher ratings.

Certain characteristics of the reporter's job might also be related to the social scientists' judgments of the story. Having a specialized beat should enable the journalist to build up a degree of expertise in a substantive field. Even though the beat was not social science (only one journalist reported his beat as social science), specialization in one field should provide continuity and insight. Beat reporters might become familiar with the stream of research in their fields and perhaps develop a certain critical sense of how to report it well. The centrality of social science content to the reporter's beat also seemed relevant. If a social science study dealt with the core of the reporter's beat, such as crime or welfare, we expected that the social science might be more accurately handled. On a more general plane, we considered the possibility that longer experience as a reporter was related to performance. Experience should lead to general improvement in reporting skills, and the reporting of social science might well profit from the higher level of journalistic performance.

Finally, we wanted to see whether reporters who took social scientists seriously as a reference group performed more ably. We had asked them a series of questions about whose criteria they took into account when writing the story with social science content about which we interviewed.

We thought it likely that the more they considered the criteria of the social scientist mentioned in the story—and other social scientists as well—the higher would be the ratings of the story. (We accepted responses that stressed accuracy as one level of such concern.)

Thus, we examined the social scientists' ratings of the story against the following characteristics of journalists:

- majoring in one of the social sciences as an undergraduate or graduate student
- coursework in economics, political science, sociology, or psychology
- number of social science fields in which courses were taken
- years of education
- academic ranking of college or university
- whether relatives or close friends are social scientists
- disposition toward the social sciences
- whether reporter has a specialized beat
- relation of social science content in story to beat
- years of experience as a journalist
- years at the current media organization
- importance reporter assigns to social scientists' criteria in writing a story with social science content

Characteristics of the Social Scientist

It was not obvious from previous research or from common lore which characteristics of social scientists would affect their satisfaction with media stories. The only relevant evidence was the finding of Tichenor et al. (1970) that scientists who were generally satisfied with science reporting were more likely to be favorably disposed to the story about their own work. And this finding was causally ambiguous: which satisfaction came first? Nevertheless, we examined the relationship. We also looked at social scientists' organizations, positions, and degrees, thinking that perhaps tenured professors in university departments would be more difficult to please. We thought it possible that those who believed that media publicity was beneficial to their careers might be more charitable in their judgments of story accuracy.

In terms of improving the quality of media stories, one hypothesis was that previous experience with the media might help. Those social scientists who have dealt with reporters before may have learned how to get their message across. The more often they have been covered, perhaps the more expert they have become in communicating with the press.

Accordingly, we examined judgments of the story in terms of these characteristics of social scientists:

- opinions of social science reporting in general
- organization (university, research organization, government agency, other)
- highest degree
- position (tenured faculty, nontenured faculty, researcher, manager)
- perception of advantages or disadvantages resulting from appearance in media
- types of advantages or disadvantages (career advancement, making message known, publicity for organization, research grants, ego satisfaction, distortion)
- frequency of prior media coverage

Characteristics of the Communication Linkage

We anticipated that stories written on reporters' own initiative would be more satisfactory than stories to which they were assigned. For their own stories, they would have more interest and commitment and therefore more incentive to get the facts straight. Following the findings of Tichenor et al. (1970) and Berry (1967), we expected that the issuance of a press release about a study would lead to a more accurate story. Reporters with a press release in hand are directed toward the most significant findings of the study, and they have a short authoritative document to use for reference. We also expected that a story would be judged better when the reporter had read the study report. Reporters are adept at extracting information through oral communication, but on subjects as complex as social science research, reading the authors' report should increase reporters' comprehension and the accuracy of the story.

Another expectation was that personal contact between reporter and social scientist (for study stories) would improve the accuracy and emphasis of reporting. When the two parties talk, the reporter has the opportunity to ask questions and surface perplexities; the social scientist has the opportunity to explain, amplify, and guide. In similar vein we thought that it might improve quality ratings if the reporter was curious enough to ask for additional details about the study's conclusions and, further, to ask for information about the methods used in the study. An interest in methodology, we thought, might signal a serious effort to comprehend the research results and the extent of their generalizability. Conversations that occurred close to press time (or air time) would, we thought, be fresher in the reporter's mind, and therefore might lead to better stories than contacts weeks before publication.

Furthermore, we expected better ratings for those cases in which the reporter gave the social scientist an opportunity to check the story before publication. If the social scientist could catch errors of fact or emphasis prior to publication, the story should be better received.

In about half the study stories in our sample an editor had made or suggested changes in the story prior to publication. In these cases it seemed possible that the editorial process had led to omission of material or shifts in emphasis. We therefore looked at editorial change against ratings of the story. We wanted to see, too, whether there was a relationship between journalists' satisfaction with the final story and social scientists' ratings.

Thus, in terms of communication between reporters and social scientists, we examined the relationship between social scientists' judgments of the story and the following linkage variables:

- story written on own initiative or not
- press release/press conference or not
- whether reporter read study report; if so, how much of report s/he read
- personal contact between reporter and social scientist
- number of conversations
- recency of conversations
- whether reporter asked for additional details on study results
- whether reporter asked about methods of study
- whether social scientist had opportunity to check story
- whether editor introduced changes in story
- extent of journalist's satisfaction with story

Characteristics of the Story

Several features of the story itself might be expected to be associated with higher quality ratings. Whether the story mentioned a study or quoted a social scientist is one. Quoting a person's remarks should be easier to get right than describing a complex study. Length of study is another. A longer story should be fuller and more complete and thus run less risk of being damned for omissions. Similarly, in stories where the social science content was not the main point of the article ("ancillary stories"), a larger fraction of the story devoted to social science should be an asset.

Prominence of placement—for example, on the front page or the first page of a section in a newspaper, or a special flag on the cover or on the table of contents page in a newsmagazine—might suggest greater commitment by the medium. On television news, use of film would have a similar connotation. Another indicator of media commitment might be the length of time the story has been in development. When editors give reporters several days or weeks to work on a story, the resulting story should show the benefit of the investment.

In the case of studies, stories that contain some reference to the research methods used can be expected to get better ratings. We should anticipate that the more information about methodology provided, the more satisfied social scientists are apt to be.

Another element of the story is the inclusion of interpretation or critique of the study beyond that provided by the study's authors. It was not usually obvious from the story how much of the discussion derived from the social scientist and how much was added by the reporter. So we asked the social scientist. In 29 percent of study stories, social scientists said that the journalist had added interpretive or explanatory commentary. Some stories included comments or evidence from other people, social scientists and nonsocial scientists. Our coding of the stories indicated that 42 percent of study stories were in this category. Some of them included criticisms, elaboration, or supporting statements; some contained references to other research studies, most of which confirmed or were compatible with the current study, but a few of which seemed to dispute the study's conclusions. It seems likely that addition of these elements should color social scientists' judgments of the story. We can expect social scientists to rate more highly those stories that provided a review of other evidence and interpretations.

Accordingly, we looked at the following attributes related to the story:

- study or quote
- length in column inches, in seconds of TV time
- proportion of space in ancillary stories devoted to social science
- special placement
- time between story idea and publication
- discussion of research methods in study story (i.e., method described/ method named but without detail/no mention)
- inclusion of journalist's interpretation of study
- inclusion of critique, alternative interpretation, or supportive or conflicting findings in study story

Results of the Analysis

Analysis proceeded in two stages. First, we looked at the relationships between each of the variables and the composite measure of story quality. The basic strategy was regression analysis. To satisfy the assumptions of regression analysis, we used the logarithm of the quality rating as the dependent variable. The first analysis showed which individual variables significantly predicted the rating of the story.

The second stage was multiple regression. The effort was to identify the *set* of variables that together best predicted the quality ratings. We tested a number of regression models to find those which explained the largest amount of variance in the ratings.

Let us first look at the bivariate relationships, starting with reporter characteristics. Only a few reporter variables were associated with ratings of the story. Some of the relationships that seemed most reasonable failed to materialize. Reporters who reported studying one or more of the social sciences in college did not write better stories (in the social scientists' judgment) than those reporters who did not. Not the social sciences generally, nor courses in economics, sociology, political science, or psychology were associated with quality ratings. Only fourteen reporters had majored in a social science, and they did no better than the others. Nor did those who had graduate degrees, studied at high-quality institutions, or had friends or relatives working as social scientists. Reporters who had a favorable orientation toward the social sciences were no more likely to produce stories that satisfied the social scientist than those whose attitudes were mixed, neutral, or negative. In fact, although the association is not statistically significant, there was a gentle trend in the opposite direction: reporters more skeptical of the social sciences wrote slightly more satisfactory stories.[2]

Reporters who had a beat did not write stories rated better in accuracy, emphasis, and completeness than reporters on general assignment. Interestingly enough, those whose beat was science did not do particularly well. The nine stories written by science writers fell in about the middle of the pack. For study stories, there was no relation between the centrality of the study to the reporter's beat and the quality ratings. Length of time with the news organization did not have an effect on story quality.

The two attributes of reporters that made a difference were the extent of their concern for satisfying the social scientist's criteria for a social science story and the length of their experience in journalism. As we have seen, relatively few reporters stated that they believed it was important to try to meet the criteria of the social scientist in the story; a much larger proportion said that what was important was to be accurate. When we

---

[2] This pattern is reminiscent of a finding in a study on interviewing. Those interviewers who reported that their rapport with respondents was close and friendly received less accurate answers (as revealed through record checks at the welfare agency, election board, and child's school) than interviewers who said their relationship with respondents was cool and businesslike (Weiss 1968–69).

compare these responses to responses indicating a disinterest in social science criteria, we find a significant relationship with story rating ($p < .01$). Reporters who were concerned with satisfying social science criteria more often succeeded in doing so.

As for experience, the longer that reporters had plied their trade, the better were their stories. The relationship was not strong ($p < .10$), but it was comforting.

Of the variables dealing with social scientists, not one was significantly related to judgments of the story. Neither the social scientists' general satisfaction with social science reportage, degree, organization, nor position made a difference in ratings. Full professors with doctorates in university departments were just about as satisfied with the story as were nondoctorates in research organizations or government agencies. There was little support for the expectation that those who believed that publicity was a boon registered more satisfaction with the story. There were no differences in quality ratings among those who believed that media attention was an advantage, a disadvantage, or some mixture of both.

Previous coverage by the media was not significantly related to ratings of the current story. Those who were being reported for the first time were no less (and no more!) satisfied with the story than veterans of dozens of earlier stories. The suggestion is that experienced social scientists have no special wisdom about achieving good treatment.

Most of the hypotheses about the linkage between reporter and social scientist also fell by the wayside. When the reporter wrote the story strictly on his/her own initiative, the story was rated no more accurate, appropriate, and complete than when the story came about through any other route. Those studies on which a press release had been issued or a press conference held were rated no better than other stories. Most reporters said that they had read the research report, either a summary that had been prepared for them (beyond the press release) or the full report. There was no relationship between their reading the report and the rating of the story—nor with how much of it they said they had read.

The sheer fact of personal contact between the reporter and the social scientist was not an advantage for the ratings. Fifty-seven percent of the reporters on study stories had talked to the researcher, but contact alone made little difference. Nor did the recency of the discussions. However, the number of times they talked about the study did show a modest relationship ($p < .10$). There was also limited support for the usefulness of discussing study findings (although not for discussing research methods). When social scientists said that the reporter had asked for details of study findings, ratings of the story were somewhat better ($p < .10$).

In only a handful of cases did the social scientist ask to check the story or the reporter offer the chance. In these cases the checking consisted mainly of the reporter's reading back the story (or a part of it) on the phone. The social scientists who checked the story were mostly satisfied, but not significantly more so than social scientists who had not had a chance to check.

Whether or not the editor had made changes in the reporter's story of a study was not associated with the quality ratings. Nor did the reporter's satisfaction with the final version of the story, regardless of whether there had been editorial intervention, show a relationship to the social scientist's rating. Of all the linkage variables, only frequency of contact and the discussion of details of research results were associated with the rating of the story, and these relationships were modest.

Characteristics of the *story* were more influential. What actually appeared in print (or on the air) was more strongly associated with the ratings that social scientists assigned to a story than were the other elements we have examined. The story, after all, is what they were rating. One important variable was type of story: quote stories were significantly better rated than were study stories ($p < .001$). Our expectation that quoting a social scientist accurately and appropriately is an easier task than reporting a study is well supported.

Another strong relationship was the inclusion of the journalist's interpretation in a study story. When journalists added their own commentary, social scientists' ratings were significantly more negative ($p < .001$). They often did not believe that journalists' gloss on their work made good sense. There was an effect, too, of the inclusion in the story of additional research findings or of interpretation by other people (social scientists or nonsocial scientists). Although we had thought that social scientists might register approval of such evidence of reporters' diligence, the relationship was somewhat different. Social scientists rated story quality highest when the story contained confirmatory comments or supportive research evidence; they gave intermediate ratings to straight reporting with no outside elaboration; they rated lowest those stories that included alternative explanations, discrepant findings, or criticism. They gave good ratings to stories that contained support and confirmation. They were least satisfied with stories that challenged their study results.

This dislike for journalists' interpretation and for critical opinion or discrepant findings from other sources has a certain ambiguity. On one level it sounds as though they are ordinary vulnerable human beings who don't like their judgments questioned or overridden by others. A more charitable interpretation would be that they have worked long, hard, and well on a piece of research and have come to considered conclusions. Along comes a journalist who takes only a few days to understand the research, and then adds a poorly informed interpretation of his/her own or quotes comments from other people who either do not understand the study or are otherwise off the mark. Under such circumstances, impatience with the story would seem to be in order.

The final story variable that proved to be related to the ratings was the description of research methods in the story. In study stories, when the journalist described or at least named the study methods used, social scientists gave the story significantly higher ratings ($p < .05$). Although most reporters gave such detail short shrift, social scientists were more positively disposed toward stories that acknowledged the relevance of methodology.

The remaining variables were not significantly associated with quality ratings. The length of the story and the prominence of placement did not make a difference, once the distinction between quote and study stories was controlled. For stories with ancillary mentions of social science, the proportion of the story dedicated to social science did not make much difference. The length of time that had been spent on story development also showed little effect. How many days or weeks elapsed between the initial idea for the story and its publication was unrelated to quality ratings.

The pattern of results raises doubts about some familiar assumptions. Attributes often assumed to improve social science reporting here show little or no effect: the extent of reporters' training in the social sciences in college or graduate school, their general disposition toward the social sciences, the availability of press releases and press conferences, whether they read the research report, whether they initiated the story or were assigned to it, even the discussion of research methods with the researcher. Above all, the specialty of a beat did not show a relationship to ratings of the story. The absence of a relationship throws into question the usefulness of specialization as a means for bringing greater knowledgeability to social science reportage. In defense of specialization, it might be argued that these reporters had the "wrong" beats. If so, it is not at all clear what the "right" beat would be. We return to this subject in chapter 8.

That no social scientist variables were implicated in the story ratings is less puzzling—and less troublesome. In one sense, the lack of significant relationships is even reassuring, in that no subcategories of social scientists gave particularly hard or easy ratings to media stories. Of course, we have not made headway toward identifying social scientist behaviors that lead to better reporting. The data do not even show a relationship between social scientists' degree of satisfaction with the current story and their willingness to cooperate with reporters in the future. In fact, three quarters of those who were most negative about the current story were willing to participate without any qualification in a future story, which was the same percentage as said they would be willing to cooperate among the total sample. The one person who was unwilling to talk to reporters in the future thought that the current story was excellent.

Multivariate Analysis

The next step in the analysis was to construct multiple regression models to identify the combination of variables that best predict story ratings. We constructed one set of regression models for all stories and, because a number of variables applied to study stories only, we constructed another set of models for study stories. We not only entered the variables that had shown significant bivariate relationships with quality ratings but also variables which, on logical or theoretical grounds or through outright optimism, seemed promising candidates. Even though they were not individually associated with story quality, they might show a relationship when other variables were controlled.

Table 4.1 shows the regression models for the total sample of stories. The variable that best predicts quality ratings is the study/quote variable. Quote stories were more highly rated, and this variable alone accounts for 29 percent of the variance in quality rating. See column I in the table. In model II we introduce the variable "journalists' concern with satisfying social science criteria" into the regression equation. The addition of this variable increases the variance explained to 31 percent. The final variable

TABLE 4.1

Predictors of Quality Ratings of Stories

	Standardized Regression Coefficient (Beta)		
	I	II	III
Whether story was quote or study	.54***	.50***	.48***
Journalists' concern with satisfying social scientist's criteria		.16‡	.17*
Journalists' years of experience			.15‡
R^2 (percentage of variance explained)	.29	.31	.33

***Significant at .001 level
*Significant at .05 level
‡Significant at .10 level

TABLE 4.2

Predictors of Quality Ratings of Study Stories

	Standardized Regression Coefficient (Beta)		
	I	II	III
Whether journalist added own interpretation	.47***	.46***	.46***
Whether story included confirmatory or conflicting data/opinion		.23*	.27**
Frequency of journalist-social scientist conversation			.18‡
R^2 (percentage of variance explained)	.22	.27	.30

*** Significant at .001 level
** Significant at .01 level
* Significant at .05 level
‡ Significant at .10 level

entered, in model III, is length of journalists' experience. With all three variables, this model explains 33 percent of the variance. No additional variable significantly increases explanatory power.[3] Thus, the analysis suggests that experienced reporters who care about social scientists' criteria (including accuracy) and quote a social scientist produce the best-rated stories.

Table 4.2 presents the regression models for study stories only. The best predictor of quality ratings is whether journalists included their own interpretation of study results in the story. If they did, ratings are strongly lower ($p < .001$). A conceptually similar variable—whether stories contained confirmation, no outside material, or critique—enters the equation in model II. (Despite their conceptual similarity, the two variables are essentially uncorrelated [$r = .02$]). Together these variables account for 27 percent of the variance in story ratings. Model III adds the frequency with which reporters talked to the researcher. More conversations yielded higher ratings. This variable is significant at the .10 level and its addition increases the percentage of variance explained to 30 percent. We tried to include other variables, such as length of reporters' experience and journalists' concern for satisfying the social scientists' criteria. No other vari-

---

[3] That variables which showed significant bivariate relationships with story rating do not survive is due to the fact that variables already in the equation explain much of the same variability.

able had a significant coefficient or significantly increased the variance explained. The additional exercises did demonstrate the stability of the regression coefficients for the first three variables across a variety of models.

The main lessons from the final model seem to be negative: if reporters want social scientists to approve their story, they should avoid inclusion of their own commentary and omit contradictory evidence or opinion from others. Talking to the social scientist several times helps a little, too. But all three variables together account for only 30 percent of the variance in the story ratings. Definition of useful practices and behaviors still proves elusive.

We can imagine three reasons for the absence of stronger relationships in the data. First, our measure of story quality is probably not a strong indicator and the sample size is relatively small. As we saw at the outset of this chapter, other studies of newsreporting, which tend to share these features, also fail to find many significant relationships. Second and more substantively, the organization of newswork and the universal conventions of reporting may tend to wash out differences among reporters. The procedures of news production set boundaries to variability in performance. Reporters who are unsure of their social science knowledge may make special efforts to consult colleagues, editors, social scientists, and other sources. Stories that fail to capture social science well may also fail to satisfy journalistic norms of clarity and plausibility and thus be rejected by the editor. Reporters without a beat may receive closer editorial supervision. Through formal and informal practices, the organization of newswork may attenuate the effects of journalists' characteristics and behavior.

Third, at this stage of knowledge, aggregate data may be too blunt an instrument to dissect the reporting process. If we want to learn how media–social science interactions work, we have to look more closely at individual journalists and social scientists and their idiosyncratic interactions. In the next section, we go back to our qualitative interviews to examine the fine-grained processes of reporting.

Concrete Examples

Let us look at specific cases in which stories were rated poorly and well to see how the reporting process played out. We hope to catch a glimpse of elements that we were unable to measure but which have consequences for the quality of social science stories. Contextual particulars may fill in the gaps about features that distinguish poor from good stories.

On many counts stories rated wrong or distorted look similar to their better-rated counterparts. Usually they originated in much the same way, just about as often involved press releases and press conferences, and involved no allegations of stupidity, purposeful bias, or withholding of information. As the statistical analysis had suggested, the processes of reporting were similar for both "good" and "bad" stories.

Unsatisfactory Stories

Only a few cases appeared to contain some special elements. One involved a journalist at cross-purposes with the social scientist. The journalist's purpose in the story was to reveal the political reasons for the government's delay in releasing a study report, and she devoted little space to the findings. The social scientist was annoyed that she "didn't care about the study," and he believed that part of her report was a misrepresentation. He did not see any political motives behind the government agency's delay; he said that clearance of a final report usually takes time. The low ratings that he assigned the story bear the marks of the divergent interests at work.

Another poorly rated story suffered from a more ideological divergence in interests. The study was reported because it was being used as justification for industry lobbying efforts to change consumer bankruptcy laws. The reporter, reporting from the consumer point of view, focused the story on the industry's lobbying efforts and mentioned the study primarily as an example of how much the industry was spending to pursue its interests. The findings of the study received one sentence in a 54-column-inch story. The social scientist found the reporting inadequate, misleading, and wrong. He objected not only to specific errors but to setting the study in a context of business versus consumer interests.

A third story showed evidence of cross-purposes between the social scientist and the federal department that had sponsored his research. The Department of Justice, the sponsor of the study, sent out a press release. The journalist read the press release and read a summary of the report, but he didn't talk to the social scientist. The social scientist disliked the emphasis of the story because it reflected the department's release. "The Justice Department press release reflected administrative priorities," he said and therefore emphasized violent offenders. The story followed suit. "If they don't contact you, there's a danger of mis-emphasis. . . . Often it [research] is misused politically and such political use deserves careful study, as in this case."

Another handful of stories were judged inadequate because of errors in reporting statistics. Several social scientists commented that journalists lacked facility with statistics. Said one, "They can write, but they can't count." In one story the social scientist had told the journalist that 20 percent of American families moved during an average year in the 1950s.

He was irked when the story read, "In the 1950s, one-fifth of families changed addresses at least once in the decade."

Another social scientist reported a more complicated error: "I told [the reporter] that for every 1 percent of whites on unemployment, 2 percent of blacks are on unemployment. The story said that for every one white unemployed, two blacks are unemployed. That makes it a 20 percent higher figure. But I'm not sure if I was not clear on the phone or if it was her. I wish she had called back to check the facts." Given the difficulty of the computation, it's hard not to sympathize with both actors in this mini-drama.

Other errors arose in the reporting of percentiles, percentage differences, and gains in test scores. A story on test scores of Army volunteers treated percentile scores as though they represented percentage of items correct. The error led to gross overstatement of black-white differences. A TV reporter explained, "What we have to do is translate scientific language into language the public can absorb in one minute twenty seconds. Scientists often have blinders on. They'll say 1 percent of eight million, and you ask them: is that one million, and they say, oh no." Her statement, inaccurate as it is, reflects both sides of the argument: the perhaps unnecessary complexity of the social scientist and the journalist's lack of ready facility with numbers.

Some of the other stories that social scientists were dissatisfied with illustrate the clash between "news values" and fair representation of the research. For a story on the effects of television the television reporter said that he had read one and one-half chapters of the seven-chapter research report, skimmed the entire report "to make sure I was on the right course," and interviewed the social scientist for fifteen minutes. According to the social scientist, "the bulk of the fifteen-minute interview was about the positive" aspects of television viewing, as was most of the report. But on the air the story focused on what was deemed newsworthy: the negative effects of television on children. The social scientist objected to the negative emphasis.

Another social scientist was dissatisfied with a story because her study received only two lines. She wished that there had been greater attention to the content and the context. This was by no means an uncommon situation, but other social scientists tended to be more tolerant of the constraints of the media. As one social scientist said, "If there were no space constraints, I would want it [the study] on the front page with my name mentioned. I would want more lengthy coverage."

Among people who were aggrieved at the story, the other main complaint was shift in emphasis. In a quote story the social scientist had talked to the journalist about studies of highway safety. He said the story was "the best so far," but he wanted to convey that "accidents could be prevented by regulation of the auto industry. [The journalist] wrote that safety would be enhanced merely by wearing seat belts. There's a great political difference there." The social scientist objected to "use of the journalistic technique of making a human interest story" of the information, so that important points "got a bit lost."

A social scientist who had conducted a study on gun control found the story factually accurate, but he objected to the inclusion of his results in the same paragraph as statements of the National Rifle Association. He said, "A fellow from the NRA told me, 'We like about 60% of your findings,'" but the placement of his results in the context of NRA statements gave the misleading impression that he and they were in full agreement.

As these vignettes suggest, even the most disaffected social scientists do not charge frivolousness or flamboyance or lack of conscientiousness on the part of the press. Nor do journalists complain of arrogance or uncooperativeness or impatience on the social scientists' side. Stories that are judged unsatisfactory reflect primarily a difference in purpose, a difference in judgment about what should be reported, or errors in presentation of data.

The most interesting aspect of this review is that the stories rated worst, with a few exceptions, do not sound dramatically different from stories rated better. Many other social scientists accepted modest misstatements or abbreviated accounts with greater equanimity, because they did not believe it was the function of the media to showcase their wares. Said one social scientist,

> *I don't think the purpose of a newspaper article is to serve the purpose of a scientific journal. The purpose is to describe what is newsworthy in the findings and how it elucidates the everyday problems people experience. It's a human interest story.*

Another social scientist said, "A report complete with qualifications is not news. You have to ignore limitations. This is a legitimate practice for the news. . . . The policy context constantly changes, so even when the report is published, the setting is already different."

With that perspective, they judged social science stories by less stringent standards.

Excellent Stories

At the other end of the spectrum, social scientists gave a variety of reasons for high ratings. One social scientist praised a *Wall Street Journal* story by saying that the material was complex and the reporter had condensed it ably. "He pulled it together very well. It's hard enough to compress into a two-hour speech, so I'm amazed how well he compressed it in the space he had. . . . It was very accurate. . . . I was very pleasantly surprised how well he did."

Another social scientist thought that a *Washington Post* story was a "superior job." It included material from a journal article that she had published, and the social scientist appreciated the fact that the journalist had taken the time to read her work. It also contained confirmatory evidence from a recent survey that she had not been aware of. The journalist's thoroughness was noteworthy.

Said another social scientist, "He had an amazing facility to quote back to me word for word. He had a machine-like shorthand, so he could get what I said nearly verbatim. . . . He is a very intelligent guy . . . chose the most important material to quote." Another said, "The study is 1500 pages and will be printed in six volumes. But the *Times'* selection of two lines couldn't have been better."

Social Science
Not Covered by the Media:
Reporting of AAAS Meetings

SO FAR WE HAVE LOOKED AT SOCIAL SCIENCE THAT THE MEDIA HAVE REPORTED. What about social science that the media ignore? How do we identify the kinds of social science that are routinely neglected? It seems important to find out whether there are patterned regularities in media attentiveness— whether, for example, coverage varies by such factors as social science discipline, kind of information, renown of the social scientist, topic of investigation, or channel of dissemination. Are there certain types or styles of social science that are likely to be reported and others that are generally excluded?

The major obstacle to addressing the question is the difficulty of constructing a comprehensive inventory of available social science. We can examine the stories with social science content that appear in the press, but with what body of social science do we compare them? How do we get an understanding of the types of social science that are underrepresented or ignored?

To deal with the question of which social science does not appear in the media, we need a bounded universe of social science to which reporters have access. We developed two plans to construct such a universe. One strategy was to look at the media fate of the social scientific papers presented at the annual meetings of the American Association for the Advancement of Science (AAAS). Another, which is discussed in chapter 6, was to collect the incoming communications in five news organizations—press releases, phone calls, magazines, announcements of meetings, invitations, etc.—and follow up on which of them led to stories and which did not.

Coverage of AAAS Annual Meetings

This inquiry examines coverage of two successive AAAS meetings—1982 and 1983. On the basis of the results of our investigation and previous studies, we predicted social science coverage of the 1984 meeting. We compare our predictions with events.

The annual meetings of the AAAS provide a known universe of social science sessions. The AAAS also subscribes to a clipping service that retrieves newspaper stories from around the country that mention its meetings. Thus, we can compare the sessions that journalists report with those that they pass over. We can also see which papers at a session they choose to write about and which themes they select for attention. Although clipping services inevitably miss a sizable number of stories, there was no reason to expect differences in completeness across subjects or across years.

The AAAS meetings have several marked advantages for our purposes: (1) Unlike the American Sociological Association, say, or the American Psychological Association, the meeting is not limited to a single discipline. AAAS meetings cover the full range of the social sciences. We can compare media coverage of one discipline with another. (2) Meetings are well attended by the press. At the 1982 meetings, for example, 838 members of the press were registered. The AAAS staff are experienced in making arrangements for the media—press conferences, offices, interview rooms, phones, taping facilities, and so on. The meeting *Program* includes summaries of the sessions, a book of *Abstracts of Papers* is distributed, and full copies of many of the papers are available to the press. (3) Since AAAS also deals with the natural, biological, and engineering sciences, we have the additional opportunity of comparing media coverage of the social sciences with the natural and biological sciences.

The choice of AAAS also has drawbacks. Most of the journalists who cover the AAAS conference are specialists in science, medicine, and related areas. They are not a representative cross-section of reporters who write on social science topics under normal routines of reporting. Because there are very few journalists in the country whose beat is social science, the reporting of social science falls on journalists who cover business, politics, crime, urban affairs, and general assignments, as well as science and medicine. Fortunately for our purposes, the AAAS Information Office notes that a sizable minority of reporters in attendance are not specialists in science reporting but are more like the reporters who generally cover social science.

Another drawback is that since our procedure was to compare the social science content presented at the meetings with published stories, we have no information on stories filed by reporters that were not printed. There are not likely to be a great many of these stories once a newspaper pays for its reporter to travel to the meeting. On the other hand, reporters who work for news services write one story which may appear in dozens of newspapers. This is particularly true for AP and UPI, but it applies to a lesser extent also to the news services of major newspapers—*New York Times, Washington Post, Los Angeles Times, Chicago Tribune, Boston Globe, Knight Ridder, Christian Science Monitor*. On both these counts it is important to recognize that our procedure provides us with a composite of reporters' choices of what to write and editors' decisions on what to publish. The number of stories that appear in the press about a particular session reflect both reportorial and editorial selection.

Finally, clipping services did not clip stories unless they mentioned AAAS. Probably few stories filed at the time of the annual meeting failed to mention AAAS since the AAAS annual meeting is the "where and when" of the report. Moreover, the prestige of the organization gives the story enhanced credibility and legitimacy. But several reporters mentioned to me that besides the daily stories they file during the meeting, they keep information they acquire there for later use. One reporter said, "I'll use what I learn here throughout the year, without mentioning AAAS." In this respect our method of inquiry understates the reporting of meeting content.

The Format of AAAS Meetings

The AAAS was founded in 1848 and now has 140,000 individual members. It has twenty-one specialized sections to which members belong, from chemistry and psychology to the history and philosophy of science. It is also a federation of scientific organizations, with nearly 300 affiliated societies. Its annual meeting is a multidisciplinary six-day scientific congress that typically registers over 5,000 scientists. Symposia cover specific scientific fields such as physics and anthropology, cross-disciplinary subjects such as biomedical technology and aging, and issues of science education, science policy, and public policy issues with a strong scientific component such as arms control. From 150 to 200 scientific sessions are held.

As an integrative organization AAAS emphasizes symposia that bring the knowledge of several disciplines to bear on a single topic. The aim is not so much to present the newest scientific results (scientists prefer to present such data at their disciplinary association meetings) as to integrate the knowledge of different disciplines around issues of public significance. Specialized sections of the association, such as Section H (anthropology), Section J (psychology), and Section K (social, economic, and political sciences), also present symposia that are more characteristic of prevailing interests in the disciplines.

Sessions at AAAS meetings are organized to appeal to nonspecialists as well as specialists. Because of the broad range of its membership, AAAS seeks a level of discourse that is accessible to scientists with very different backgrounds. As a consequence, discussion of social science at the meeting is likely to be understandable to journalists who lack special training, probably more so than meetings of separate disciplinary associations. As one reporter at the meeting said to me, "Journalists don't have to be hotshots at the frontiers of research to do a good job reporting here."

The 1982 meeting took place in Washington, D.C., on January 3–8. There were a total of 164 symposia on the program. Of these, 37 symposia, or 23 percent, had substantial social science content. In 1983, for the first time in over a century, AAAS changed its meeting from the period around the New Year's holiday to the end of May. The site of the meeting was Detroit. Attendance was down markedly. From over 5,000 registrants in 1982, registration fell to just over 2,500 in 1983. The number of journalists registered at the meeting also dropped, from 838 in 1982 to 310 in 1983. The 1983 meeting had 152 symposia on the program, of which 31 (or 20 percent) had social science content.

The Extent of Press Coverage

Table 5.1 presents the ten symposia that received the greatest attention from the press in 1982. Four of them dealt primarily with social science. (The symposium on the evolution of the human diet may look out of place, but it was co-arranged by a social scientist, included anthropologists among the speakers, and was sponsored by the anthropology section of AAAS.) Whereas sessions with social science content made up 23 percent of all sessions at the meeting, they took four places of the top ten in news

TABLE 5.1

Press Coverage of Symposia at the 1982 AAAS Meeting

Rank Order	Symposium	Number of News Stories	Press Conference?	Social Science?
1	Subjective Science?	298	Yes	—
2	Terminal Cretaceous Extinction	213	—	—
3	Control of Dental Caries	191	—	—
4	Enduring and Reversible Effects of Early Experience	182	Yes	Yes
5	Stratospheric Modification, Carbon Dioxide, Climate	170	Yes	—
6	Chemical and Biological Warfare	152	Yes	—
7	Critical Issues in Crime Control Policy	150	Yes	Yes
8	Evolution of the Human Diet	137	Yes	Yes
9	Nuclear Magnetic Resonance	117	—	—
10	Mathematical Performance by Males and Females	108	Yes	Yes

Notes: Total number of symposia: 164 (30 symposia held more than one session); press conferences held: 25; sessions with more than marginal social science content: 37; press conferences for symposia with social science content: 6.

coverage. To look at the data another way, 11 percent of the social science symposia received top coverage compared with 5 percent of non–social science symposia. Social science was disproportionately well covered.

Table 5.2 shows the equivalent data for 1983. (Only the top nine symposia are listed, because there was an abrupt fall-off in number of stories after the ninth.) Again, the social sciences were particularly well reported. Sessions with social science content, which were 20 percent of the total sessions, received three slots in the top nine. For the total meeting 10 percent of the symposia with social science content and 5 percent of those without social science content received high coverage—almost exactly the same as in 1982.

Dunwoody (1982), who analyzed press coverage of the 1977 and 1979 AAAS meetings, found that the social sciences were well covered at the earlier meetings as well. She speculates why science reporters, who "profess to dislike social science research," "consider it to be 'soft' research," and "have a difficult time evaluating it" (1982:19), nevertheless give it good play. She suggests two reasons: many social science stories have obvious reader relevance, and social science is easier to understand than other

TABLE 5.2

Press Coverage of Symposia at the 1983 AAAS Meeting

Rank Order	Symposium	Number of News Stories	Press Conference?	Social Science?
1	Global 2000 Revised	248	Yes	Some
2	Chemical and Biological Warfare: Detection, Control, and Disarmament	241	—	—
3	Emerging Technologies for the Disabled	157	Yes	—
4	Sodium, Potassium, and Essential Hypertension	110	—	—
5	Stress in Children and Families	104	—	Yes
6	Control of Mammalian Sex Ratio	83	—	—
7	Future of American Mortality: Social, Biological, and Policy Aspects	76	—	Yes
8	Science of the Automobile	48	—	—
9	Prenatal Diagnosis	47	—	—

Notes: Total number of symposia: 152 (26 symposia held more than one session); press conferences held: 24; symposia with more than marginal social science content: 31; press conferences for symposia with social science content: 3.

scientific research. Reporters in a hurry to meet a deadline may be drawn to papers they can readily comprehend.

Two additional reasons can be offered for the amount of social science coverage. The original premise of reporters' discomfort with social science may be outdated. As Dunwoody's paper shows and the AAAS Information Office confirms (Wrather, personal communication), the anti–social science attitudes of the science writers' "inner club" (Dunwoody 1980) have dwindled. At the 1983 and 1984 press conference I attended, and in many conversations with reporters at the meetings, there was little more questioning or criticism of the social sciences than of the natural and biomedical sciences. When reporters talk about their skepticism about social science, which they do, it sounds much like their attitude toward other subjects that they report—from medical research to politics. Reporters seem to take pride in their "show me" approach to the world.

A second consideration is that stories that appear in print represent not only the decision of the reporter to file a story, but also the decision of the editor to print it. It is that composite decision process that results in the higher level of reporting of social science than of other AAAS subjects.

Editors, who tend not to have backgrounds in science, are probably more engaged by the relevance to readers and ease of comprehension of the social sciences.

Subject Matter of Press Coverage[1]

As Table 5.1 shows, the three most widely reported symposia at the 1982 meeting did not concern social science. The first—"Subjective Science?"—included four papers that discussed cases in which preconceived notions or sociopolitical attitudes influenced lines of scientific investigation. It seems like an intriguing subject. However, almost every one of the 298 stories centered on a small point in one talk, namely, the effect of aspirin in reducing blood clotting and thereby possibly preventing strokes and death. The stories played the theme of health care. A press conference had been held, and Estelle Ramey, who mentioned aspirin, was one of the two session participants who spoke at the press conference. Nevertheless, she was surprised at the coverage. She said, "It just shows that anything that has to do with longevity gets attention" (Bishop 1982:7).

Stories on the second most widely reported session—"Terminal Cretaceous Extinction"—dwelt on reasons for the disappearance of dinosaurs. Reportage of the third session—"Control of Dental Caries"— stressed the point, made in a paper by J. B. Brunelle and A. J. Miller, that there has been a 32 percent decline in tooth decay over the last ten years.

The session that ranked fourth in press coverage, and first among the social science symposia, was "Enduring and Reversible Effects of Early Experience." A press conference was held which four of the speakers attended. Five papers were presented at the session. Yet all the news stories centered on one paper, by Jerome Kagan, and all emphasized the biological or hereditary aspect of shyness. The word "shyness" or "shy" appeared in all headlines, most of them saying it may be inherited. Most (147) of the 182 published stories came from an AP story, which included the social scientist's caution that the findings about the persistence of shyness were drawn from a study of one small group. When the AP story was shortened in some newspapers, the caution was usually dropped. Reporters and editors seemed to be attracted to a subject that would be relevant to many readers, and to the unexpected possibility that a quality like shyness could have a biological basis.

Ranked second among social science sessions and seventh overall,

---

[1] This section draws on a master's fieldwork paper by Walton B. Bishop, "Analysis of News Coverage for the 148th Annual Meeting of the AAAS," College of Journalism, University of Maryland, 1982.

"Critical Issues in Crime Control Policy" showed the same pattern of journalistic selection. The symposium featured five papers, yet 135 of the 150 stories that appeared in the press highlighted S. A. Mednick's paper, which suggested a biological basis for criminal behavior. An AP story accounted for 80 of the stories, and it focused exclusively on Mednick's claim of the heredity of crime. Two other reporters, who accounted for 29 of the published stories, also highlighted the heritability of crime but included opposing viewpoints in their stories, citing social scientists who disagreed with Mednick's position. Their accounts were among the very few instances at the meetings in which reporters referred to scientific positions or research findings not presented at the meeting. Overwhelmingly, reporters limited their stories to the day's "news," ignoring conflicting or supportive views from other sources. Even for sessions which specifically took issue with earlier research, most reporters were content to report the current statement without discussion of the view that was being refuted. Review of the coverage of the meetings gives a strong sense that news is what is being said today. Relatively few reporters put today's news in a larger scientific context.

A minority of the stories on the crime control symposium (thirteen) focused on Herbert Edelhertz's paper, which dealt with white collar crime. All of these stories discussed the likely upsurge in white collar crime arising from growing computer use, changing economic patterns, and the transfer of functions from federal to local governments.

The third best-reported social science session was "Mathematical Performance by Males and Females." The subject was both controversial and timely. A paper published in *Science* in December 1981, just before the meeting, had shown that males performed significantly better than females and suggested that mathematical ability was biologically determined. The papers at this session reported research indicating that mathematical performance is not determined by sex but mediated by a variety of environmental factors. Almost all of the 108 stories that appeared in the press emphasized the theme of the session: Biology is not mathematical destiny. Reporters were seemingly attracted by the widespread relevance of the topic to readers, the conflict with other recent research reports, and the abiding interest in male-female differences and similarities.

Thus, the social science that received the greatest media coverage seems to be controversial. Papers that disputed the accepted wisdom and those that disputed specific prior studies captured journalistic attention. Oddly, in all three cases in 1982, the central issue concerned heredity as an explanation for social behavior.

In terms of press coverage the next social science symposium ranked fifteenth, with sixty-three stories. This was "Influence of Hypnosis and

Related States of Memory: Forensic Implications." Five papers were presented—by psychologists, psychiatrists, and a law professor. No press conference was held. Most media stories emphasized that reliance on hypnosis in court cases is risky. They reported findings presented at the session that hypnotically induced memory can be manipulated or mistaken. Again, the press seemed to like the challenge to the accepted wisdom.

Ranked sixteenth over all, "Aging from Birth to Death: Biosocial Perspectives" received sixty-one stories in the media. Almost all of them derived from the *Washington Post* news service. The theme of the story was that people can live longer if they follow certain specific prescriptions. With its practical advice and optimistic tone, the story can be assumed to have universal appeal. There was no press conference.

In 1983 fewer reporters attended and fewer stories appeared in the media. The number of reporters registered fell by 63 percent, but because so many newspapers run wire service stories, the decline in press attendance did not translate into a corresponding decline in published stories. The number of stories fell by only 31 percent.

The top story of the meeting, as shown in Table 5.2, was "Global 2000 Revised." This symposium was specifically organized to refute the contentions of the Global 2000 report issued in 1980 and its update at the 1982 AAAS meeting. The original Global 2000 report to President Carter was a massive government study of world trends in population, resources, and environment, which reached pessimistic conclusions about the direction in which the world is heading. Half a million copies of the three-volume report were sold, hundreds of articles were written about it, and it was discussed at the Venice Summit Conference of world leaders. The 1982 AAAS meeting had devoted two symposia to it, one an update and the other a discussion of implications for American education. The 1983 symposium, organized by futurist Herman Kahn and economist Julian Simon, was an all-day meeting featuring ten papers, some dealing with economics and demography and classified as social science, as well as others on agriculture, energy, and so forth. All of the papers disputed the gloom and doom scenario of the original report. A press conference was held.

The intent of the symposium was to generate controversy. It did; 248 stories appeared in the press. Almost all of them focused on the message that conditions are getting better, not worse. As one reporter told me, "The standard view is that the world is going to hell. The session contradicts what everyone thinks."

The second best-reported session was "Chemical and Biological Warfare: Detection, Control, and Disarmament." Five papers were presented on this highly significant topic, and 241 stories were published, but every news story reported a comment by Matthew Meselson, the discussant, who did not present a paper. He alleged that "yellow rain," which the United States had charged was the result of biological warfare by the USSR in Laos, Cambodia, and Afghanistan, might in fact be nothing but bee excrement. This was the theme of stories written by the AP, *Los Angeles Times, Washington Post,* Knight Ridder, Hearst News Service, and *New York Times.* Follow-up stories by the AP, UPI, *Los Angeles Times,* and *New York Times* reported that the State Department discounted the allegation about bee feces. Some papers treated the story lightly, giving it frivolous head-lines, but Meselson was serious.

The AAAS had not scheduled a press conference for the symposium, but at Meselson's request it allowed him to give a nonofficial press briefing. According to Joan Wrather (letter, 1984) of the AAAS Informa-tion Office, when Meselson arrived in Detroit, he had "a full-time press relations person" with him, and the press briefing was standing room only. Thus, it was not so much the regular symposium as the extracurricu-lar activities of a determined spokesman that accounted for the high press coverage—plus, of course, the lure of the subject, on both serious and frivolous levels.

Third on the list of press coverage was "Emerging Technologies for the Disabled." A press conference was held, and 157 stories appeared in print. All were drawn from AP and UPI stories. The theme was robots' abilities to do household chores for the crippled and elderly.

The social science symposium that was best reported after Global 2000 was fifth on the overall list; "Stress in Children and Families" re-ceived 104 published stories. All stories focused on the report by Bernard Brown that stress lowers IQ scores among children. The topic seems to have reader appeal; it is unexpected and counterintuitive. In addition, Wrather notes that before the meeting began, Brown contacted several media people and informed them of the paper he was to present in Detroit. *USA Today* ran the story on page 1 prior to the meeting, and the wire services picked it up. Wrather writes, "I think the story would have gotten good coverage anyway, but it is really not a fair test of a social science session that appealed to the press with no outside help" (Wrather 1984).

The other social science session on the list (see Table 5.2)—"Future of American Mortality: Social, Biological, and Policy Aspects"—ranked seventh for the meeting and had stories in seventy-six newspapers. The stories stressed increases in life expectancy, sex differentials in longevity, costs associated with the increasing life span, and the possibilities for equal mortality rates (a "square distribution") up to the ages of 90–95. A column by Edwin Feulner, president of the Heritage Foundation, used the information on sex differentials in mortality as a basis for opposing the pending Fair Insurance Practices Act (to equalize men's and women's insurance premiums). His column appeared in nine papers, accounting for 12 percent of the session's coverage. The fact that the American mortality session was among the best-covered sessions at the meeting again seems to demonstrate the attraction that the subject of longevity holds for journalists and editors.

Press Noncoverage

What about social science sessions that did not receive much reportage? Do they differ in patterned ways from better reported symposia?

First, it is important to recognize that *most* sessions—natural science and social science—went unreported or received scanty coverage. Of the eight symposia held in 1983 under the general heading "Economics and Industry" (four of which we classified as social science), only "Plant Closures: Corporate Disinvestment and Economic Succession" was covered at all in any U.S. newspaper. Two stories appeared, both of which mentioned a suggestion made in one presentation for increased public participation in plant closing decisions. Of the nine symposia held under the heading "Sociology and Anthropology" (eight of which were classified as social science), only the session on the future of American mortality received more than two press stories, and four of them received no coverage at all.

In 1982, when reportage was greater, nine symposia were listed in the program under the heading "Sociology and Political Science," and only two of them received more than four stories. These were the sessions, discussed above, on crime control policy and aging. The symposium that received four stories was "Ethological Approaches to the Study of Politics," at which a speaker compared politicians' gestures during political campaigns with the behavior of monkeys. The comparison was the subject of all four stories. The other six symposia on sociology and political science received little or no coverage.

What characterizes social science sessions that received little coverage? Can we identify particular kinds of social science that the media avoid? To some extent we can. Mainly, they are symposia that sound highly specialized, even esoteric, and seem targeted to other specialists. If the subject has no obvious counterattraction, such as controversy or relevance to readers, the press is likely to ignore it.

Primarily, sessions with low reportage did not appear to present unusual findings which challenged the customary wisdom; they did not deal with topics already high in news value; they did not have obvious relevance or importance to readers; they did not deal in controversy or conflict.

However, there were some sessions at both meetings that seemed to meet one or more of these criteria and still did not receive heavy coverage. This was as true for non–social science symposia as for those concerned with social science. Examples of sessions that would seem to qualify for media attention were those on fraud and dishonesty in science, efficacy of psychotherapy, and deregulation of electric utilities. Yet fraud received only twelve stories, psychotherapy had six stories, and deregulation had no stories. Our criteria for coverage obviously do not sort symposia infallibly into high and low reportage categories. What else is going on?

There is a hint that some symposia deal with overly dramatic topics which reporters see as too violent and unpleasant for reader consumption. Their topics are interesting, bordering on the sensational, and have elements of conflict, but still are poorly reported. Examples in this category deal with violence or misery. "Torture, Medical Practice, and Medical Ethics" (1982) had papers on the extent of torture, torture victims, and their psychosocial rehabilitation. AAAS held a press conference on the session, but only sixteen newspapers printed stories. In 1983 "Adolescent Despair, Suicide, and Violent Death," despite the dramatic title and content of the papers, received only six stories in the press. Perhaps reporters who expect to be reporting on a scientific meeting are not drawn to topics as lurid as these. "Management of Pain and Symptom Control in Terminally Ill Patients" (1983) received similarly limited coverage.

Probably the most viable explanation for why seemingly newsworthy sessions are missed is sheer shortage of time and attention. Reporters are likely to file no more than six or seven stories during the meetings, and they have to ration their attention in order to do a responsible job of reporting on the stories they select. Out of 150–200 sessions, they have to narrow down rapidly to a few, guided by a quick take on what sounds interesting, their prior knowledge and interests, the availability of a news "angle," and the ease of translating the information into language understandable to a lay audience.

Unlike much reporting, stories written from and about a scientific meeting have to be filed quickly. They are tied to a specific time and place. They are due right after the paper has been given or the speech has been made. Whereas reporters often take days or weeks to develop a story on social science (see chapter 2), meeting stories have to be written fast. Therefore, few reporters search beyond what is obvious and readily accessible.

Press Conferences

To help them, AAAS holds a series of press conferences at each meeting. Press conferences make the maximum amount of information available in the shortest amount of time and at the same time clarify points that are obscure or confusing. Obviously the choice of symposia on which to hold press conferences signals to the media which sessions AAAS considers worthy. Some writers have charged that, through its press conference structure, AAAS "manages the news."

Each press conference runs for about an hour (there were 25 in 1982 and 24 in 1983) and focuses on one session in the program, usually one scheduled for later the same day or early the next day. From two to four of the scheduled speakers give brief summaries of the papers they will present. Their reports tend to be conversational, without many scientific or technical terms, and are designed to be clear to reporters. After brief introductory statements, the conference is devoted to questions and answers. In the interchanges reporters' questions are answered, their interpretations are tested, and collateral issues are explored. Having attended about two dozen of the press conferences, I find it an attractive way to learn a great deal about new subjects rapidly and enjoyably. Many reporters tape record the proceedings, for use either in radio broadcasts or as back-up for print stories.

I talked with the AAAS staff who decide on the topics for press conferences about their criteria for selection. In part, they try to predict which symposia will hold the greatest attraction for the media, and in part they respond to the imperatives of their own organization. These are the characteristics that they report taking into consideration as they winnow through the 150–200 symposia in the program:

- subjects in the news, the scientific as well as political news
- controversy
- subject that was the focus of a press conference at a previous AAAS meeting, particularly if opposing viewpoints are now being presented
- big names
- scientists who are hard to reach without such an occasion
- subjects that "should be covered better than they are," such as handicapped or minority scientists, emerging technologies for the disabled (a press conference provides a "captive audience" and "raises consciousness" [Wrather 1983])
- balance among disciplines (AAAS has twenty-one specialized sections, and the press office tries to achieve adequate representation)

- cooperation from symposium arrangers (reporters complain if too many of the paper presenters speak at the press conference; AAAS tries to limit speakers and relies on the symposium arranger to select three or four to appear; if the arranger will not choose, AAAS may drop the symposium from the schedule)
- willingness of paper presenters to meet the press conference schedule (this was a major problem for the first-day sessions at the Detroit meeting, because the press conference would require speakers to arrive early; several conferences could not be held because of speakers' unwillingness to comply)

Other characteristics of a symposium militate against selection for a press conference. These include:

- symposia that are sponsored by an interested outside group, such as the pharmaceutical industry
- symposia in which key participants object to giving publicity to the session (this sometimes happens when an important scientist who is giving a paper at the symposium disagrees with its major theme, such as fraud in science)
- symposia that AAAS knows are pet subjects of the press (for example, the press is fascinated with dinosaurs and the reasons for their extinction; although the Information Office decided not to hold a press conference for the 1982 symposium on this topic, it was the second best reported session anyway)

Overall, 15–16 percent of the scientific symposia are the subject of press conferences. For the social sciences, press conferences were held on six of the thirty-seven social sciences symposia in 1982, or 16 percent, just about the same proportion as all symposia. In 1983 press conferences were held on three of the thirty-one social sciences symposia, down to 10 percent.

The Influence of Press Conferences

How much influence do press conferences have on coverage? As we have seen, AAAS staff say that they balance three types of considerations in their selection of topics. They try to *anticipate* which topics will appeal to reporters; they try to *steer* them to topics that the organization considers important; they have to *cope* with a variety of organizational constraints and participant vagaries. Even if there is a relationship between the holding of a press conference and the amount of press coverage that a session receives, it would be difficult to say whether this means that AAAS is effective at anticipating or effective at steering media interest.

In 1982 seven of the ten symposia that received the greatest coverage had been the subjects of press conferences. All of the social science symposia with heavy coverage were the subjects of press conferences. (See Table 5.1.) In 1983 only two of the top nine symposia had had a press conference, including only one of the three symposia with social science content. (See Table 5.2.)

Table 5.3 shows data for all social science symposia at the two meetings. In 1982 the six social science symposia that held press conferences collected 515 stories, or an average of 86 stories each. These 515 stories constituted 77 percent of all the coverage on social science at the meeting. Only nine other social science symposia received any media coverage at all, and they received an average of seventeen stories each. On the average in 1982 a social science symposium with a press conference received seventeen times as much coverage as a symposium without a press conference.

In 1983, on the other hand, press conferences made little impact. The total number of stories for social science symposia with and without press conferences was almost exactly the same. Six times as many social science symposia *without* press conferences received media coverage as those with press conferences. Although the average number of stories was steeply higher for sessions with press conferences, one symposium is responsible. The session on Global 2000 accounted for every social science "press conference" story except one (which went to a symposium called "The Technology of Peace Making"). If we eliminate Global 2000 from the count, the average number of stories for press conference symposia with coverage would be one, compared with seventeen for non–press conference symposia with coverage.

Press conferences, it is probably reasonable to conclude, play some part in directing attention to the sessions that AAAS puts on the docket. While the choice of press conferences is partly anticipatory—an attempt to foretell which sessions journalists will want to learn more about, the press conference itself reinforces journalists' interest. There is no evidence that scheduling a press conference for an unpopular topic will foster coverage. In fact, some conferences are attended by only a handful of journalists and no stories result. But the convenience that the conference offers for busy reporters, the comfort of knowing that other journalists have attended and see news value in the subject, and the assurance that the reporter is in step with the pack—all exert an effect. In a few cases, the same result was accomplished by determined participants who held informal briefings for the press.

TABLE 5.3

The Influence of Press Conferences on Press Coverage of Social Science Symposia*

	1982		1983		1984		Total	
	Press Confer-ence	No Press Confer-ence	Press Confer-ence	No Press Confer-ence	Press Confer-ence	No Press Confer-ence	Press Confer-ence	No Press Confer-ence
Social Science Symposia	6	31	2	28	4	36	12	95
Total Stories	515	151	1	224	163	661	679	1,036
Symposia with Stories in Press	6	9	1	13	3	10	10	32
Average Number of Clippings for Symposia with Any Stories	86	17	1	17	54	66	68	32
Average Number of Clippings for All Symposia	86	5	0.5	8	41	18	57	11

*Excludes 1983 symposium on Global 2000 Revised.

Reporters also take the initiative themselves. Twenty-two of the thirty social science sessions covered by reporters in these two years did not come to notice via the press conference route. Reporters attended the sessions, read the papers, talked to the presenters, or all three. The number of stories on these sessions tended to be smaller; the average number per session was seventeen. Overall, they accounted for a third of total social science coverage over the two years.

Other Factors Affecting Amount of Coverage

Names are news. Celebrities should merit play in the press. However, reportage of the two AAAS meetings shows little evidence that famous names generated particular attention.

Science celebrities abounded at the meetings. But in the sciences even Nobel Laureates' names are not household words. Only in one or two cases did the name or reputation of the scientist seem to affect the extent of reporting. The late Herman Kahn may have been one case, although his Global 2000 symposium was notable for other reasons as well. George Keyworth may have been another, although he was not so much a celebrity in his own right as recognizable as the President's Science Advisor. His address on the future of the space program, not included in our tables because it was not a symposium, was the subject of 291 news stories in 1982. In no other instances is there a discernable link between heavy press coverage and prominent names. Some of the most eminent of the scientists and social scientists at the meetings were barely mentioned in the press.

Proximity is another common news value. Newspapers favor stories about local events and local people. Here, AAAS reportage confirms expectations. Newspapers serving the metropolitan region in which the meeting was held published more stories on the meeting. For the Detroit meeting, the *Detroit News* and the *Detroit Free Press* averaged almost a story a day, and the *Ann Arbor News* published five stories on one day. Also, papers from the hometowns of speakers sometimes ran a story about the speech. A Eugene, Oregon, paper published a story about the paper presented by a University of Oregon professor, a New Jersey paper ran one about the paper given by a president of a local college. These hometown stories were sometimes the only stories that a session received.

In terms of total coverage, local stories made very little dent. They represented a small proportion of stories about the meeting.

We were interested in whether the specific social science discipline made a difference in the amount of reportage. Analysis indicates that there were differences. Sociomedical sciences, psychology, and sociology received considerably more coverage than political science, anthropology, and economics. Economics received the least coverage of all. It was the subject of six symposia in the two meetings, which together received a total of two stories. This is a very different picture from the main content analysis (see Part II), in which economics received by far the highest level of media attention.

The explanations are obvious. Regular reporting of economics in the media is made up largely of items that have become familiar—statistical indicators, such as cost of living and unemployment statistics, reviews of current conditions, predictions by economists about the future state of the economy, and similar items that have become routinized through repetition. The AAAS sessions, in contrast, dealt with unfamiliar topics. Even for economists, the subjects were fairly specialized. Examples: assessment of forecast uncertainty, risk analysis, formulation of national industrial strategy. It was easier for reporters to ignore these sessions than try to translate them into interesting and understandable stories. The difficulty was compounded by the fact that few reporters whose beat was business or economics would choose to attend the AAAS. For the science reporters and general reporters at the meeting, economic subjects must have looked especially abstruse and forbidding.

Health topics, including psychosocial aspects of health, were well covered. Information on the types of behaviors that improve health status was particularly welcomed on grounds of its relevance to readers. Here, coverage was probably abetted by the numbers of medical and health writers in attendance. But attention was selective. Of the three social science symposia listed under "Health Care and Public Health" in the 1983 program, one—"Stress in Children and Families"—ranked fifth in coverage at the meeting, with 104 stories; another—"Adolescent Despair, Suicide, and Violent Death"—collected six stories; the third—"Optimum Utilization of Knowledge in Search of Health," which ran for two sessions, morning and afternoon—received no coverage at all.

Sociological and psychological sessions also received reasonably good, but selective, attention. Among the issues that reporters and editors chose were crime policy, stress, and trends in mortality.

Discipline was not the determining factor. As we saw in the interview study, reporters are much more interested in the *topic* with which social science deals than they are with the discipline from which it derives.

Another question that we put to the AAAS data was whether the type of social science information presented had an effect on amount of coverage. Were quantitative data better received than qualitative data? Were data from longitudinal series given more attention than cross-sectional data?

Were data from records preferred to interview data? Did large sample sizes increase the appeal? A few reporters at the meeting said that they paid attention to issues such as these, but I could not find evidence in the reportage that they made any difference at all. Some minimally substantiated statements received heavy play, whereas much solid research was ignored. Again, the appeal of the topic appeared to overwhelm all methodological considerations. As one general assignment reporter said about the speakers, "If they're here, I assume they know what they're talking about."

An Attempt at Prediction

It is one thing to generalize about what the media do and do not cover after the fact. But if we really understand reporters' and editors' selection criteria, we should be able to predict press coverage in the future. Accordingly, I took this analysis and the two earlier studies of AAAS coverage by Bishop (1982) and Dunwoody (1982) and attempted to predict the coverage of social science at the 1984 AAAS meeting in New York.

What I had at hand were the meeting program, the volume of abstracts of papers, and the schedule of press conferences. My first step was to identify the symposia that qualified as social science by virtue of the content of the papers, the disciplinary affiliations of speakers, and/or the sponsorship of the symposium by AAAS's social science sections. There were forty social science symposia in 1984, about 22 percent of total symposia. For information about the news appeal of each symposium, I relied primarily on the program, which listed the names of speakers and titles of papers and gave a capsule description of the session theme.

Given the earlier analysis, I was particularly alert to sessions that promised controversy on either of two dimensions: conflict with accepted knowledge and belief or conflict among current studies and scientists. I also looked for sessions with obvious reader interest, such as those on health issues, and for topics already in the news. I took note of press conferences with their sometime pulling power. (But Dunwoody [1982] had found that press conferences on days 1, 5, and 6 of a meeting led to fewer stories than press conferences on days 2, 3, and 4. In 1984, three of the four press conferences scheduled for social science sessions were being held on day 1 or day 6 of the meeting.)

The prediction took the form of a listing with three sections: sessions with high probability of coverage (ten symposia), sessions with a moderate likelihood of coverage (nine symposia), and those with little or no likelihood (twenty-one symposia). I purposely overloaded the bottom category to keep the game sporting, because a number of sessions were so technical or specialized that they were obviously improbable candidates for reportage. For each of the forty symposia, I wrote a brief explanation of my reasoning, and I mailed the statement to colleagues before the New York meeting began.

In general, the attempt at prediction was successful. Table 5.4 presents the predictions and the actual coverage of social science sessions. Of the ten symposia that I rated most likely to succeed, seven actually were among the top ten in coverage. I had listed all of the top five, and these five sessions captured 712 stories, for 86 percent of all press coverage of the meeting. The ten symposia on my top ten list accounted for 91 percent of all stories about the meeting. The other three sessions that received high coverage were all in my middle category. For the twenty-one sessions that I had classified as least likely to be reported, a total of three stories appeared, two about one session and one about another. To put it another way, 70 percent of the sessions in my "high" category made the top ten, 33 percent of the sessions in the "middle" category, and 0 percent of the sessions in the "low" category.

I overestimated the attraction of three sessions. The session on teenagers' contraceptive behavior seemed a natural. My note on the prediction statement explains why I thought it would get attention: "Daily living; controversy. Sex. New contraceptives, comparison with Swedish teenagers." Similarly, I thought that election polling would have more appeal in a presidential election year, particularly with Adam Clymer of the *New York Times,* Burns Roper of the Roper Organization, and other well-known experts on the panel. There was a press conference to boot. But neither of these sessions collected a single story.

The three sessions from my middle group that made the top ten had solid credentials. "Technological Prospects and Population Trends" dealt with life expectancy, which I noted is a "popular topic." "Increasing Participation in Science and Mathematics During the Precollege Years" was a topic in the news, "important," and related to "daily living." "Psychological Testing and American Society," with its press conference, had a clear claim to attention. The topic, I noted, was "interesting and controversial," but the session was scheduled for the last day of the meeting, when Dunwoody's research showed that many reporters would have left, and the papers dealt with historical rather than contemporary issues. Nevertheless, the stories that were filed on the session were picked up by a fair number of newspapers.

Three of the four symposia with press conferences in 1984 wound up among the ten most-reported sessions. But even more than in earlier years, the influence of the press conference was equivocal. Only one of these sessions was in the top five in coverage (coming fifth), and among them, press-conference sessions received only 20 percent of all news stories on the meeting. When we add the data on 1984 press conferences into Table 5.3, we find that the relationship of press conferences to coverage, which seemed strong in 1982, is further attenuated. The totals for the three meetings combined now show that more stories appeared in the press about sessions for which no press conference had been held (1,036) than about sessions with a press conference (927 if we include Global 2000 and 679 if we exclude it). For those symposia which were covered by the press, sessions with press conferences obtained about two and a half times more coverage. But three times as many non–press conference symposia were reported.

Summary

The exercise in prediction gives greater confidence that we can identify the characteristics that attract reporters and editors to certain social science subjects. Although the prediction was far from perfect, and journalists' behavior will inevitably elude perfect forecasts, we have discovered much about the kinds of social science that are favored by the media and the kinds that are disregarded. We have learned that the criteria that journalists bring to social science are very much the same criteria that they bring to all news.

The attributes that appear most important in attracting media attention to social science are challenge to accepted beliefs, controversy, and relevance to readers, on topics already in the news. Sessions that presented information at variance with familiar expectations were likely to capture media attention. So, too, were sessions where there were strong differences of opinion among scientists, such as the Global 2000 forecasts and the link of mathematical performance to gender. Our data tend to confirm the statement by Stocking and Dunwoody (1982:156) that "something is more likely to become news if the information conflicts with everyday expectations or if it contains elements of disagreement or opposition among parties." Presumed relevance to readers' concerns was another appeal. Much of its strength was evidenced in sessions on health, longevity, and topics related to children (shyness, IQ).

In addition, the holding of a press conference was related to amount of coverage. This was more true in 1982 than 1983, both for science and social science, and 1984 saw a further attenuation of the relationship. While a press conference makes reporting easier and more convenient, it also in part represents AAAS's prediction of which topics will appeal to

TABLE 5.4

Predicted Versus Actual Coverage of Social Science at 1984 AAAS Meeting

	Press Conference Scheduled	Actual Coverage		
		In Top Ten?	Rank Order	Number of Stories
Predicted High Coverage				
The Oldest Old: Multidisciplinary Implications	No	Yes	1	157
Health Prospects for American Women	No	Yes	2	154
Mental Health in Social Context	No	Yes	3	144
The Polygraph Test: Detecting Deception in 1984	No	Yes	4	142
Knockdown-Dragout on the Global Future	Yes	Yes	5	115
Achievement in Science: The Second International Science Study	No	Yes	7	32
Gentrification: Alternative Explanations and Polar Policies	Yes	Yes	10	4
Whistleblowing Examined	No	No	12.5	1
Election Polling: Early and Last Minute	Yes	No	—	0
New Thoughts About Teenagers' Contraceptive Behavior	No	No	—	0
Predicted Middle Coverage				
Technological Prospects and Population Trends	No	Yes	8	20
Increasing Participation in Science and Mathematics During the Precollege Years	No	Yes	9	8
Psychological Testing and American Society	Yes	Yes	6	44
Reassessing Personnel Supply and Demand in Scientific and Technical Occupations	No	No	—	0
Moving Ideas and People	No	No	—	0
Cognition, Computing, and Interaction (2 Symposia)	No	No	—	0
Cognition Development and Disciplinary Knowledge	No	No	—	0
New Perspectives on the Prevention of Nuclear War	No	No	—	0

TABLE 5.4 (*Continued*)

	Press Conference Scheduled	Actual Coverage		
		In Top Ten?	Rank Order	Number of Stories
Predicted Low Coverage				
Frontiers of the Social Sciences	No	No	11	2
Dilemmas in US Agricultural Research Policy in the 1980s	No	No	12.5	1
Urban Poor in Less Developed Countries	No	No	—	—
Evaluating the Impact of Foreign Aid	No	No	—	—
General Systems Theory and the Analysis of Political Systems	No	No	—	—
Impact of Women on International Development	No	No	—	—
Heterogeneous Populations and the Limits of Multivariate Statistics	No	No	—	—
Punctuated Equilibria	No	No	—	—
Can Game Theory Model Real-World Conflicts	No	No	—	—
Modeling the Welfare State	No	No	—	—
The Cultural Selection of Risk	No	No	—	—
Hard Decisions and Soft Data	No	No	—	—
Anthropology and the Emerging World Order	No	No	—	—
Peer Review and Public Policy	No	No	—	—
The Bargaining Problem Revisited	No	No	—	—
Funding and Knowledge Growth	No	No	—	—
Motor Development in Children	No	No	—	—
Agricultural Research: Approaches to the Integration of Socioeconomic Studies	No	No	—	—
Agricultural Research Policy: Selected Issues	No	No	—	—
Ethnography of the Laboratory	No	No	—	—
Credible Approaches to Nonexperimental Science	No	No	—	—

journalists. There is no evidence that a press conference in itself can convert non-interest into reportage.

Some attributes that seemed plausible candidates for distinguishing well-covered from noncovered sessions turned out to have little influence on reportage. These included the prominence of the scientists, type of information, and methodological rigor of research. There were differences in the amount of reporting by discipline, with sociomedical sciences, psychology, and sociology outpulling political science, anthropology, and economics. However, it was not discipline but the topics under discussion that accounted for the differences. To the extent we were able to judge, the scientific importance of the information did not enter into reporters' story decisions.

If we had hoped for some dramatic breakthrough from this analysis, the results are anticlimactic. Intuitively, we knew them all along. Because we are ordinary readers and viewers, constantly exposed to the media in the United States in these last decades of the twentieth century, we have a good sense of what the media report—and ignore. But when we think about social science, many of us forget our daily experience and look for different categories and different criteria. Perhaps the most instructive lesson from this excursion to AAAS is the reminder that social science is nothing special to the press. To get reported, social science has to meet the ordinary standards of news.

$$6$$

Social Science Not Covered:
Incoming Media Communications

IN OUR SECOND EFFORT TO IDENTIFY THE SOCIAL SCIENCE NOT REPORTED IN THE
media, we made arrangements with journalists in five news organizations
in Boston during the summer of 1983 to save all their incoming (nonper-
sonal) mail and keep track of incoming phone calls for two consecutive
days.[1] Lynne Sussman, research assistant, spent those two days observing at
each office. The organizations were the daily *Boston Globe* and the Boston
bureaus of *Newsweek, Time,* the Associated Press, and United Press International. The reporters who were asked and agreed to participate in the
study were those most likely to receive press releases or other material
about social science studies, either directly or through organizational rout-
ing. Eighteen reporters and editors participated at the *Globe*—including
those associated with the Living section and the Sunday magazine, and
those who wrote on medical news, race relations, health, education, learning, science and technology, economics, and metropolitan news. At the
wire services and newsmagazines, journalists participated who were present on the two survey days.

At each office we collected all the incoming material. We retrieved all

---

[1] The days for each organization ranged from July 7–8 at UPI to September 19–20 at the
Boston Globe.

the items that journalists threw out and photocopied items they saved. We ourselves classified the material as social science or not.

Then we read the media carefully for two weeks to see whether stories based on social science intake were published. Ten months later we went through the *Globe* index to see whether later stories had used any of the social science that journalists had saved during the observation period. We also checked with reporters at the *Globe, Time,* and *Newsweek* to find out whether they had subsequently written stories on any of the social science items that they had saved, and we reviewed the news-magazines for the period.

None of the reporters at AP or UPI saved any material for possible later use. Although some of them said that they would like to write feature stories, they have limited opportunity. For AP and UPI we assumed that the daily wire included any social science story that was going to be written. As a UPI reporter said, their criteria for stories are "accurate, readable, and on the wire fast."

Press Releases

During the observations at every media office, reporters stated that press releases were among their least important sources of stories. At AP one reporter talked about being bombarded with press releases "like mos-quitoes." A reporter at the *Globe* talked about the incoming mail as "an albatross" and explained that story ideas "come more from talking with people on the beat or in general." The word at UPI for press releases was "junk." These metaphors sound much like Golding and Elliott (1979:87) who write about "the miscellany of invitations, press releases, advertising free-sheets and decorative hand-outs that drop like confetti on newsrooms everywhere." Yet reporters usually sift through them, although rapidly and skeptically.

Most press releases have to do with upcoming events (a few of which are filed for future coverage) or organization and personnel (appoint-ments, promotions, honors, fund raising campaigns, corporate earnings). Certain regular releases from government, such as the local unemploy-ment rate, are published routinely. But it often takes a follow-up phone call about a press release to gain attention. A *Globe* reporter said that if a release is really important, it will be sent over by cab and followed up by a phone call. Several reporters complained about the public relations bar-rage that they get from some organizations to publish their releases. An AP reporter said, "These people's jobs are on the line and so they keep after me. . . . I'm as likely to reject a story with persistent PR out of irritation." Yet during the observation period we saw one previously rejected press release retrieved and turned into a story after a phone call to an AP editor. Of course, many phone calls are fruitless, too.

Reporters disparage press releases and emphasize that they originate stories through their own knowledge and contacts. A *Globe* reporter said that she seeks stories, they don't come to her; reporting is an "active creative process." But to the extent that they alert reporters to specific events or expert sources, press releases can be a valuable adjunct to the ongoing pursuit of news. Reporters acknowledge that some of them are worthwhile, particularly when they "flesh out an idea" that the reporter is already working on or considering.

Reporters have a variety of other sources to tap for news. At the bureaus of AP and UPI, they get many of their stories from local newspapers and radio. They clip articles from papers in the area, and they keep the local news station tuned in all day. Several reporters work out of the Massachusetts State House and cover legislative and executive events. Stringers, many of whom are associated with small papers and radio stations, phone in news. Reporters attend conferences, talk to sources, call other bureaus. At AP there is a science writer who does stories about articles from the Boston-based *New England Journal of Medicine,* as well as other "hard science" originating locally. The wire services keep up with developments minute by minute in stories they are following, and send the latest update out on the wire.

The *Boston Globe* moves to a slightly slower rhythm. Especially among the specialty reporters with whom we were dealing, there is less emphasis on the breaking story and more cultivation of contacts. Reporters are expected to develop their own "enterprise" pieces, and they spend a large part of the day on the phone talking to sources as they craft a story. They read other newspapers and magazines, attend meetings, and talk to colleagues. They are always alert to new ideas for stories in their field.

At the newsmagazines writers develop story ideas over periods of months. They gather material from magazines, specialized journals, books, conferences, interviews, phone calls, personal experience, conversations with experts and with friends. Their focus is on analysis and trends. Ruth Galvin, one of the pioneer social science reporters in the country, has an office in *Time*'s Boston bureau, where she maintains extensive files on story ideas that she is developing. Newsmagazine reporters in the bureaus recommend stories to the editors and writers of the specialized sections of the magazine in New York. When a story idea is accepted, originating either from this bureau, other bureaus, or the New York staff, the New York editors define the shape of the article. They integrate the contributions from various sources, sometimes sending specific queries to the bureaus for follow-up, and they write the final copy.

Other Incoming Communications

Given reporters' scorn for press releases, we expanded our analysis to include other types of incoming mail. Accordingly, Lynne Sussman collected all the material that was accessible—newsletters, magazines, journals, clippings from other newspapers, and announcements of various kinds. Through observation and conversation, she also tried to keep track of incoming phone calls that had a social science focus. Our intake goes far beyond press releases to encompass the variety of communications that came in to participating reporters. After we collected the information at each news organization, we classified the items which qualified as social science by the selection rules used in the content analysis (see Part II). The total intake for all five organizations was 590 items, of which 90 dealt centrally or peripherally with social science.

The 90 items with social science content were a diverse assortment. Just over half were directly about social science. These included reports of social science studies, release of data, publishers' notices about new books, announcements of upcoming conferences, journals, and university bulletins about retirements, visiting professors, faculty activities, and new research programs. Some examples: The National Opinion Research Center of the University of Chicago reported a drop in public support for return to the military draft, based on its General Social Survey. The U.S. Bureau of Justice Statistics released a report on the criminal careers of a nationwide sample of offenders in state prisons. Scholastic, Inc., the educational publisher, announced a grant to New York University for a research project on the effects of microcomputers on the life and learning of children. From Oxford University Press came an announcement of the publication of the proceedings of the World Conference on Gold, *The Gold Problem: Economic Perspectives;* from William Morrow an announcement of a new book by sociologists Philip Blumstein and Pepper Schwartz, *American Couples;* from Crown Publishers word of a book by anthropologist D. B. Owen, *Love Signals: How to Attract a Mate;* from Perigee Books notice of a book by three psychologists on "psychologists' secrets for getting ahead in business."

Northeastern University announced a scheduled conference, "Freud and Man's Soul: The Impact of Language on Psychotherapy." Wellesley College announced an upcoming conference, "Women's Psychological Development: Theory and Application." The Fletcher School of Law and Diplomacy at Tufts University established a research center to analyze trends in international business. Boston's Museum of Science described an exhibit developed by a University of Pennsylvania psychologist that allows visitors to experience for themselves how older people hear, see, smell, and taste.

Other incoming mail was more peripherally related to social science: for example, an announcement of a conference or lecture series at which social scientists were scheduled to speak, even though the conference topic was not social scientific. Thus, social scientists were on the programs of a University of Southern Maine lecture series on black culture and a conference held by Women In Cable, a professional society. There were releases about non–social science activities of social scientists, such as a sociologist who opened a museum exhibit on early California aviators and a psychologist who criticized an exhibit at the Museum of Fine Arts for excluding black artists.

Advocacy groups used social science data in many of their releases as support for their message. The National Coalition to Ban Handguns gave data on crime rates by size of city. The American Association of University Women included estimates of lifetime earnings for men and women. The Planned Parenthood League of Massachusetts cited surveys that showed public support for sex education. The National Committee for Citizens in Education reported studies on the impact of educational programs funded under Chapter 2 of the Educational Consolidation and Improvement Act.

Journals and magazines that arrived at the Boston organizations included the *Journal of Comparative Psychology, Journal of Personality and Social Psychology, Archives of General Psychiatry, Anthropology Newsletter, New Society, Science, Science News, Discover, Harvard Educational Review,* and *Japan Report.*

Journalists' Responses to the Mail

In tune with their verbal disparagement of press releases, journalists threw away most of the mail that reached their desk. Nine of them explained the reasons for discarding, saving, or using items. (This is very much in the tradition of the "Mr. Gates" studies in which a wire editor explained his criteria for choosing stories from the wire for his newspaper [White 1950; Snider 1967; see also Gieber 1956].) The reporters whom we spoke to gave these reasons for rejecting items: space limitations, not broad enough appeal to readers, not a hot topic, too academic, not news, too public relations–oriented, too specialized. They also rejected items when they didn't know the news source or considered it unreliable or self-interested and commercial. They were not interested in items if they could not find an angle from which to construct a story. They explained that they needed a new angle when the item as it stood was dull.

Other reasons related to the specific media for which the reporters worked. All the media had a strong preference for local stories—the bureaus of the wire services and newsmagazines because their explicit charge is local news and the *Globe* because it conceives of itself as a regional rather than a national newspaper. One *Globe* reporter talked about a press release from the University of Illinois on social science research, saying that it might be suitable for the *New York Times,* but it doesn't suit the *Globe's* definition of itself.

Internal division of labor also made a difference. Reporters disregarded items when they believed they belonged in the bailiwick of another desk or department. They were not interested in items on which stories had recently been done. They kept some items because the paper ran a regular column into which they might fit.

The reason they most often gave for saving a press release or article was that they had plans for a story to which the item might relate. *Newsweek* had a story in the works on medical costs, and *Time* was working on one about domestic violence. Writers in both media saved relevant articles. *Globe* reporters, too, kept material on subjects that they thought they might develop in the future.

Table 6.1 shows the number of incoming items, the number of stories written, and the number of items saved for later use. The upper part of the table shows the breakdown by media, and the lower part shows the same data by type of social science information.

Stories Based on Incoming Mail

Three stories were written on the basis of the material that came in, and twenty-four additional items were saved for possible later use. All the stories were written by the wire services, and all were done immediately. AP wrote a story based on two Bureau of Labor Statistics releases about declines in employment in the Boston area and high Boston pay rates. The story was written straight from the releases. The second story was based on a report from the business cycle dating committee of the National Bureau of Economic Research, which was phoned in to UPI with a press release following the next day. It indicated that the recession had bottomed out and recovery begun the preceding November, according to analysis of output and sales figures. The third story gave the results of a poll conducted by a local radio station (not exactly mainline social science, but fitting the rules developed for the content analysis [see Part II]). Staff of station WBZ phoned AP with the responses of the constituents of a local congressman who had been censured by Congress for homosexual relations with a congressional page. These three stories, two of which were phoned in, represent the full "take" from the social science releases.

Two additional stories, both in the *Globe,* were based on material that appeared in the mail we collected. However, the stories were written by reporters on the paper who had not participated in our inquiry. They had

TABLE 6.1

Social Science Items That Arrived at Five Boston Media
in a Two-Day Period

	Incoming Items with Social Science Content	Stories Written	Additional Stories[a]	Items Saved
Media				
Globe	43	0	2	3
Time	21	0	0	19
Newsweek	6	0	0	2
AP	15	2[b]	0	0
UPI	5	1[b]	0	0
TOTAL	90	3	2	24
Type of Social Science				
Study	42	1[b]	1	14
Data	16	2[b]	0	1
Social Science Organization	8	0	1	4
Social Scientist	23	0	0	4
Theory	1	0	0	1
TOTAL	90	3	2	24

[a] Stories written by reporters who did not participate in our inquiry, based on duplicates of press releases received by participating reporters. Since we did not collect all incoming items from writers of these stories, counting the stories would give an overestimate of the effect of press releases.
[b] Two stories, one by AP and one by UPI, were based on phoned-in information. One was a poll for which there was no press release; one was an analysis of data where a press release followed the phone call.

received duplicates of the press releases that came in to the reporters whom we studied. To count these stories as resulting from incoming mail seems reasonable, but since we did not collect all the other press releases that these writers had received and rejected, counting them would give an artificially high estimate of the power of press releases. We present them separately in Table 6.1.

One of these *Globe* stories was an analysis of municipal debt in the cities and towns of Massachusetts, done by a Boston bank. It appeared—on page 25—the day following the release and was written by a reporter who covered the Massachusetts State House. The other was a story about the new Rockefeller Center for the Social Sciences at Dartmouth. Announcement of the dedication came in to the *Globe* about a week prior to the ceremony, but the story did not appear until two weeks afterward. It was published in the section on regional news in the Sunday paper.

We called the journalist to find out why the story appeared so late. He said that he had the "intellectual beat" on the *Globe,* a loose assignment to cover higher education, ideas, ideas in politics—jocularly called the "egghead beat." He was among several people at the paper who had received the release about the Dartmouth dedication. They discussed coverage, and it was decided that the "upcountry reporters" in New Hampshire would do the story. However, there was confusion about the assignment, and they did not file. The *Globe* printed a short wire service story[2] the day after the event. Tom Winship, the paper's editor, wrote a memo to the National Editor asking why someone hadn't been assigned and telling him to get a story. "As the guy on the intellectual beat, I was asked to do the story. So I drove up there." It wasn't the press release, but the editor's displeasure over the neglect of the event, that triggered the story.

Although we watched the newspaper and newsmagazines and checked with reporters again after ten months, we found no additional stories based on material that had come in during our inquiry. There were no indications that the items that reporters saved had made their way into stories. Nevertheless, two reporters said that the information provided useful background. Ruth Galvin of *Time,* who herself kept nineteen of the twenty-four items, notes that she keeps active files on scores of story ideas. She adds relevant material as it becomes available against the day when New York gives the go-ahead for a story. Ten months after the period covered in our observation, she had expectations that a couple of the items she had filed away might still be used.

What can we conclude? Three stories written out of ninety social science items is a 3 percent "success rate," not a particularly high return on investment. Moreover, two of the stories were actually written from phoned-in information. One of them, the poll of constituents of Representative Studds, was *at the most* only marginally social scientific. The only written release that made it on its own was the Bureau of Labor Statistics data, and BLS releases about local economic conditions tend to be routinely reported. In terms of the central foci of the social science disciplines, the stories selected seem to be a haphazard and offbeat lot. Only the National Bureau of Economic Research (NBER) story on the end of the

---

[2]We do not include the wire service story in our count, because observation at the AP took place on different days, and the press release did not arrive during our period of observation.

recession is somewhere near mainstream social science. The additional stories in the *Globe,* on the Dartmouth Center for the Social Sciences and Massachusetts cities' municipal debt, are also somewhat tangential. The municipal debt study was done by the Bank of Boston's economics, trust, and public finance departments and probably falls on the social science borderline. The Dartmouth Center for the Social Sciences story told almost as much about Dartmouth alumnus Nelson Rockefeller for whom the center was named as it did about the kinds of social science that the center would undertake.

Yet marginally social scientific as most of the stories are, they are typical of many stories that fell into the content analysis (see Part II). Many social science stories that the media report have the same kind of borderline contours. Only a small proportion are "core" social science studies.

What primarily distinguished the stories that derived from incoming communications in this inquiry is their local character. All were about New England, except the NBER analysis of the recession, and that was done by a local research organization. Given the regional media with which we were dealing, this feature is understandable.

The other notable feature is the importance of personal contact. Except for the BLS story, stories would probably not have been written had there not been telephone calls providing information.

The most surprising element is that the stories were all wire service stories. It is generally assumed that newsmagazines and newspapers are more receptive to social science than the hard-news, fast-paced wire services. *Time* and *Newsweek* have an interest in behavior and "living" and trend stories in the back-of-the-book sections. The *Boston Globe* is considered a "writer's paper," which encourages reporters to develop and write "soft" stories rather than just transmit information. Yet in our inquiry the three stories that were published came from AP and UPI. However, the scope of our inquiry is too small to sustain much generalization.

It is worth noting that several of the press releases disregarded by the Boston media received extensive play from media elsewhere. As we have seen, one release was about Blumstein and Schwartz's sociological analysis *American Couples.* Although no story was written about the book in the media we examined, Blumstein and Schwartz spoke at the 1984 American Sociological Association meeting about the heavy coverage that they and their book received across the country.

Perhaps the most important lesson from the inquiry is that trying to interest the media in a social science study via written communication alone is usually fruitless. Reporters told us repeatedly that social scientists who want attention for their studies have to learn more about the media than their mailing address. They have to learn who the reporters are, what subjects they write about, and which types of stories they favor, and they have to learn to provide information by phone and by press release in ways that make a good story for them. If the journalist is interested in following through, the social scientist can work with the journalist to shape a story that fits the requirements of the media without sacrificing social science integrity.

If social scientists have information that would make a good story, they have to undertake its transmission to the press with the same kind of effort and care that they devote to the research itself. Most of the time, even intense and sophisticated communication will not pay off. But at least it will shorten the odds.

It is not news that "knowledge transfer" rarely occurs effectively through the shuffling of paper. The same lesson has been learned in industrial research laboratories, international development projects, consultation for government policymakers, and many other sites. Dissemination of information is enhanced by personal contact with the "users" and by sensitivity to their needs and organizational constraints. It is not surprising that the same strategies apply in the domain of the media.

A Survey of Journals

Given what we learned about AAAS coverage and the use of press releases, have journalists missed anything important? Since there is little consensus among social scientists about what is important, the question is difficult to answer. We made another foray into studying it, by looking at the spring 1986 issues of five major social science journals. We selected the first ("lead") article in the issue and looked to see whether it received media coverage. The journals were the *American Economic Review, American Political Science Review,* the *American Sociological Review, American Anthropologist,* and *American Psychologist.*

The results are unsurprising. Neither the articles' authors nor the journal editors had heard of any coverage. The editors further said that they knew of few instances of media reporting of any articles that had appeared in the journals. To the extent that the major disciplinary journals represent the social science that the disciplines believe is important (and that appears to be a reasonable measure), the media miss it in its entirety. Several of the editors of these journals believe that if they could have "translated" the articles into "journalistic language" (one talked about "being a Boswell"), the material would have been newsworthy. But what is in the major journals is not news.

Whether the media missed any methodologically sound studies on topics important in the society is, of course, a much harder question. We can not answer it empirically. Our strong hunch is that they did. While they seem to be alert to big social science, especially to studies supported by federal funding or promoted by active advocacy groups, and to studies on topics already high on the media agenda (such as cocaine use and consumer behavior), studies on "dull" topics and "important" only to poorly represented segments of society probably go unnoticed.

Conclusions

Our efforts to uncover the types of social science that the media do not report have yielded important clues. First, under the most favorable circumstances, the vast majority of social science goes unreported. Even when an organization like AAAS provides reporters with press conferences on social science sessions, copies of papers, ready access to speakers, and the universal lubricant of coffee, many sessions receive little or no coverage. This was especially notable at the 1983 meeting when two of the three social science symposia on which press conferences were held received a grand total of one story between them in newspapers throughout the United States. When social scientists mail press releases to media offices, reportage is very low. Coverage of social science is the exception; media neglect is the rule.

Of course, social science is not unique in this regard. The world is full of events and people pushing for media attention, and the media have to filter out the overwhelming number of claims. Social science probably gets much the same treatment accorded most other subjects.

Second, within the accepted limits of newsworthy material, reporters have considerable choice of which social science to report. At the 1982 AAAS meeting, variability was reduced—both because press conferences seemed to influence reporters' selection and because journalists exhibited a fair degree of consensus on which topics were newsworthy by virtue of controversy or reader appeal. At the 1983 meeting, press conferences had considerably less influence on channeling reporters' attention, reporting ranged more widely across sessions, and reporters' selection criteria became more problematic. Nevertheless, predictions of coverage of the 1984 meeting accurately tagged the large majority of stories. In the incoming communications inquiry, the media had neither the "event" of a meeting to direct their attention nor the aid of briefings, paper abstracts, and so on. It was impossible to find decision rules that determined which social science found its way into print. Choices looked idiosyncratic.

Third, the influence of reporters' own interests and initiative became more visible here than it was in the interview study. While reporters not infrequently told us in the interviews that stories—stories about studies, that is—were their own idea, we were usually able to find the source that stimulated the idea. We classified only a quarter of the study stories as originating strictly from the reporters' initiative and search for information. In the incoming communications inquiry, the influence of the reporter comes through more strongly. While reporters may actually originate the subject of stories in only a minority of cases, they exercise enormous influence through the process of selection. They decide whether to report on the releases, mail, and phone calls with which they are bombarded.

Thus, the interactive nature of the reporting process stands out more sharply. Sociological books on journalism over the past decade have stressed reporters' active role (and the influence of their organizations) in "deciding what's news" (Gans 1976; Roshco 1975; Tuchman 1978; Golding and Elliot 1979; Fishman 1980; Epstein 1973). These writers and others (for example, Schudson 1978; Gamson 1984) have stressed the protean nature of reality, the multitude of ways in which reporters can shape "the blooming, buzzing confusion" into news, and the salience of the journalist and the news organization. When we focused on the social science *sources* of study stories, this significant point was blunted. In our broader look at incoming communications, we see the manifold social science "realities" available for reporting and the latitude that reporters have for selection.

That they also have considerable latitude in choosing the angle, the peg, the theme of a story is emphatically true. As we saw in some of the AAAS reportage, they can go for the "aspirin" angle rather than write about the effects of existing commitments on the direction of research; they can pick out the issue of heredity in criminal behavior and give short shrift to white collar crime. We see the newsmaking potential that reporters exercise. We see the influence of their news sense and their own particular interests. That the structure and operating procedures of the news organizations in which they work strongly guide their choices is obvious, but we cannot add much on this score from these two investigations.

A fourth finding from the inquiries is that the categories that are salient to social scientists are not good predictors of story choice. Variables such as social science discipline, type of information, mode of research (for example, quantitative or qualitative, longitudinal or cross-sectional), reputation of social scientists, and renown of institution do not exert much influence. Reporters' criteria for selection of social science do not fit these categories. As we discovered in the interview study, topic is the key sorting variable, and topics that are important in the larger world drive the choice of social science. This was further underscored in the reporting of AAAS meetings and in the selection of items from incoming mail and calls. What appears in the main journals of the social science disciplines is not news.

7

The General Pattern
of Social Science Reporting

AS WE HAVE SEEN, SOCIAL SCIENTISTS CITED IN THE MEDIA WERE PLEASED WITH THE
stories about their work. About 85 percent believed that the story was
generally accurate, about 80 percent believed that the emphasis was appropriate, and, even with the limited page space and air time available,
fewer than 30 percent believed that essential parts of their work had been
omitted. A fair number of respondents qualified their answers with allusions to the stringent constraints under which journalists work, noting that
they take these constraints into account in judging the stories that appear.
They recognize that the media are engaged in a different pursuit from the
social sciences and are not designed for the purpose of transmitting social
science to the public, and thus they do not hold them accountable to the
canons of the academy.

At the same time, these social scientists were less enchanted with the
reporting of social science in general. Almost a quarter believe that reporting in general is inaccurate, and another third are unwilling or unable to
generalize. The percentage of social scientists characterizing the general
reporting of social science with some variation of "accurate" still outnum-
bers the percentage responding with any version of "inaccurate," but it
remains a more skeptical assessment in the general than in the specific
case.

In chapter 2 we suggested a number of possible explanations for this pattern of response, from the elite character of the media we studied to social scientists' appreciation for the career advantages that coverage brings. There is another possible explanation: that social scientists mean exactly what they say. They believe that most individual stories are reasonably good in their treatment of social science but that the pattern of reporting leaves something to be desired. Several people said so explicitly. For example:

> *My concern is not accuracy, but the selection of which stories to report. That's true of all news, not just social science. . . . Accuracy is a relatively trivial concern of mine compared with a more representative selection of all the important findings available.*

Although they had no cavil with the way in which the reporter quoted them or their results, they were uncomfortable with the overall picture of social science that went out to the public.

In this chapter we focus on complaints that social scientists registered about the overall structure of reporting, no matter how good-humored or resigned they were about it. We take off from social scientists' responses and analyze the conditions of newswork that are responsible for the deficiencies that they identify. We come to see that there are important difficulties in the reporting of social science that are connected to basic practices in contemporary journalism.

Complaints about Social Science Reporting

Social scientists level five major charges at the reporting of social science. They are:

oversimplification of social science complexities

undue closure and certainty in the reporting of research results

fragmentation, with no attempt to relate an individual story to a whole body of research

inadequate scrutiny of the quality of social science studies and of the expertise of quoted social scientists

biased selection from the range of social science available

Each of these criticisms has its analog in complaints about political and general news reporting. Observers have long bemoaned the press's addiction to short, simple driblets of stories, without context or interpretation, and to its uncritical acceptance of news from official sources. Thus, the complaints we hear about social science reporting fit into grooves worn by earlier critics, but the nature of social science gives them a special tilt.

We take note that none of our respondents outlined what proper and unbiased reporting of social science would look like. (To be sure, we didn't directly ask them.) The social scientist quoted above came as close as anyone: a *representative* selection of *important* findings. But representative of what? Important to whom? These are questions with which we skirmish again later in the chapter.

Oversimplification

Oversimplification was the criticism most frequently leveled at the media by the social scientists whom we interviewed. Social scientists said about the stories in which they figured:

> *If I had to say it in ten words or less, I might choose those words. What was given were very brief statements tucked together like sardines that didn't do anybody very much justice.*

> *It's a classic kind of situation. . . . A large and complicated study is reduced to a few sentences. It is not the truth the public deserves. It suffers more from underexposure than from inaccuracy.*

> *What gets lost are the complexities and qualifications I always insist on, and which make life hard for reporters. I'm a complexifier. Simplifiers get reported fairly. These are social scientists with simple views. They are getting reported fairly, but social science is not.*

A reporter agreed with this point. He said: "When writing for newspapers you have to leave out subtle detail and state positions more dramatically than perhaps you would like. That's a difference between social science reports and media reports, because you want people to read what you write."

The basic structure of the media imposes this condition. They have a limited amount of space and time, a limited "news hole," so that only the most salient elements of a story can be told. Reporters are writing for a lay audience, most of whom are unacquainted with social science concepts, so they have to engage in what one of them called "the perilous enterprise" of translating social science into everyday language. They bring clarity to the complexities and nuances of social science, often at the sacrifice of precision and depth. Furthermore, as the reporter quoted above notes, the media have to grab the attention of their audience. They want people to read what they write; they need people to buy what they sell. Unlike social scientists, who are often satisfied with the readership of a few dozen colleagues engaged in the same specialized field, journalists' job is to engage the reader and the viewer and then get their story across in perhaps forty seconds on television or a few minutes in print.

Several social scientists whom we interviewed understood. Said one, "I don't think the purpose of a newspaper article is to serve the purpose of a scientific journal. The purpose is to describe what is newsworthy in the findings and how it elucidates the everyday problems people experience. It's a human interest story."

The task of journalists is to write short, clear, interesting stories that appeal to a mass audience. They have to find "what is interesting in the findings" and make it into "a human interest story." The demands of the media for brevity, speed, clarity, and communication create an enduring tension with social science.

Undue Closure and Certainty

Another inherent strain between reporters and social scientists is the tug between finality and uncertainty. Reporters want a sense of closure on research results. In science reporting this leads to the "breakthrough" syndrome: reporters dramatize each new study as a scientific breakthrough, whereas scientists see the study as a blip on a long curve. Similarly, in social science, reporters tend to overemphasize the certainty of the current conclusions. Social scientists have a sense of continuing inquiry, a realization of the truth in the old cliché that more research is needed.

Social scientists said:

> I think [news reporting of social science] is generally slightly sensationalized. That's not quite the right word. It tends to present everything as the last word. "So and so proved such and such." I don't believe that's ever true, at least in the work I do.

> Articles in the media always sound more definitive than they are. As if it is truth until further notice.

> [News reports of research] are generally overblown as if it was all engraved in stone. . . . [Journalists] lack a sense of ongoing inquiry. They want final conclusions simply put.

The reportorial push for conclusiveness grows out of the conditions of journalistic practice. Reporters strive for impact. They need to make a story dramatic and conclusive enough to get past the editor and into print. They are competing with their colleagues for page space or air time. To win the competition, they have to make the story sound significant. They add drama, and they sacrifice the sense of cumulative and collective inquiry.

Fragmentation

A corollary of the "finality" of each story is that there is almost no cumulation of research results over time. In the media each story is discrete, unique, isolated.[1] One social scientist said: "My study was just out there, sitting there. It didn't have any tie-in to the whole body of research on [the subject]." Even if the same paper ran a story on directly related research a few weeks or months earlier, the *new* story almost never mentions it. *That* research is not new; therefore, it is not news. There is little effort to go back and compare or synthesize. For example, during our inquiry *Time* ran a story about an NIMH report on the link between children's viewing of television violence and subsequent aggressive behavior. A few months later *Time* ran another story on the (positive) effects of television viewing on children. No mention was made of the NIMH report.

The media have few incentives to review previous research. Media practice focuses on the new. To expect them to imitate the literature review of a scientific article is unrealistic. Newsroom procedures push toward timeliness, impact, significance, uniqueness. Each report is a "story" in itself.

When a new story on social science research contradicts earlier reports, the divergence is only occasionally mentioned. Even when the new research is presented in an adversarial context—to refute earlier studies—reporters often omit any explanation of the earlier work. For example, the Global 2000 symposium at the 1983 AAAS meeting was designed as a rebuttal of the pessimistic analyses of the original report. Most

---

[1] Robert Merton reminds me that an opposite phenomenon also occurs. In handling a continuing story, one that unfolds over a period of time, the media tend to retain the original "frame" in which the story was set. Even when developments veer in unexpected directions, subsequent stories are still likely to retain the original thematic structure and to repeat selected elements from earlier stories (Klapper and Glock 1949). Adler (1986:50) notes that the same pattern occurs *across* media. She writes that "once a journalist has been the first to publish certain 'facts' amounting to a 'story' all other journalists tend to go after the *same* story . . . it is exceptionally rare for a story in one publication to contradict, or even to take the mildest exception to, a story published in another." However, the discussion here is not about the development of a single story but about a sequence of separate stories. Although they may deal with the same topic, they arise from different sources and are often written by different reporters. No effort is made to give them a common frame—or even to develop linkages among them.

reporters at the 1983 meeting concentrated on the accounts presented by the scientists on the program without describing the original work. Of the thirteen reporters who filed stories on the session, eight barely alluded to the original analysis; the stories by the AP, UPI, *Chicago Sun-Times,* and *Los Angeles Times,* among others, referred only to the fact that current analyses were more optimistic. These stories received the bulk of the circulation. Of the major papers and news services, only the *New York Times, Washington Post, Chicago Tribune,* and *Christian Science Monitor* also gave information about the premises and conclusions of the original Global 2000 report. Only three journalists went beyond the juxtaposition of conflicting positions and tried to understand the basis for the discrepancies—syndicated columnist Joan Beck from the *Chicago Tribune,* Robert C. Cowan of the *Christian Science Monitor,* and Ethan Allen.

Accordingly, what the public is given is a hodgepodge of stories, some seemingly in agreement and some in conflict. Several social scientists have worried that the media are giving the public an unflattering picture of social scientists as a squabbling crowd who cannot agree among themselves. A consequence of media modes of presentation, they say, may be the erosion of public support for social science research.

Of course, criticizing the media for revealing disagreements within the social sciences is akin to blaming the messenger for bringing bad news. As one of our social science respondents said, the problem of conflicting findings is not the media's doing: "I don't think findings in sociology are terribly important. Over the last twenty years, they have contradicted each other every five years. They are more contradictory than the press."

Words that Walter Lippmann wrote in 1922 about political institutions may apply equally to the social sciences:

> *The press is no substitute for institutions. It is like a beam of a searchlight that moves restlessly about, bringing one episode and then another out of darkness and into vision. Men cannot do the work of the world by this light alone. . . . It is only when they work by a steady light of their own, that the press, when it is turned upon them, reveals a situation intelligible enough for a popular decision. The trouble lies deeper than the press, and so does the remedy.*
> *[p. 229]*

It is too much to expect journalists to compare the results of studies or the views of social scientists and try to reach synthesis. That is a task for social scientists. It is a difficult task and one that is not being well or widely done. Several journalists said that they wish the job were done better. Said one: "Social science is of immense value, but its single pieces are never put together. There are no holistic overviews."

Inadequate Scrutiny of Quality

A few social scientists in our interviews complained that reporters were insufficiently critical of social science both in their choice of studies and in their selection of experts to quote. They complained that reporters accepted too much on faith, that they assumed the quality of studies even when quality was poor and accepted the expertise of people who were in fact not expert enough to deserve media attention. Said one:

> *An expert's opinion is not always based on sound research. The journalist can't distinguish between sound research and opinions. If they get someone forcefully quoting an opinion, they think, "He sounds like a Nobel Prize winner." They're interested in "Did you say this or didn't you?" They're not interested in whether it's true or not.*

Said another social scientist, "Reporters attribute expertise too easily." And another, "I have a jaundiced view of economic science. The media has not done enough work to show up the problems with economics as a science. I think the media has been deficient in exposing the fact that there's not much there."

Since the social scientists we interviewed had done the research and given the quotes reported in the recent stories, it is interesting that this theme surfaced. Our own look at the stories and our interviews with social scientists suggest that a few of the studies that made their way into the organs of national news were based on frail evidence, and one or two studies had obvious flaws.

Research quality is not a matter of major concern to journalists. As we saw in chapter 2, the quality of a research study is not a main criterion by which reporters select which studies to cover. Only 19 percent of the reporters mentioned research quality as any part of the basis on which they select a study. Nor is methodological competence something which most reporters feel qualified to judge. As generalists, they cannot develop the specialized knowledge and skill to evaluate evidence in the many domains with which they deal. They have to rely to a considerable extent on experts. When research looks controversial, the primary way in which they judge whether it is well done is to ask other social scientists.

One journalist remarked that it is his general practice to talk to other social scientists about a study he is reporting on, even if he doesn't use their opinions in the story. He believes that this is important to do because "it's an awfully thin pancake that doesn't have two sides." Another journalist who reported on a study said, "I talk to people. I ask them 'What do you think of this?' Let them knock it down. I'm not a specialist. . . . Every week is a new term paper you write. You live and die by how good your sources are."

The organizational pressures of the media allow reporters the luxury of checking a study out with other sources only when the story is big enough or important enough to warrant the effort. In our investigation reporters checked with other social scientists 20 percent of the time. One journalist explained that

> *if [the study] is obviously controversial, for example, showing that a particular substance causes cancer, then I would check it out with several other sources and not take it at face value. But if it's a matter of showing that the crime rate is such and such, then I don't.*

For most studies they were reporting, they made do with the press release or study report, a conversation or two with the researcher, a quick reading of available material, and their own good sense. For most stories that was good enough. But in at least two cases which we looked into in some detail, fairly shoddy social science was given éclat through exposure in the national media.

For quote stories the question is which social scientist to quote. Chapter 2 describes the manner in which reporters located expert sources. Media practices encourage returning to sources who have been useful in the past. As one social scientist told us:

> *[The media] have a stable of experts who are called on for these sorts of stories. . . . I recognize names or not, but I'm damn sure they're not good examples of the field as a whole. . . . They tend to be good staid academic types who have worked with government, who are "recognized experts." . . . Reporters accumulate quotable experts who feed their biases.*

The first part of this statement—that the media tend to go to establishment types with appropriate academic credentials—is fairly well substantiated in our data (see chapter 2). That they return to experts whose opinions are compatible with their own and who "feed their biases" also sounds plausible but is harder to test. We make an effort to look at bias in the next section.

When reporters did not have an appropriate social scientist available or wanted to change the cast of characters, they undertook new searches. They asked colleagues, took names from published papers or books, talked to other social scientists, and called university news bureaus. The search was usually done in a hurry, by telephone, and seemed relatively haphazard, but almost all the social scientists felt qualified to speak on the subject.

Several of the media that we studied have an in-house survey operation staffed by social scientists, and reporters at the *New York Times, Washington Post,* CBS, and NBC can turn to the resident social scientists for information and opinions about sources. Many reporters call a series of social scientists and discuss one person's position and credentials with the next. We found only one or two cases of the kind that Shepherd and Goode (1977) complain of, where reporters went to bureaucratic superiors or department chairmen of the researchers who had actually done the relevant work. The notion that people in higher positions in a hierarchy are inherently more knowledgeable does not appear to have unduly afflicted our sample. They do, however, seem drawn to "good staid academic types" in universities who have reassuring credentials.

Several journalists explained that it takes several years to learn their way around social science, finding out which people they can turn to and trust on which subjects. One journalist said, "I have a source book, which I've compiled over fifteen years, of people whose judgment has proven fairly accurate in all fields—law, politics, psychiatry." Reporters also talk of the reading they do to "background" a story, which also serves to turn up names and check credentials. But by and large, they say that they have to rely on the judgments of others in choosing the "right" source.

The basic dilemma remains. Reporters want to do a responsible job of reporting social science, and some social scientists want to encourage them to do it more critically. But they do not have sufficient knowledge to exercise critical selectivity in the many areas of social science that come their way. Or, if they acquire enough knowledge, they may not have enough confidence in their judgment—or their editors may not trust their judgment enough—to forgo the need for social science counsel.

The issue of critical judgment becomes particularly salient when social scientists disagree. When studies come to conflicting conclusions or social scientists offer opposing interpretations, reporters make one of three choices. First, they can give the latest news and ignore previous statements. That, as we have seen, is common. Second, they can report the conflicting viewpoints side by side. This procedure accords with journalistic norms of "objectivity" and "balance," where objectivity means neutrality and balance means letting both sides (or the several sides) of an argument be heard. In a balanced story reporters make no effort to explain the bases for the differences, nor do they try to give the reader grounds for deciding who has a better case. They treat social science as they treat other news: They present a variety of perspectives from experts and keep their own hands off. A third option, used much less frequently, is to make the controversy itself the focus of the story. A reporter highlights the conflict between sociobiologists who see a biological basis for human inequality and social scientists who see environmental conditions as paramount.

That there is a fourth way of writing the story about social science conflict rarely occurs to reporters, but several observers have wondered whether reporters couldn't take a more active—and critical—role. They might explain reasons for discrepant research results and conflicting forecasts. They might describe the different assumptions that social scientists make, the different measures, populations, definitions, or time periods they use. Even if reporters did not try to adjudicate the conflict themselves, they could give the reader a basis for understanding the differences among social scientists and perhaps even help the reader decide who is right.

Reporters do not see this type of critical reporting as their job, any more than they see it as their job to explain why politicians hold opposing views. When I raised the question in a discussion with the Nieman Fellows at Harvard in June 1983, one reporter said that if social scientists think they have problems with the press now, "this would all be child's play compared to the fur that would fly" if reporters undertook to decide which social science was right.

Fairness and balance, not the validity of research, are issues that engage reporters. In television this bent was reinforced until recently by Federal Communications Commission (FCC) rules, which defined fairness as the presentation of opposing views on an issue. Epstein (1973) writes that networks, therefore, solicited opinions from spokesmen with opposing views. Neither person's arguments were questioned, nor was the weakness or superiority of either side exposed, "for even to appear to favor one side might be construed as an unfair presentation by network executives. . ." (Epstein 1973:265). Therefore, policies did not encourage correspondents "to attempt to resolve controversial issues in favor of one side or another by conducting their own investigations" (Epstein 1973:265).

Neutrality, which in the case of television has had the added sanction of the FCC, is a pervasive norm in print media as well. The same attitudes and cast of mind that discourage independent determination of which political position is right also tend to limit independent determination of which social science is right. Only two reporters with whom I discussed the subject at a AAAS meeting believe that they, as science writers, have a responsibility to uncover the differing assumptions that underlie discrepant scientific estimates and make them visible to the public. It is probably no accident that they are science reporters.

Goodfield wrote an interesting book on the reporting of science, which grapples repeatedly with the issue. She asks, ". . . should the journalist take on the role of critic?" (1981:88). She quotes John Ziman: "The good technical journalist can acquaint himself with the essential expert opinions and draw attention to the most significant features of a complex argument. If he really knows his stuff, he can distinguish between genuine expertise and bogus authority" (1976:794). But Goodfield comments, "Yet there are, of course, dangers in relying only upon the journalist. . . . [Their reports] are not altogether to be trusted . . ." (p. 14). Her final assessment is ambivalent:

> *So the journalist has the added role of both presenting equitably and intelligibly the views of scientists who disagree with each other and helping the public understand and decide between them. In coming to terms with this situation, journalists must decide (i) whether they will play this role, and (ii) what criteria they will apply to these matters . . .—and to do that journalists are going to have to get very solidly educated in these issues. [p.92]*

She advises scientists to offer full cooperation and candor in this endeavor.

Social science reporting is probably even more problematic than science writing, which the media recognize as a specialty that requires extensive training and preparation. The reporting of social science is seen as something that any journalist can do, and few of them have the incentive to become thoroughly knowledgeable in social science. To expect them to provide "the prerequisites for [public] debate, that is, a thorough independent assessment of scientific discoveries" (Goodfield 1981:13) is to expect more than the current organization of newswork can sustain.

What would be desirable is more attention to the assumptions and definitions that underlie conflicting research findings. Reporters could explain the grounds on which one social scientist says poverty is decreasing while another says poverty is increasing. The *Times* story mentioned in Part II is a good illustration of reporter's clarification of seemingly contradictory findings. In reporting a National Academy of Sciences study on the link between diet and cancer, the reporter indicated that an earlier "contradictory" report referred to the relationship between fat intake and heart disease, not cancer, and that the earlier report reflected the opinions of biochemists concerned with evidence of cause and effect whereas the National Academy panel included epidemiologists and public health experts who relied more on statistical correlations to reach conclusions. It is a sophisticated and useful analysis. What no doubt is not wise is to leave in the hands of the press the determination of which social science is right and which is wrong. As Richard Rovere wrote about probably the most blatant case in which reporting "the facts" led to misguided news, the press coverage of Senator Joseph McCarthy:

> . . . *I suspect there is no surer way to a corrupt and worthless press than to authorize reporters to tell the readers which "facts" are really "facts" and which are not. Certainly in those countries where this is the practice, the press serves the public less well than ours does. [1959:166]*

We agree. Yet we have a system where reporters choose which news is "news." In the social sciences they decide which studies are worth reporting and which people are worth quoting. We echo Goodfield's hope that more journalists will become "solidly educated," but without changes in newsroom values and practice, education alone will not resolve the dilemmas.

Biased Selection

That the media select social science by criteria different from those of social science journal editors is indisputable. Whether in so doing they ignore bodies of research that social scientists would like the public to know about seems a reasonable question. Certainly the media ignore almost all work related to the development of theory, historical reviews, and almost everything on methodology except for occasional reports of change in the calculation of major indicators such as the unemployment rate or consumer price index. As we saw in chapter 6, editors of the major social science journals know of few articles that have ever been picked up by the press. The media are uninterested in studies that have no obvious link to the public's interests—in daily living, economic conditions, social trends or political events. Their universe of attention is bounded by topics that can be expected to engage the attention of a reasonably well-informed U.S. adult with no special concern with the esoteric doings of social science.

Given these limits, it is difficult to second-guess the media's choice of social science. What *would* be a reasonable allocation of attention? What is a representative selection of important findings? It is difficult to imagine an answer that could gain a consensus from social scientists—either by discipline, by topic, by orientation to public issues versus private interests, or on any other dimension. Perhaps the best we can do is posit a few notions about media imbalance and see to what extent our sample of stories supports them.

The possibilities we examine are: (1) the media select quantitative studies over qualitative studies; (2) the media select social science, particularly social science research, that supports rather than challenges the major institutions of society; (3) the media, being "vaguely liberal," as one of the social scientists we interviewed put it, select liberal-leaning social science.

Quantitative Studies. The stories about research studies are over-whelmingly about quantitative research. Of the 76 study stories about which we could judge, 69 provided numerical data or strongly implied that numbers underlay the results. Most stories did not describe the research methods that were used, but when methods were described, they were usually surveys. Occasionally econometric models were cited, there were a few cases in which institutional or program records were analyzed, and there were two experiments.

Quantitative data have obvious attractions. They sound authoritative. There is something reassuring about a crisp "57 percent" that is lacking in a "majority." Reporters, like the rest of us, have become accustomed to the quantitative apparatus of test scores, census projections, election polls, and so on, and they use numbers to lend credibility to a story.

In an important sense the preference for quantitative research is counteracted by the use of social scientists in quote stories. Several of the notable social scientists who were quoted, such as David Riesman and Digby Baltzell, are known for qualitative and historical research. The quote stories themselves stress insight over data. While most of the journalists who wrote quote stories said that the quoted social scientist based his/her statements on research, they appeared to give as much credence to qualitative and historical analysis as to quantitative research.

Support for Societal Institutions. Only about 60 percent of the stories had implications for either support or challenge to major institutions of society. Of those stories which did, almost three times as many of them suggested a need for change—modest change—as supported the existing institutional system. For example, one story reported the relatively low impact of recent civil service reform. Another described a variety of programs for delinquents, none of which was effective in deterring crime. Another reported that college students know little about world geography and foreign cultures. Another described the limited representation of women and minorities in positions of labor union leadership. Still another reported on the extent of sexual harassment of women in the army. The media's traditional emphasis on controversy makes these kinds of stories more appealing than stories oriented toward the status quo.

Relatively few stories gave clear-cut support to political or social institutions. The closest were studies and quotes dealing with uptrends in the economy, but they were outnumbered by stories of unemployment and inflation. Challenge was more common. Perhaps the greatest challenge came from two stories: one reporting a link between television violence and children's aggressive behavior, a challenge to television, and the other about children's fears of nuclear war, which might be construed as a challenge to the military establishment, U.S. foreign policy, or the current system of international relations. The prevailing theme was the need to reform institutions.

Liberal Leanings. We define liberal in terms familiar since the New Deal as involving support for the underdog (for example, women, racial minorities, prisoners) and support of government intervention (for example, economic regulation, action against lead poisoning, government-supported day care, job training). Most study stories did not have a liberal-conservative dimension, but of the 29 that did, liberal leanings outweighed conservative 18 to 11. That studies would tend to have a liberal cast is not surprising, since most social scientists hold liberal beliefs (Orlans 1973; Lipset and Ladd 1972). Much social science research has a humanitarian bent and deals with "social problems" in the broad sense of the term, and many research findings have implications for government intervention.

What we know of elite journalists' political opinions suggests that they, too, are liberal (Barton 1974–75; Lichter and Rothman 1981), although a more accurate characterization might be the one that a large proportion of journalists adopt for themselves: independent. Gans has noted that few journalists are ideologically oriented, and it is difficult to classify them on a left-right axis. He writes, "In reality, the news is not so much conservative or liberal as reformist" and much akin to the Progressive movement of the turn of the century (1979:68). Journalism has a great deal in common with Progressivism, including a strong emphasis on objectivity, a belief in the virtues of professionalism, and an expectation that the public good will be served through the exposure of social and political evils (Gans 1979:205). That much of the social science which journalists report has strong undertones of the reformist impulse suggests the strength of this insight. The muckraking tradition in the journalism of the early 1900s still colors reporters' orientation to news.

Herrnstein (1982) has alleged that the media give biased coverage— at least on the issue of the heritability of intelligence—by suppressing or distorting evidence that supports the "conservative" position, namely, that IQ has some genetic basis. On the left, social scientists voice similar criticism of media silence and/or distortion. Observers who look for neo-Marxist or even social-democratic perspectives in reporting find little to observe. The media, they say, are inhospitable to such ideologies (Tuchman 1978; Gans 1979).

Our data do not provide systematic evidence on either score. Reporters' descriptions of their work suggest that they tend to be suspicious of social science with any political or ideological overtones. Several of them reported checking out study results that had possible political connections "to see if [the researcher] had a vested interest" or if the sponsoring organization "may have financed the study" because it had a stake in the results. The operative norm remains objectivity, and the basic position seems to be the eastern establishment version of middle-of-the-road consensus.

The Transformation of Social Science into News

Over all, the reshaping of social science is less ideological or political than it is stylistic. Reporters treat social science much as they treat news from other sources, and they incorporate it into the traditional repertoire of journalistic forms.

Robert Darnton, in a perceptive paper reflecting on his five years as a newspaperman, says that there is a stylized pattern for shaping a news story out of the swarm of daily events. Every reporter learns how to manipulate "standardized images, clichés, 'angles', 'slants', and scenarios, which will call forth a conventional response in the minds of editors and readers" (Darnton 1975:189). He emphasizes that stories are patterned on a "traditional repertory of genres" that goes back hundreds of years through seventeenth century news-sheets, French *canards,* English chapbooks, broadside ballads, nursery rhymes, penny dreadfuls, "as if they were metamorphoses of *Ur*-stories that have been lost in the depths of time" (p. 189). The writing of news is profoundly influenced by stereotyped images and a standardized structure for what a news story should be. Darnton writes that "newspaper stories must fit cultural preconceptions of news" (p. 192) and that stories must be written "within the conventions of the craft" (p. 191). The traditions that lie behind the construction of today's news stories, hard news as well as features, "probably derive from ancient oral traditions" of story telling (p. 191). (See also Lippmann 1947 [1922]; Rosten 1937; Breed 1955.)

More prosaically, Lapham (1981:34) writes of a veteran newsman who kept in his desk drawer, along with a bottle of bourbon, "a looseleaf notebook filled with stock versions of maybe fifty or sixty common newspaper texts. These were arranged in alphabetical order (fires, homicides, ship collisions, etc.). . . . The reporter had left blank spaces for the relevant names, deaths, numbers, and street addresses."

Reporters approach the reporting of social science with the set of journalistic conventions in mind. They fit social science to the available story-telling forms, and the genre helps to shape their presentation. One of the social scientists whom we interviewed captured this insight: "Surprisingly, newspaper people have trouble understanding what you say unless it fits their template."

Journalists' Story Frames

Analysis of stories with social science content shows that reporters use a series of frames to make a story out of social science. These are the frames that are most commonly used:

Make an Event of the Study's Release.   No reporters were on the scene when the social scientist made sense of the data or reached the "aha!" stage of understanding. The moment of discovery, if there was such a moment, cannot be reported like the launching of a space shuttle. It took place in the recesses of the researcher's mind or in the interactions among members of the research team. News in effect "happens" when the journalist interviews the source, attends a press briefing, or is given a handout. Reporters make an event out of the release of the study. Whether the social science report was released at a press conference, presented at a professional meeting, published in a book or journal, or publicized through a written circular to the press, reporters capitalize on the sheer fact of its release. With that as event, they can proceed to cover the story.

This was the most common convention for reporting the research studies in our sample. Thirty-one stories used the news peg of release. Typical phrases that appeared in the lead sentence were: "just released," "reported today," "new survey," "yesterday released a report," "has just written a new best-seller," "spoke at a symposium," "a new study."

Attach the Study Results or Other Social Science Content to a Hard News Peg.   This convention takes an event that is already in the news and attaches social science to it. For example, a reporter writes a lead about congressional action on cost of living adjustments for Social Security and then introduces a study about the poverty status of the aged. The congressional action sets a frame for the study results. Similarly, a reporter writes about administration plans to drop requirements for bilingual education and incorporates results of a study on the effectiveness of bilingual education into the account.

In some cases the reporter seems almost to "manufacture" the event as an excuse for presenting the social science, or at least latches on to a not particularly newsworthy occasion as a way of leading into the social science and giving it immediacy. A long analytic piece about the slump in the construction industry was pegged to a convention of the National Association of Home Builders. An analysis of child support payments used the occasion of the publication of regulations by the Department of Health and Human Services. In other cases the reporter is covering hard news, such as the visit of the Egyptian president to the United States, and draws on social science to provide depth and substance.

Seven of the stories in our sample used a hard news peg. In about half of them the peg seemed more of a justification for the story than a real event.

The possibility of integrating social science into hard "breaking" news has considerable appeal. If social science were used to provide background and analysis for hard news, it could contribute to understanding of political, social, and economic developments in the world. For example, if Congress cuts the food stamp budget, a reporter could draw on evaluation studies of the program to indicate probable effects of the cuts.

However, coverage of that sort would make heavy demands. It requires more resources, greater specialization, different organization of newswork, and a change in prevailing values. Reporters would have to have the expertise and time to keep up with relevant research on a regular basis so that they could draw on it when events break, and they would need a well-stocked and well-indexed library that would make research rapidly retrievable. Since hard news has to be reported fast, it is too much to expect extensive reporting of this type under current conditions. More possibilities exist in the newsmagazines, the Sunday sections of newspapers, columns, news analyses, and television news documentaries. Later in the chapter we look at feature stories that incorporate social science, a form that seems more feasible for integrating social science into media accounts.

Attach Social Science Content to Cyclical Events. Some reports use a cyclical event as a news peg, such as Father's Day, Valentine's Day, or school graduations. These events come around regularly and predictably, and the media traditionally write about them. Psychologists who have studied interpersonal attraction know that the phone will begin ringing off the wall in early February as reporters get ready for Valentine's Day stories (Rubin 1980).

Five stories in our sample were pegged to cyclical events. "On this day before Father's Day," began one, and cited research on older fathers. Another story reported, ". . . this week, thousands of gowned seniors will shuffle down the aisles" and discussed data on school dropouts. Other events to which social science was attached were a city's 300th birthday and—a more "constructed" event—the tenth anniversary of Nixon's visit to China. The key characteristic of cyclical events is that reporters have time to plan appropriate stories in advance and to seek out relevant social science. But very few studies, even with high journalistic imagination, can fit this genre.

Frame Social Science in a Human Interest Context.   To put a study into human terms, reporters sometimes start with a vignette from real life. They set a scene. For a study on unemployment a reporter might interview a woman standing in line at the local unemployment office, asking her about the effects of unemployment on her family; the interview provides a lead-in for the research findings. This frame puts the findings back into the realm of human experience from which the social scientist extracted them in the first place. Warm, breathing individuals lie beneath the numbers, and the journalist makes them visible.

In our sample fourteen stories began with a human interest anecdote. One story begins, "Like many Japanese, Hiroshi Nakamura still remembers vividly. . . ," followed by an analysis of U.S. trade restrictions. Another story begins, "A married account executive begins flirting with his boss at the ad agency," and then presents research on moral ambiguities. One story puts the reader into the position of survey respondent: "Picture this. You're sitting in your livingroom relaxing. The doorbell rings. It's a public-opinion pollster. . . ." The death of two teenagers in a car crash opens a story on highway safety. The refusal of half the employees of a local firm to move when the company changed locations introduces an analysis of relocation.

This is a fetching convention and one that reporters tend to use well. But it runs the risk of oversimplification. By dramatizing the experience of one or two people the reporter can undercut the variety of experience that the study has revealed. Nevertheless, this frame can satisfy the criteria of both reporters and social scientists. It works well on television.

Make the Social Science Itself a Human Interest Story.   Eighteen stories in our sample used social science for its human interest. Topics included the effects of beauty on people's personal and professional lives, divorces among blacks, responsibilities of the children of single parents, attitudes of teenagers toward parents and friends, suicide, births among women in their 30s, people's behavior when someone breaks into the line ahead of them, sexual harassment, attitudes of confidence/cynicism, and balancing marriage and career responsibilities. These kinds of stories often appear on what used to be called the women's page and is now called "living," "style," or "behavior." They relate to people's everyday lives, and they usually try not only to entertain but also enlighten.

Dramatize "the First, the Biggest, the Most Expensive, the Most Comprehensive." In this convention key phrases such as these appear at the beginning: ". . . the most extensive study . . . ever undertaken, both in terms of the number of people studied and the number of years she followed them"; ". . . broadest review . . . ever undertaken in this country by a scientific group"; ". . . the first such comprehensive survey . . ." Whereas other stories will mention factors like this later in a story to enhance credibility, stories in this category make a news peg of firstness and mostness.

In our sample three study stories were reported using this frame. While all of them appear responsible, the form also lends itself to distortion. It can exaggerate the uniqueness of a study and accentuate the non-cumulative tendencies of newsreporting. Stories that stress the cost of a study are sometimes a not-too-subtle put-down. Who needed to spend $200,000 to find out that victims of crime are subsequently afraid to go out after dark? Still, stress on specialness resonates with journalistic traditions.

Emphasize the Paradoxical, the Ironical, the Unexpected. Reporters look for unexpected, counterintuitive, "man bites dog" stories. Social science that challenges the accustomed wisdom is likely to gain their attention. We saw this in reportage of the AAAS meetings, where journalists reported on papers about the inheritance of shyness and the unreliability of testimony given under hypnosis. The existence of a "gender gap" in support for the Reagan Administration, with women considerably lower in support for the administration's policies than men, marked a shift from long years during which male and female opinions followed similar patterns. That was news.

As a convention for storytelling, reporters sometimes construct a paradox, a strawperson. They set up a lead of the taken-for-granted variety, and then they explode it. An example from our sample: "Staying fit has become a national preoccupation. . . . It's ironic, then, . . . more and more American women are abusing their [health]." The story continues with a discussion of data on drinking and smoking. Another story plays up the social scientist's surprise over her findings: ". . . [she] is startled by the results of questions she sent to 5,000 households. . . ."

Emphasis on the unexpected appeared in almost a dozen stories in our sample, but it was the primary reporting convention for four stories.

Focus on Differences. Controversy is an archetypical journalistic value. Paletz and Entman (1981:16) observe that drama is such an urgent requirement for news that "journalists have been known to highlight if not concoct conflict and to find characters to symbolize its different sides. One reason: to attract an audience that is thought to have little patience for the abstract, the technical, the ambiguous, the uncontroversial."

For social science reporting the convention of controversy can lead to highlighting differences among social scientists or between social scientists and other public figures. Both varieties appeared among the five controversy stories in our sample. Two stories focused on differences among demographers in forecasting population trends. (After our observation period there was a similar story on differences among pollsters in election forecasts.) Another story aired disagreements and self-doubts among social scientists under the headline "Social Sciences: Why Doubts Are Spreading Now." Another story reported that industry spokesmen were challenging prevailing economic theory about the relationships among government deficits, inflation, and growth.

A substantial number of other stories in the sample reported the differing views of social scientists on a particular issue. In an effort to provide fair and balanced coverage reporters often line up pro's and anti's. What distinguishes the stories in the controversy category is that the conflict itself was the focus of the story.

During the period that we monitored, no story had the visibility given the criticisms by other social scientists of James Coleman's studies on desegregation, white flight, or public and private schools, nor did any story focus on the divergent views of economists regarding monetary and fiscal policy or other policy issues. The most notable recent case of social science controversy was probably Australian anthropologist Derek Freeman's attack on Margaret Mead's work in Samoa. News stories in early 1983 focused on his criticisms of the adequacy of Mead's fieldwork and more broadly on the vulnerability of methods of anthropological inquiry. Hundreds of stories appeared in the media worldwide. The story had almost everything—the well-known public figure of Margaret Mead, an attack on a tradition of scholarship, an exotic locale with waving palm trees and nubile teenagers, and a focus on sexual behavior. For the media it was first and foremost a story of controversy, with critics of the late Margaret Mead on one side and her supporters on the other.

Use Well-known or Colorful Personalities. A few social scientists are well-known figures in their own right, but not many. James Coleman and Milton Friedman, like the late Margaret Mead, are candidates for "personality status." When social scientists are not well-known or colorful, the media can attempt to create a colorful image. A story in the *Boston Globe* about sociologist Paul Starr, following his receipt of a Pulitzer Prize, played up the contrast between his student activism in the 1960s and his scholarly work at Harvard in 1984.

In our sample no stories focused on social science personalities, and only one used a political personality as a frame for introducing study results. In this case it was former Secretary of Health and Human Services Joseph Califano who gave the study visibility.

Analyze Public Policy Issues.   Thirty-nine stories in our sample did not fit any of the news frames we have identified, but twenty-eight of them made a fairly homogeneous category of their own. They were interpretive analyses or features on public policy issues. Most of them were serious efforts at analysis, examining the causes and effects of significant issues, such as high medical costs, gas price decontrol, and farm surpluses. They explained the history of an issue, who was affected, and its second-order consequences. Most of these stories dealt with economic issues, although there were also stories on social issues, such as crime, and governmental issues, such as making the federal bureaucracy more responsive. The reporter defined terms, explained interrelationships among elements— such as interest rates, borrowing, business growth, and government deficits—and sometimes tried to relate the phenomenon to "you, the reader."

Social science was almost always used in ancillary fashion. Reporters drew upon a study or a quote to provide evidence for a point or as judgment and interpretation. The intent of the story was to make sense of a complex phenomenon, and social science was used when and where it was helpful.

This category of news analysis, or trend analysis, has been developing in the media since the 1930s when economic crisis and the rise of Nazism made apparent the need for more interpretive news reporting (Schudson 1978; Roshco 1975). Reporters and editors also became aware, in those years and thereafter, of how the media were being manipulated by the new public relations industry and its glossy handouts and constructed "events." The standard news format of the press made it easy game for public relations specialists. Never was this more evident than with the advent of Joseph McCarthy, who knew how to make news of his charges of Communist activity and how and when to get maximum play and allow minimum time for rebuttal. A news framework geared to "timeliness" and "objective reporting" had little way to protect itself. The media felt impelled to broaden the analytic component in the news.

Signed columns on political affairs began in the 1920s (Schudson 1978:150) and by the 1930s they were syndicated, providing greater breadth of analysis to newspapers across the country. The weekly news-magazines, unable to compete in up-to-date coverage with newspapers, inevitably took a somewhat more analytic look at events. On radio and TV there were news documentaries, with Edward R. Murrow a notable pioneer. More recently, syndicated columnists have been joined by writers of op-ed pieces, and reporters on major papers are given the time and resources to explore issues in depth.

The trend toward greater emphasis on news analysis has been hailed on and off since the 1940s as an important step in putting the news in perspective. Analysis has grown, particularly in syndicated columns, the Sunday sections, the newsmagazines, and TV news specials, but there is strong counterbalancing resistance. Too much interpretive reporting threatens to turn into the "new journalism" of the late 1960s and early 1970s with its anti-establishment flavor, its personal and particularistic bent. Such reporting runs the risk of sacrificing the trust of the mass audience. Golding and Elliott (1979) note: "It also challenges the basic values of factuality and objectivity by inviting comment in the guise of analysis, partiality in the guise of background, and for these reasons is unpopular among journalists."

The old style of "objective," "eventistic" reporting helps reporters and editors resolve such intrinsic dilemmas of newswork as deciding what news is and how to present it (Tuchman 1978). They are loath to abandon it too rapidly for fear of having to confront the thorny old issues again.

Currently the major media support a certain amount of interpretive reporting by the news staff. The media provide resources and room for interpretation of public issues, and reporters who write analytic pieces aim to do so within the tradition of objectivity. They marshal facts, give balanced representation to opposing views, and cite acknowledged sources.

The use of social science within analytic stories seems to be one of the more promising directions for the reporting of social science and, to an extent, for the news as well. When social science is embedded in serious journalistic analysis, it escapes the episodic hit-and-run character that dogs it elsewhere in the media. The journalist puts it into context. While the context is quite different from its context of origin, it is the context of the subject matter—decentralization of authority from the federal government to the states, the causes and effects of falling interest rates. Often policy implications are highlighted. On occasion, the journalist uses social science from several disciplines, overcoming the obsolete barriers between the social sciences and crafting interdisciplinary approaches to issues. When journalistic analysis is well done and its use of social science responsible, it creates informative interpretation for a large audience.

Of course, journalists can also make poor use of social science, yoking it to inept analysis, misinterpreting or distorting social science evidence to suit the case they are making, or using social science as window dressing. Not all journalists doing interpretive reporting have sufficient knowledge of social science (including a rudimentary knowledge of statistics) to choose appropriate social science sources or to extract significant themes.

Good interpretive reporting does not, of course, require the use of social science. There are other ways to make sense of the world, ways with longer traditions and, some would argue, greater power. Still, when journalists use social science well in analytic stories, they not only disseminate social science to a wider public (which social scientists are likely to appreciate) but they also broaden the range of evidence and ideas available to the public.

Conclusion

Despite social scientists' satisfaction with the individual stories that appeared in the media, some see serious shortcomings in the pattern of social science reporting. We have looked at criticisms that (1) reporting is oversimplified, (2) it is overdramatic and allots too much certainty to provisional findings (and all social science findings are in a sense provisional in today's changing world), (3) it fragments social science into slivers and shards, and (4) it is insufficiently critical toward social science authority, failing to subject it to adequate review and abjuring any responsibility for clarifying inconsistencies or disagreements among social scientists. To a considerable degree, each of these criticisms is true. Nor is their prevalence the result of ignorance or caprice. Rather they arise from the structure and values of newswork. The organization and standard operating procedures of journalism push in these directions. The shaping of social science into news drags along behind it, like old tin cans tied to a newlyweds' car, a series of clattering impedimenta.

We also looked at the charge that the media select a biased subset of social science for presentation. The notion of bias assumes some true standard, some distribution that is representative of all social science or of its "important" studies. Perhaps the appropriate standard is methodologically sound studies on important subjects that are of interest to significant elements of the public. We have difficulty figuring out how to construct such a population of studies. Almost no social scientist we spoke to thinks that the media should be interested in all of the vast social science array that the disciplines publish for their own purposes in their own journals. Nearly all social scientists recognized the limited range of public attention and the responsibility of the media to be relevant to their audience. So the definition of which social science should be reported remains shrouded in mist.

If there is little consensus on an ideal body of social science in the media, criticism can still be constructive by identifying gross bias. As has been said about pornography, even if you can't define it, you know it when you see it. Perhaps social scientists can point out the most glaring deviations from the straight and true. Some social scientists who see bias in media coverage say the bias is toward controversy, drama, and excitement. Some say it is ideological, with a tilt toward the left. We looked at three hypotheses about bias, namely, that there is a bias toward quantitative social science, toward social science that upholds major social institutions, and toward left-liberal social science. The media tend to report studies that are quantitative, but they are receptive to commentary based on qualitative evidence as well. Ideologically, we found that where there is a political penumbra, the primary impulse seems to be reformist. Journalists tend to report on social science that shows a shortfall between intent and achievement and thus a need for incremental improvement.

Perhaps the most pervasive influence on the reporting of social science is the necessity for fashioning it into a "story" that fits journalistic story-telling conventions. Several journalists whom we interviewed commented on the grayness of social science and the need to reshape it.

> *[Social scientists] are terrible writers, very boring. They don't use flesh and blood, they use graphs and bar charts. They should ham it up. If they're writing about failing financial institutions, they should talk to a failing financial institution. Make it into drama. They have no talent for telling stories.*

> *The problem with sociology is that it requires study footnotes and leaves out human experience.*

Reporters undertake to remedy the shortcomings. As they do, they jettison much of the social science paraphernalia—authors' names, journal source, descriptions of research methods, and so on (see Part II). Yet let us remember that social science writing is also based on a set of conventions and these reflect the purposes and structure of the social sciences. Although the conventions differ from those of news writing, they impose an equally artificial structure and an equally tight choreography on communication. Ziman (1968:34) has written:

> *The work as published is no mere chronicle of the research as it took place; it is a much more contrived document, with its logical teeth brushed and its observational trouser seams sharply creased. It is written in a curiously "impersonal" style, deliberately flat and unemotional, as from one calculating machine to another.*

Journalists tend to see the social science paper as written at such a high level of abstraction that it retains little sense of living people and human institutions. It also leaves out the human aspects of the author. As Merton (1968:4) notes: "Typically the scientific paper or monograph presents an immaculate appearance which reproduces little or nothing of the intuitive leaps, false starts, loose ends, and happy accidents that actually cluttered up the inquiry." He observes that scientific communication actually conceals the process of investigation, exaggerating the rational aspects of the work.

The two formats, those of journalism and those of social science, are both creatures of convention. Journalistic narrative forms, descending as Darnton suggests from popular balladry and Mother Goose, have the virtue of being familiar to the public. We have identified ten story forms that journalists use to turn social science into news. Each of them puts a certain "spin" on the story. The most common convention is to make an "event" of the release of study results. Perhaps the most interesting to social scientists is the use of social science as supplementary material in interpretive features on public issues. Although social science can be poorly used in the service of reporters' analyses, it can also be used to enrich and amplify reporters' understanding and to improve the depth of interpretation that reaches the public.

The number of stories using social science as ancillary material in the media we examined has risen significantly (see Part II). This suggests that reporters are increasingly drawing upon social science studies, quotes, and data in their analytic reporting. Hess has called the phenomenon "social science journalism" (1981:118) and describes it as "serious, dealing with cause, and predictive . . . it deemphasizes personalities and events" (p. 119). These may sound like positive descriptors to some of us, but Hess is less sanguine: "Social science journalism may be a worthy goal. But it also requires considerable preparation time, library and research facilities, and page space and air time to do justice to complexities. There must also be an audience that has the interest as well as the leisure to read and listen" (p. 119). He is not sure that such conditions exist or that reporters would be equipped by temperament or training to take advantage of them if they did. "The best journalists always have been story-tellers, not theoreticians, Homers, not Aristotles" (p. 120). Better a good chronicler of events than a bad social scientist.

Hess's analysis raises an important issue. Increased coverage of social science has costs for the media and risks for the social sciences as well as benefits. Do we—social scientists and journalists alike—want to encourage increased reporting of the social sciences under current conditions? If so, can improvements be made in the process and the product? That is the subject of the next chapter.

8

In Which We Conclude, Seek to Improve, and Take Stock

THERE IS AN OLD STORY ABOUT A GAMBLER WHO WENT TO THE CASINO EVERY NIGHT to play roulette. Every night he played and every night he lost. Finally, a friend took him aside and said, "Don't you know that wheel is crooked?"

The gambler said, "Sure, I know."

The friend said, "Then why do you keep on playing?"

"Because," said the gambler, "it's the only wheel in town."

If the social sciences want to get their messages to a mass audience, then the mass media are pretty much the only wheel in town. Although there are wobbles and glitches in their functioning, our data show that they are nowhere near as crooked as many social scientists have feared. Given the fact that the odds always favor the house, the media tend to give the player a pretty fair shake.

But the media are not a neutral conduit to the public. The media channel influences which messages are carried and what is transmitted. The media pick and choose, shorten, shape, reorder, and alter. They do not often distort, according to the social scientists in our inquiry, but they are not a popularized and readable version of the *American Sociological Review*.

In this chapter we return to the hypotheses about media reporting with which we began (see chapter 1) and see how they have fared. We examine which of them are supported by the data and which need revision. Next we take up the topic of improving social science reporting. In this cause we pass on advice from our respondents on how social scientists can get more and better coverage, and we examine the utility of a number of prescriptions for longer-term reform. Finally, we take a hard look at whether reporting of social science in the mass media, on balance, is a good thing. We look at its value for the social sciences, for policymakers, and for the public.

The Fate of the Original Hypotheses

We began the inquiry with five hypotheses about the reporting of social science. The first stated that journalists treat social science much as they treat any other subject. The second was that journalists use social science in part to legitimate their accounts and validate their interpretations. The third, more problematical but in good currency in some social science circles, held that coverage is determined to a considerable extent by the entrepreneurial activities of those social scientists who seek media attention. A fourth hypothesis was that most journalists are insufficiently knowledgeable about social science theories and methods to report adequately. Finally, we expected the organization and practices of newswork to be largely responsible for the ways that social science is played. We are ready now to take stock.

The assumption that social science is treated much like other news is well supported. Journalists tend to select social science by the usual criteria for news: it is interesting; it is new; it is related to subjects in hard-news events; it is important; it is controversial. As one reporter told us:

> *I don't think of things as social science. The criteria are the same as any damn story: Is it important? Is it interesting? And to some degree, is it new? They're the same criteria I use when I'm writing about the Democratic National Committee.*

When reporters find something newsworthy, they report it, and in the process, they reshape it to fit the conventions of news writing. Accuracy is one of the norms of news writing, so stories overwhelmingly adhere to the social science facts. One of our main findings is social scientists' satisfaction with the stories in which they figure. But stories on social science also tend to be simplified, dramatized, short of context, fragmented, and crafted into an available story form. In short, social science news is much like other news in the media.

Regarding the use of social science to provide credibility for journalists' accounts, we see that journalists do use research data and quotes from social scientists as ancillary material in stories they are reporting. A few journalists said explicitly that social science provides legitimacy. One reporter in our study put it this way: "You people put a stamp of approval on what we all know. You package it. Americans, perhaps, are too reliant on studies, but you give justification even if we already know the facts as common knowledge."

A social scientist made the same point in more elegant language:

> Social scientists have a role in the modern world rather like theologians had in the past. They are the intellectualizers of widespread beliefs they seldom originate; rather they clarify, criticize, and shape them into articulate doctrine. There is a weighty sense of being ultimate authorities, of saying "Yea" or "Nay" out of disciplined investigation to what others merely opine or want to believe. [Sutton, quoted in Robinson 1984:80]

The quest for legitimation, however, seems only incidentally to be the purpose for drawing on social science. Reporters often value data for its informational contribution (as well as the sense of hard factuality), and they call on social scientists because they are well informed or interesting or dispassionate or offer a deft turn of phrase. They seem to use social science more for the information and ideas it provides than for its legitimating services. While most reporters are favorably disposed toward the social sciences, they are not particularly respectful, let alone deferential. They like social science when it does what they need done—provide information, a point of view that needs covering, or a colorful quote. Occasionally they turn to social science to support a position or perspective that they are developing in a story, but they may use government officials or other sources in the same cause.

The suspicion that coverage is strongly influenced by the self-promotional activities of social scientists receives relatively little support. Of the 80 studies in our inquiry, authors of 15 said that they had contacted members of the media, but in only 5 of these cases could we trace the story back to the social scientist's contact. Among the 47 stories that quoted social scientists, none arose through the social scientist's initiative. Granted that social scientist entrepreneurship might have occurred at earlier times, still it does not appear that the promotional activity of *individuals,* for whatever noble or ignoble purposes, is excessively influential. Rather it is agencies—sponsoring agencies, particularly governmental sponsors, research organizations, and publishers—that were behind most of the press conference and press release activity. Organizational promotion meshes well with the beat system in journalism; beat reporters cover agencies and they maintain regular contact with sources in organizations. Although reporters respond to only a small fraction of the claims on their attention, when they do, it tends to be to the claims of organizations.

The hypothesis that reporters are inadequately prepared in the social sciences receives support from their reports of sketchy social science course work in college and graduate school. Most of them do not feel well enough trained to make independent judgments of the validity of social science, but they do not see that as their job. When confronted by the need to judge the quality of research or the competence of social scientist sources, they rely on social scientists' institutional affiliations and reputations, a few phone calls to other social scientists when controversy looms, and their own common sense. In the main, they manage to choose studies and sources well. Their success is attested to by the caliber of most studies they report, the fact that social scientists who were quoted felt qualified to talk on the subject, and the correlation between frequent visibility in the media and frequency of citation by peers in social science journals. There were a few poor choices in our sample of stories, but not many.

Whether their collective choices yield an ideal configuration of social science in the media is another question. We found it difficult to imagine an ideal pattern of social science reporting and equally difficult to imagine the methods by which one could construct such an ideal.

The final hypothesis was that the organization and practices of news organizations are largely responsible for the way journalists report social science. In many ways we saw that structural conditions set the journalistic ground rules. To assure a sustained flow of stories, editors assign some reporters to beats expected to have a high story yield and hold other reporters available for assignment to nonroutine and unexpected events. Social science does not have the characteristics that would lend itself to a beat. This leads to the engagement of dozens of different reporters in writing stories with a social science component, few of whom have the time, resources, or motivation to become expert in social science.

Similarly, the need to bring order into the production of news leads to a certain reliance on press releases and press conferences to filter demands for media attention. Reporters express irritation at the constant stream of mail, but they riffle through it because it is an efficient means to locate the few items worth attending to. Our data show that the "take" on press releases is low, and even convenient and well-publicized press conferences held for journalists already in attendance at AAAS meetings didn't consistently generate stories. Nevertheless, the media need ways to systematize and routinize the gathering of news (an intrinsically chaotic commodity), and they find press releases and press conferences useful procedures for finding items that meet news criteria.

Another structural feature is the limited page space available in print media. This constraint engenders competition among reporters to get their stories into print. Since stories are judged on interest, importance, and congruence with themes already dominant in the news, reporters are tempted to play up drama, overstate conclusiveness, and fit the story to familiar simplified molds. On television, news time is more stringently limited, and once the leading stories of the day are covered, producers seek stories that not only meet the same criteria but also come with high-quality action footage. Social science rarely satisfies such standards and thus is rarely seen on network news.

Commitment to neutrality and objectivity is a pervasive element in the journalistic credo, helping to justify the special status of the media in our society. The commitment to neutrality provides one motive for quoting expert opinion, which is sometimes social scientist opinion; reporters need not draw conclusions themselves and they can use quotes to present the "balance" of contrasting views. Accuracy is another journalistic value. Reporters' respect it for it leads to the pattern of overwhelming satisfaction we saw among social scientists with stories about their work.

The bottom line is that the commercial basis of news organizations requires stories that interest a large enough audience to pay the toll and thus puts a premium on human interest and simplicity. Not only are the kinds of people who are attracted to journalism likely to be uncomfortable with abstractions and to enjoy the human and concrete, but the conditions of their work reinforce such predilections.

Still, within the rules and procedures that the organization of news-work sets, journalists have wide latitude. They can search for social science or ignore it; they can play it as news or as the basis for an analytic feature; they can include details of methodology and reference to earlier research or not; they can write two paragraphs or 20 column-inches. In many ways they decide what's news and what kind of news it is. The climate of some of the media in our inquiry, most notably the *New York Times,* appears to favor the kind of serious reporting that academics prefer.

Advice on Dealing with the Media

Several of the social scientist respondents in the inquiry offered advice on how to deal with reporters. Since they are people who have been covered by national media, they apparently know whereof they speak. A few journalists made suggestions, too. The advice for those seeking not only to be reported but to be reported well is:

1. Know your local reporters. Find out who writes on the subjects with which you deal, what they usually write about, and which themes engage them. When you mail press releases, address them to reporters by name, not to "editor." Send them information that will interest them and send it in brief, readable form. Phone them and offer further interpretation and data. Make yourself available to them when they are stuck for information, references, or the names of sources to contact. Cultivate a relationship. Since stories in local newspapers may be picked up by other media and the wire services, the fruits of cultivation can extend beyond the local scene.

2. When reporters come to you, listen to them. Try to understand what they are asking and what their assumptions are. If you believe that their angle is off-base, try to help them find a better approach to the story. If they ask questions you cannot answer, say so. And, of course, treat them with courtesy and respect.

3. Write research summaries that are brief, lucid, and suitable for lay readers. Don't try to cover every finding in your study; concentrate on two or three points. Couch your findings in the frames of journalism, not of social science.

4. If you foresee areas of possible confusion or misunderstanding, confront them directly. Say not only what the findings mean but also what they do not mean, and why. Two of the reporters whom we spoke to said that they are more likely to trust a research report if it "admits inconvenient facts," so a certain amount of candor may be rewarded.

5. Present not only your own research but also a discussion of how your findings relate to other research in the field. (This may not attract reporters to the story, but if they decide to write one, this will help them do a better job.) Where your findings disagree with earlier results, try to put the conflict in context and give possible explanations. Reporters may include the explanation in their stories and thus provide the context of the broader research field.

6. Marshal the resources of your institution's public affairs office. The staff probably have journalistic training and experience in writing good press releases and, even more useful, ongoing contacts with journalists.

One of our respondents suggested sending out press releases that are embargoed, that is, not for publication, until two or three days later. The interim gives reporters time to call, read, get further information, and become more knowledgeable. One social scientist recommended to those facing TV cameras that they repeat the key point they want to make in every sentence, complete with qualifications or caveats. In that way no 20- or 30-second clip can misrepresent the message.

This is short-term advice culled from our discussions. But if we want to go beyond the current state of social science reporting with its mix of good and not-so-good elements, we must look to longer-term improvements.

Improving the Reporting of Social Science

Over the years observers have offered a number of recommendations for improving the reporting of social science. Some focus on responsibilities of the media, some on actions that social scientists can take, and some suggest boundary-spanning services to link social scientists and journalists. As we consider their possibilities, we take into account the findings of our investigation.

Responsibilities of the Media

The most frequent prescriptions for the media are specialization—that is, a beat in social science—and better education for specialist-reporters. A social science reporter, like a science reporter, will presumably become expert in social science matters and give consistent and competent coverage. Without much attempt at defining what a "social science beat" should cover, advocates of this approach assume that it would lead to better-educated, more skillful journalists covering a range of sound research developments in the social sciences, to the edification of a wide and receptive audience.

The fact that the major national media have only the barest trace of a social science beat after all these years, and that what there is concentrates on personal relationships, suggests that journalists have made a different news judgment. Editors and news executives apparently see little need for coverage of social science per se. In fact, it is hard to conceptualize a beat that would sensibly cover the range of social science that is being reported, namely, economics, political science, sociology, psychology, sociomedical sciences, and more. Not only would the jurisdictional lines be blurred (when is a story social science and when is it crime or education or politics or the economy?), but the demands on reporters' knowledge and talents would be formidable. If a beat were limited to sociology and psychology, it would still run athwart the divisional lines that make sense to journalists. Perhaps even more important, it is not obvious that a large and attentive readership awaits. While entertaining stories from social science may capture attention, readers of only a few quality media are likely to be receptive to serious coverage of the issues that engage mainline social science.

Given the existing beat structure, our data show that reporters with beats do not produce more satisfactory stories, not even when the social science subject in the story is central to the beat. Although this finding says little about a possible social science beat, it does tend to jar our confidence in specialization as a solution.

Advocates also underestimate the costs that such reorganization would entail, not only in money but in decreased flexibility. It would take a well-to-do organization to tie up a reporter on a subject as specialized as the social sciences. Reporters, no matter what their beat, are expected to be able to fill in at short notice and cover a wide range of stories. As news issues change, editors need to be able to drop old beats and assign reporters to emerging topics. Editors are concerned, too, that reporters too closely identified with a single subject will become co-opted by their sources and adopt their priorities and jargon, losing touch with readers and readers' interests. Moreover, few reporters are likely to want to make a firm commitment to a social science beat. They may not want to be stuck in the backwaters of social science for very long, perhaps not even long enough to absorb full knowledge of the leading figures, research methods, criteria of judgment, and emerging developments. They may see little journalistic future in such an arcane specialty. Papers and magazines will no doubt continue to report on trends in "living," "relationships," and "behavior," but such coverage is hardly likely to satisfy the glossier vision of a professional social science beat.

Another step that is sometimes urged is better education in the social sciences for journalists. As we saw in chapter 2, many journalists have skimpy college preparation in the major disciplines. As Rosten (1937:240) said long ago, reporters deal with the "concrete rather than the abstract" and respond as "persons to persons, rather than persons to ideas." Breed (1955:331) noted that reporters "analyze their society in terms of personalities rather than institutions comprising a social and cultural system" and are ill at ease with abstractions. Social scientists would certainly enjoy seeing journalists learn more about social structure and about the configuration of theory, research knowledge, and angle of vision that the disciplines bring to bear on current issues. Special fellowship programs for mid-career journalists, such as the Nieman Fellowships at Harvard and the Bagehot Fellowships in Economics at Columbia, can help to broaden their understanding. On more specific matters, several newspapers have arranged to have their reporters attend courses in statistics, and some have provided seminars in polling and survey methods for reporters and editors. The *Detroit Free Press,* for example, has brought in experts from the University of Michigan Survey Research Center to run seminars, and the *Detroit News* has had a University of Michigan methodologist as a consultant in residence.

But journalists deal in much besides social science. If specialists from other fields had their way, journalists would also be exposed to history, philosophy, law, the sciences, and the arts. There is a limit to how much didactic training we can expect them to value and to absorb. And as we saw in chapter 4, our data show no relation between the amount of social science education reporters have had and the quality of their social science stories.

Moreover, education in the social sciences is not going to alter the character of journalism, with its focus on events, power, controversy, and important people. That is what journalism is about. Society needs a good chronicle of daily happenings pursued with the special talents that reporters bring to the job. Golding and Elliott (1979:214) cite a former chairman of the BBC who said that he "would rather take my chances with journalists than have the news chosen by academics." As they note, if news were based on other than conventional news values, it wouldn't be news but something else. All the efforts being advocated to infuse social science into journalism—specialization, education, mid-career programs, professional associations' public information efforts, social science consultants to news organizations, op-ed pieces by social scientists, media-run surveys— are not going to change basic news values. All that these infusions can do is support whatever drive toward social science reporting reporters and editors themselves generate. Unless they see incentives for making greater use of social science, there is little that outsiders can accomplish. Where they do recognize a need for social science knowledge, these kinds of inputs may help them to make—perhaps not more, but better—use of it.

Responsibilities of Social Scientists

Advice to social scientists generally urges them to take more responsibility for media coverage—learn how to attract the attention of reporters and editors, how to make their research accessible and interesting, how to work effectively with reporters and provide responsible information. The advice that our respondents offered above is very much in this genre.

There may also be a role for social scientists who are popularizers of social science. Economist Lester Thurow writes for *Newsweek;* psychologist Robert McCall writes for *Parents Magazine.* Skilled interpreters convey a body of information, often stressing a particular point of view. In addition, journalists might welcome syntheses of research on timely topics, something on the order of literature reviews published in social science encyclopedias and journals, but written with a mass audience rather than a social science audience in mind. A crucial aspect of such reviews would be critique and quality control, sifting shoddy evidence from sound. Another requirement would be that choice of topics would be determined by subjects in the news, not by social science subfield. Many news events are scheduled well in advance. If the Supreme Court is going to decide a case on affirmative action, if the state legislature is going to debate health care cost containment, if international arms control talks are on the docket, these issues could become the subjects of research syntheses. Instead of a litter of separate stories that add little to public knowledge of either the topic or the disciplines, syntheses might promote coherent presentation of the best evidence on timely topics. However, experience suggests that review and synthesis are arduous tasks and little rewarded in the disciplines. Few social scientists are likely to be attracted to the job, particularly for a lay audience, without external incentives.

Linking Institutions

This brings us to the category of intermediary organizations, brokers between social science and the media. One possible model is the Scientists' Institute for Public Information (SIPI), which runs a media resource service in natural science fields and publishes a periodical, *SIPIscope*. In 1985 five professionals staffed the media resource service, responding to about 35–40 media requests a week. Even though their services are more responsive to requests and less preplanned than the previous paragraph suggests, the operation is highly regarded. Scientists who participate are favorably impressed with the stories that result (*Chemical and Engineering News,* February 3, 1986). It is also expensive. It is supported by grants from foundations, including Ford, Rockefeller, and MacArthur, and from the media themselves.

The American Psychological Association (APA) does something similar for psychology. The largest and wealthiest of the social science associations, it has the most active program of public information (O'Leary 1983). As of July 1986, the public information office had a staff of seven full-time people. They write about forty press releases a year, hold press conferences, and maintain a file of over 1,000 experts on a wide range of psychological specialties to whom journalists can be referred for comments and quotes. Science writers on staff summarize articles from the journals that the APA publishes (O'Leary 1983). The association gives six awards for the best interpretation of psychology in newspapers, magazines, books, television documentary, radio, and, most recently, television entertainment/drama. They work with television networks on the development of documentaries and dramas on such topics as incest and homosexuality. The public information office provides kits of materials to individual psychologists and to sections and regional associations giving advice on dealing with the press (APA 1984). According to public information officer Donald Kent (personal communication, 1984), their aim is not so much to peddle psychology as to figure out what journalists want to know and then make available the best psychological knowledge. In one of its most ambitious moves the APA acquired the monthly magazine *Psychology Today* and has spent large sums of money on it in order to convey sound psychological information to the public.

Other social science associations have more modest programs of activities. The American Political Science Association (APSA), according to Thomas Mann, its former executive director, does not believe that political science has a problem. "The press gravitates to political science. Our meetings are well covered, national reporters do stories. . . . The press regularly call our staff asking who to talk to or seeking substantive information. In fact, they call so often that it interferes with other things" (personal communication, 1984).

The association's stance is not to seek increased coverage of political science but to choose topics on which political science has something special to contribute and concentrate on those. A television course on Congress and a bicentennial magazine on the Constitution are prime examples. Said Mann, "Some of our social science colleagues think that if the public knew us better, it would increase our status and our influence. That's not obvious to me. With more reporting, there would be an increase in negative as well as positive coverage."

The American Economic Association (AEA), according to executive officer Elton Hinshaw, undertakes no activities with the media since they cover economics frequently and well. Economics reporters "do some first-rate stuff." Many economists themselves write for newspapers and magazines. The AEA is not particularly concerned about coverage of the association as such and thus sees no reason to get involved.

The American Sociological Association falls between the APA with its extensive set of activities and the AEA with none. Periodically over the years the association has become interested in improving media coverage of sociology. Rhoades' history of the association (1981) records the establishment of a Press Relations Committee in 1938, with a budget of $50, whose aims were to "reach the columns of popular periodicals, the speeches of popular leaders, and the discussions of Everyman." The committee noted that "to a large degree, the future of our science and of our profession depend upon the sort of personality-stereotype popularly held of *the* sociologist and the sort of institution stereotype popularly held of sociology" (Rhoades 1981:21).

The present period marks another upswing in attention to the media. After a lapse of many years a task force on sociology and the media was set up in 1983, and in 1984 an active public relations program began with a small budget and a part-time staff member. William D'Antonio, executive officer, talks about the need to increase the visibility of sociology and the public's understanding of it.

For the social sciences it would take major drive and major funding to establish effective links with the mass media, and except for psychology and the APA, the social science associations are not likely to devote the necessary resources to the task. Nor is it obvious that it is in their institutional self-interest to do so. Science writing, for all the efforts of SIPI's media resource center, the AAAS, and such natural science groups as the American Institute of Physics (Likely and Kalson 1981), produces not only admiring accounts of new discoveries but also grim stories of acid rain, toxic waste, and Chernobyl. In the social sciences, without a corps of specialist-reporters and with intermittent editorial interest, it is uncertain whether a serious effort at transmission would have more than occasional effects. The conclusion of the 1970 panel, quoted in chapter 1, that it is premature for the establishment of a social science service to channel a flow of sound research information to the press, still sounds reasonable. The social sciences may be better served by extending their reach to magazines of specialized appeal. Publications like *Society, Psychology Today,* and *The Public Interest* already offer social science to an informed audience, and more channels of this sort may need to be nurtured— perhaps articles in such magazines as the *Atlantic, New Yorker,* and *Harper's.* The transition from quality magazines to the popular press is a relatively well-traveled route.

The Value of Social Science in the Media

Prospects for major changes in social science reporting appear dim. Given the current pattern, is it worthwhile supporting more of the same? We examine the value of social science reporting for three major groups: for the social science disciplines, for policymakers, and for the public.

The Value for Social Science

Most social scientists who receive coverage are pleased. They cite advantages such as career advancement, increased visibility for their organization, and the opportunity to get their message to the public. Relatively few mention disadvantages. But it is problematical whether the disciplines reap collective benefits from news reportage. The hope that news from the social sciences will enlighten the public about what social science is and what it does, and lead to greater public support, is extravagant. Current reporting may be as likely to trivialize social science as to enhance understanding.

Reporters—and readers, too, I would imagine—ingest social science without recognizing it as social science. They are not concerned with sociology but with changing male and female roles or the effects of unemployment on marital stability. Only in the most general way is it likely that more exposure to disconnected bits of social science news will create an informed constituency for the disciplines. Perhaps the most we can hope is that readers will come to learn more about the specific topics that social scientists study and the special perspectives that they bring to their work.

To the question of whether it is good for the social sciences to be reported in the media, we respond finally with a loud and decisive "Maybe." We have noted that social science in the news takes on the coloration of journalism and becomes absorbed into reporters' frames. Newsworthiness and reader interest displace concern with theoretical relevance or methodological quality. If, as some social scientists whom we interviewed suggest, career advancement and research funding are influenced by visibility in the media, then the values of journalism may be seeping into arenas where social science criteria should prevail. If social scientists become seduced into playing the media game, they themselves may succumb to media standards and, to a greater or lesser extent, weaken their commitment to the standards of social science. (For analysis of the encroachment of media standards into areas such as politics, sports, and religion, see Altheide and Snow 1979.)

A rather different objection to the appearance of social science in the media is the frailty of social science evidence and the possibility of inconsistent and contradictory reports appearing on the same subject. Because controversy is a tried-and-true news value, some observers worry that journalists may highlight inconsistencies—for example, among political polls or economic forecasts. Although this was not a common genre of reporting in our inquiry, these observers are concerned that a focus on discrepancy will leave the audience skeptical of the worth of the social sciences.

We do not have much sympathy with the argument that the social sciences deserve special treatment because media exposure will reveal their inadequacies to the public. Neither the fault nor the remedy lies with the media. If the social sciences have anything to contribute, they will be reported, warts and all. At the present stage of social science development, it may be useful for the public to learn something about the limits as well as the contributions of social science.

Although it is doubtful whether social science reporting benefits the institutionalized interests of the disciplines, still on a symbolic level the media do the social sciences a service. By including social science in their repertoire, they give it the stamp of legitimacy. Just as they occasionally use social science to validate their own stories and analyses, they symbolize the importance of social science in the order of things by including it in the news of the day. One social scientist said, "Attention means people think it's worthwhile. Sometimes you work in a vacuum, and it confirms that what you're doing is of value." The media are the arbiters of what is important. Their attention to social science signifies its legitimate place in contemporary society.

The Value for Policymakers

Whatever the effects of reportage may be on the social sciences, it still provides benefits to the audience. We are especially interested in the policymaker audience, which pays close attention to the press, and for which policy-oriented social science should have special relevance. The media, as Kingdon (1984:63) writes, "act as a communicator within a policy community. . . . So one way to bring an idea to the attention of someone else, even someone who is a fellow specialist, is to be covered in the pages of the major papers." He reports the words of an analyst in a congressional support agency: "We can write reports and papers and they don't read it. But if the *Times* or *Post* picks up our report and does a story on it, they do read it, and it gets their attention" (p. 63).

Policymakers in government, industry, unions, political parties, and advocacy groups can gain three types of benefits from media coverage of social science. First, they can learn new facts. The media report the proportion of the population that has been out of work for fifteen weeks or more, characteristics of high schools which have the highest drop-out rates, reasons given by voters for choosing candidates. These kinds of data become accessible and help to inform policy debates.

Second, the media provide the *signal* that new information is afoot. Policymakers can find out the names of social scientists who are doing work in areas relevant to their issues, and they can then call upon them to testify at hearings, to serve as consultants, to serve on blue ribbon panels. They can also send for the unabridged reports and books that the experts produced. (One of the reasons for concern about the incompleteness of citations in media stories, noted in Part II, is that it makes retrieval of the original report more difficult. However, we found during our interviewing that, with a few phone calls, it is almost always possible.)

Notice in the media also signals to policymakers that other members of the policy community have heard about the report. If it deals with their business, they cannot afford to ignore it. Report of a study on bilingual education in the *Washington Post* set wheels spinning in the education subcommittees of the House and Senate, the Department of Education, state departments of education, local school boards, and Hispanic organizations (for example, Berke 1980; Boruch and Leviton 1983; Weiss 1984). The major news media are the interdepartmental memoranda that notify policymakers what other policymakers know and are doing. When social science is part of the message, it is likely to get attention.

Third, the attentive policymaker can gain "enlightenment" (Crawford and Biderman 1969; Janowitz 1970; Weiss 1977, 1980). Here it is not so much social science data as the ideas and generalizations drawn from data that come into currency. A business reporter with good grounding in recent economic thought is likely to write more sophisticated stories; a crime reporter well versed in criminological research is likely to write with richer understanding of developments in prisons and courts. In direct and indirect ways journalists pass along new concepts and new formulations.

Since the media can provide these social science services to policymakers, we pondered whether social scientists would be well advised to concentrate their dissemination activities on the media and forgo alternative channels. The evidence suggests that such a course would be unwise. The media can be a useful conduit, but they function erratically. They pick up some social science, but primarily when it deals with a topic already on the media agenda and when it comes from an established source. Much social science falls outside those boundaries. Even inside the boundaries, only a tiny percentage of available social science can fit into the news hole. Which social science gets chosen on a particular day is the resultant of multiple procedures, pressures, choices, and idiosyncratic events. Some good and important social science is inevitably going to wind up on the cutting room floor. Social scientists interested in reaching policymakers need to pursue other routes as well.

The Value for the Public

At last, we come to the basic question. Can media reporting do the public any good? Since we did not explore public *intake* of social science reporting, we cannot say what readers and viewers actually see, hear, and remember. But we can analyze what is there for the taking. Our judgment is that social science reporting, on balance, is a benefit to the media and, through them, to the public.

Let us grant the frail basis of much social science research; let us acknowledge the degree of indeterminacy in research results; let us applaud the critical skepticism about social science which some reporters voiced (in chapter 3) although less often put into practice in their reporting (see chapter 2). But with all their limitations, the social sciences have a solid tradition of inquiry that expands the range of understanding. They are based on disciplined investigation, systematic methods of data collection and analysis, independent replication, and continual challenge and testing of conclusions. They represent a mode of scholarship that collectively builds a body of knowledge. Thus, they provide more rigorous analysis of social phenomena than competing sources of information. For reporters whose horizon tends to be limited to the immediate present and available sources, social science provides a more comprehensive source of understanding. Joslyn et al (1984:565), in their analysis of TV reporting of election returns, found that journalists attributed results arbitrarily to "single factors," "confused cause and effect," and relied on "monocausal hindsight reasoning." Social science can help them do better. It can provide data on human beings and their institutions, and models and theories for making sense of the data. It can help put news in historical perspective. Social scientists can add to the depth of both straight and interpretive reporting, just as reporters can give a context of current news relevance to social science.

Perhaps most important, the use of social science broadens the sources from which news derives. One of the endemic limitations of news—and news analysis—is that reporters get so much of their information from government officials. The beat system reinforces their dependence on politicians, bureaucrats, and official spokesmen. Sigal (1973:124–25) found that three quarters of page 1 stories in the *New York Times* and *Washington Post* came from U.S. or foreign government officials and only about 14 percent from nongovernment Americans. To find another point of view takes effort and investigation, and reporters don't always know where to turn. The common tendency is to contact the countervailing bureaucracies—corporations, labor unions, state governments, and interest-group associations. Thus, there is a heavy establishment, status quo loading.

Social scientists offer the possibility of a different viewpoint. Not only do they often have well-supported evidence and a broader view of issues, they are also likely to take a less predictable position. Since reputations in academia tend to be built on originality as well as on sound research, social scientists will often say something novel. They are also more apt to challenge existing policies and taken-for-granted assumptions and to question the existing social order. When reporters begin looking to social science as a regular source of news, they widen the variety of viewpoints in the media. Almost regardless of whether social scientists are right or wrong, they provide alternative visions to the familiar ones of politician, bureaucrat, and interest-group spokesman. That is not an inconsiderable contribution.

The challenge to social science is to produce something worth reporting. We need social science that works on relevant public questions in these dangerous times. More, we need venturesome social science, not content merely to improve the technical sophistication of its apparatus but willing to entertain new speculations and take chances with new ideas. Social science must challenge the accepted commonplaces of our time, including the orthodoxies that have undergirded so much of social science itself. It should also be able to systematically explore the consequences of ideas old and new, from whatever sources they derive, to illuminate possible paths to the future. Such social science will be newsworthy.

Over sixty years ago Walter Lippmann, a journalist who knew and valued social science, advised journalists

by criticism and agitation to prod social science into making more usable formulations for the extension of reportable truth.
[Lippmann 1947 (1922):361]

Perhaps mutual criticism and prodding, of the sort represented in the interviews we have presented, will help move in the desired direction— toward sound, independent, and relevant knowledge that is well and wisely reported.

PART II
Content Analysis

Eleanor Singer

with Phyllis Endreny

for our parents

⑨

How Much Social Science
Do the Media Report?

THE FIRST PART OF THIS BOOK HAS BEEN BASED LARGELY ON THE PERCEPTIONS OF THE actors involved: social scientists who are cited in the news, or whose research is reported there, and some of the journalists who do the reporting. They talk about what they do, why and how they do it, and how satisfied they are with the results. But from the outset, we recognized that there is another source of knowledge about social science reporting, since the actors' perceptions may not tell the whole story. Consequently, we were also interested in the patterns of social science news that emerge from an analysis of what actually appears in print and on the air.

We started our investigation with certain preconceptions, nourished in part by other writers (Stocking and Dunwoody 1978; Cole 1975; Olean 1977) and in part by conversations with other social scientists. These preconceptions were (1) that there is more social science reporting now than there used to be and (2) that it has improved. In this chapter we examine the first assumption in some detail; the second is reserved for chapter 11.

For our purposes the reporting of social science in the national media represents a "best case." These media have large resources, specialized staffs, and a reputation for excellence and responsibility. They are read (and watched) by well-educated, affluent audiences, and we would expect their reporting of social science to be the best there is. While it would have been informative to study the performance of a more diverse sample of newspapers, the costs and complexity of the task convinced us to limit our attention to this sample.

In this chapter we address three broad descriptive questions about social science coverage in the news media. First, what is the *extent* of such coverage, and how does it vary among media and among types of media? Second, how *visible* is this coverage? And, finally, what are the *topics* of those stories that contain some social science content? In the final section we look at variations in the way different media deal with the "same" social science event.

Because of the dearth of data on current reporting as well as on changes in the quality and quantity of reporting over time, we built a comparative frame of reference into the study, examining social science coverage in 1982 and during a comparable period in 1970. The three descriptive questions in this chapter are, therefore, looked at in the context of change (or its absence) from 1970: Has the amount of coverage increased? Has it become more visible? Have the topics of stories into which it is incorporated changed?

Before beginning the analysis of change, we will briefly review some essential features of this part of the study and describe the characteristics of the data on which this analysis is based.

During the five months of 1982 in which we monitored every third week of media coverage (a total of seven weeks), every story that met our definition of social science (see chapter 1) was systematically analyzed. The unit of analysis was the story—that is, the discrete item. For each item we coded a set of media variables—the media name and date, the amount of space or time devoted to the item, the prominence with which it was featured, and so on. For each item we also coded a set of content variables, including such information as the topic of the story and whether it was a news story, book review, obituary, and so on. The remaining information coded varied depending on the particular social science element involved. For research reports, treated in detail in chapter 11, we coded such information as the institutional origin, the discipline of the investigator, whether or not the investigator was named or identified as a social scientist, whether or not information was given about the methods used in the study. For social scientists, discussed in detail in chapter 10, we recorded such information as discipline, institutional affiliation, whether or not a quotation was used and, if so, whether it reflected expert knowledge.

During the period in 1982 in which we monitored the media we

TABLE 9.1

Distribution of Social Science Items by Media, 1982

Media	Focus Items[a]	Ancillary Items	Total Items	Number of Items per Page[b]	Number of Items per Issue
New York Times	305	538	843	0.15	17.20
Wall Street Journal	176	249	425	0.25	12.14
Washington Post	234	395	629	0.13	12.84
Boston Globe	175	313	488	0.12	10.02
Newsweek	17	47	64	0.09	9.14
Time	12	55	67	0.09	9.57
U.S. News & World Report	24	63	87	0.14	12.43
Parade	4	7	11	—	1.57
CBS	17	19	36	—	0.73
NBC	16	17	33	—	0.67
ABC	14	4	18	—	0.37
TOTAL	994	1,707	2,701		

[a] Includes letters, columns and book reviews by social scientists, even if on non–social science topics. Over all media about 70 items fell in this category.
[b] Exclusive of Sundays; based on matching four-week subsample only.

recorded more than 2,000 news items that made some reference to social science—a number that at first seems staggeringly large. The *New York Times* had a far larger absolute number than any other medium; the television newscasts, the fewest (see Table 9.1). On average, each 1982 issue of the *Times* contained 17.2 items that mentioned some aspect of social science; at the other extreme, one would have to listen to more than one evening TV newscast in order to encounter even a single social science reference.

Because the print media differ greatly in size, we also computed the average number of news items per page which contained some reference to social science. According to this measure, and excluding Sunday editions from the calculation for newspapers, it is the *Wall Street Journal* rather than the *Times* that has the most visible social science content—0.25 items per page, though many of these are very short (Table 9.1, col. 4). There is, in fact, little difference among the *Times,* the *Post,* and the *Globe,* and all of these have more social science content than *Newsweek, Time,* or *U.S. News & World Report.*

But the total number of social science stories obscures the great diversity in the kind of coverage represented by individual items. In the first place, as already mentioned, we selected for analysis not only "focus" social science stories but also those containing ancillary references to social science in the context of a story about some other news event.

An example of a "focus" social science story is "Effects of TV Violence" (NBC, May 5, 1982), focused on the National Institute of Mental Health (NIMH) report on television and social behavior; a story about changes in television programming, on the other hand, might bring in an "ancillary" reference to the NIMH report. Of the total number of social science items, a little more than one third were focus, and the rest were ancillary.

The relative proportion of focus and ancillary items varied between print and electronic media. Whereas ancillary references consistently outnumbered focus social science stories in the newspapers and newsmagazines in our sample, the proportions of such stories were virtually equal on NBC and CBS, and focus items largely outnumbered ancillary references on ABC. The prevalence of short news stories, many of them about economic indicators, accounts for the relatively greater proportion of focus social science stories on the evening TV news. To the extent that social science receives attention at all on these newscasts, it is likely to be the focus of attention—albeit a brief focus.

Furthermore, a sizable proportion of social science items—some 20.5 percent—was made up of stories whose *only* social science content consisted of an ancillary reference to one or more bits of data[1]—for example, the unemployment rate or the weekly money supply—or to one or more economists employed by a business organization (for example, a bank or a brokerage house). Because such stories were so numerous and so peripheral, they were selected for our sample during the first and fifth weeks only, when they swelled the average weekly count from 301 to 402 items. About two thirds of these stories were included because they contained a reference to data; one quarter because they contained a reference to one or more business economists; and the rest because they contained a reference to both data and economists.[2]

---

[1] The types of data included in our sample were either developed by social scientists or collected by social science methods and were selected as important social indicators after consultation with a number of social scientists. Coders were presented with a list of such indicators (see methodological appendix), and only mention of one or more of the listed indicators qualified a news story for inclusion.

[2] These stories have been weighted by a factor of 3.5 to bring them into proper relationship with the other 1982 social science stories. All analyses are based on the weighted sample, with a 1982 N of 2,701 and a 1970 N of 915. (Such stories were monitored for one week in four in 1970 and weighted by a factor of 4.0). The design effect resulting from this weighting procedure is 1.29. Accordingly, we have used 71 percent of the printed chi-square values when analyzing the ancillary data only, and 77 percent of the chi-square values shown for the total sample. When statistics other than chi-square were involved, we have required a p-value of .02 (instead of .05) to indicate statistical significance; 20.5 percent is the proportion of the weighted sample made up by these items.

Because of the fundamental difference between social science as the focus of a news story and social science as a generally minor element introduced to provide perspective or commentary or subsidiary information, each of these two story types is examined in its own right in what follows.

Although it may be obvious, we should also point out that not all 2,700 (weighted) social science items represent accounts of different underlying events. Some events—for example, the monthly unemployment rate or the weekly money supply figures—are reported in most of the media in the sample; hence, one event accounts for multiple news items. Later in this chapter we discuss in greater detail the kinds of social science events that are likely to receive multiple coverage and the kinds of patterned variations that exist among the media in our sample. But for the time being we simply want to call the reader's attention to the fact that the figures for individual media are a better indicator of the amount of social science to which a reader/viewer is potentially exposed than are the composite figures for all the media combined.

Changes in the Amount of Coverage

Like so many common assumptions, the belief that media coverage of social science had increased dramatically in the last decade received little support when subjected to systematic analysis. True, our comparisons were limited to three newspapers—the *New York Times, Wall Street Journal,* and *Washington Post*—and three newsmagazines, and so we cannot generalize them to all media.[3] But among these six only the *Wall Street Journal* (and, marginally, the *Washington Post*) had significant increases in the total number of social science stories between 1970 and 1982 (see Table 9.2). Although the *Times* showed a small increase, this was not

---

[3] Coverage in 1970 was monitored for one week in three during a three-month period, from March 23 to June 1, for a total of four weeks. Comparisons are reported for the corresponding three-month period in 1982, which constitutes a subsample of all 1982 coverage. Comparisons of coverage during these four weeks with the remaining three weeks in 1982 showed few, if any, significant differences, leading us to conclude that the four-week subsample was representative of the total 1982 sample for purposes of the over-time comparisons. However, totals for 1982 are shown in most tables, along with figures for the subsample.

Because of the difficulty and expense of obtaining old transcripts, we did not include TV in the over-time comparison. We are aware of the widespread belief that economic reporting has increased measurably on TV since the oil crisis of 1973 (see, for example, Adoni and Cohen 1978).

statistically significant, and *Time* actually had a larger number of social science items in 1970 than during a corresponding period in 1982.[4]

As can be seen from Table 9.2, however, the absence of large overall change in five of the six media obscures different trends in the two types of social science stories. Whereas the number of focus stories remained virtually unchanged in the *Washington Post* and the *New York Times,* the number of stories which included some reference to social science elements in the context of other reporting increased significantly in both papers. (The *Wall Street Journal* showed a significant increase in both categories.) In all three newsweeklies the number of focus stories actually declined between 1970 and 1982, while the number of ancillary stories remained the same or, in the case of *U.S. News,* increased.[5]

Although there is no evidence that the reporting of social science, as a distinct news topic, increased in these media during the period of our

---

[4]Cole's study (1975) shows an increase in social science coverage, relative to other science news, between 1961 and 1971. The newspapers studied were the *New York Times, Washington Post, San Francisco Chronicle,* and *Minneapolis Tribune.* Since the mid-1960s, the United States has also witnessed the rise of popular science and social science publications (some of which have since disappeared from view) as well as science columns and sections in established newspapers and magazines. News of social science has, thus, entered new channels, which may account for the perception of its increased coverage in the mass media.

[5]In an effort to see whether changes in our application of selection criteria as the study progressed were responsible for the smaller number of 1970 social science stories (which were selected after the 1982 sample), we examined a randomly selected subsample of about 30 stories from each of four weeks in 1982: March 1–7, April 12–18, March 22–28, and February 8–14.

Of the 137 stories rechecked, we would have deleted four (and did, in fact, delete these four). Consequently, some 3 percent of the stories would probably have been deleted if we were selecting the 1982 sample after more prolonged experience. This reduction is obviously not large enough to account for the difference between 1970 and 1982 social science reporting where it exists.

One additional factor that may have reduced the number of 1970 stories was a *New York Times* pressmen's strike from March 30 to May 24, 1970. The paper reduced its coverage, though it did not suspend publication. The effects of the strike were minimal during the week of April 14–21, one of our sampling weeks, but were more serious during the week of May 4–11, which also fell into our sample; 797 columns were lost between April 1 and May 24, and though most of what was lost seems not to be relevant to social science, we cannot rule out the possibility that for the *Times,* the 1970 count of social science items is smaller than it would have been without the strike.

Changes in the number of pages between 1970 and 1982 cannot account for changes in the number of social science items, either for those media, like the *Wall Street Journal* and the *Times,* which increased in size, or those like *Time* and *Newsweek,* which decreased in size. But increases in the number of nonadvertising pages may, in fact, account for most if not all of the increase in the *Times* and the *Washington Post.* Between 1970 and 1978 the average number of *nonadvertising* pages in daily newspapers increased from 19.8 to 22.6, or 14.1 percent; the total number of social science items increased by 14.7 percent in the *Times* and by 17.5 percent in the *Post.* (Figures on nonadvertising space are based on comparisons of 109 dailies measured in both years by Media Records; see Bogart 1981:33–34.)

TABLE 9.2

Change in Social Science Coverage, 1970–1982[a]

Media	Number of Stories	
	1970	1982S[b]
New York Times		
Focus	147	140
Ancillary	234	297 [c]
Total	381	437
Wall Street Journal		
Focus	34	89 [c]
Ancillary	56	142 [c]
Total	90	231 [c]
Washington Post		
Focus	106	117
Ancillary	197	239 [d]
Total	303	356 [d]
Newsweek		
Focus	6	3
Ancillary	22	26
Total	28	29
Time		
Focus	15	2 [c]
Ancillary	29	32
Total	44	34
U.S. News & World Report		
Focus	20	14
Ancillary	20	34 [d]
Total	40	48

[a] Coverage in 1970 was monitored every third week for a three-month period, from March 23 to June 1; comparisons are based on a corresponding subsample of total 1982 coverage. Excluded from the category of focus stories in both years are letters and columns written by social scientists about non–social science topics. In 1970 these items numbered 10, 5, 9, 4, 1, and 0 for the *Times, Journal,* and so on; in 1982 the corresponding numbers were 28, 15, 13, 4, 0, and 0. Reviews of books written or reviewed by social scientists were included even if they dealt with non–social science topics; there were only eight and thirteen such reviews, respectively, in all six media in 1970 and 1982.
[b] 1982S denotes the subsample of 1982 coverage which matches the 1970 sample period.
[c] $p < .05$; chi-square goodness of fit test.
[d] $p < .10$; chi-square goodness of fit test.

study, certain structural changes that took place in the media at that time are reflected in changed social science reporting. CBS launched its own polling operation in 1967 and now collaborates with the *New York Times;* ABC did so in 1981 and collaborates with the *Washington Post;* NBC began polling in 1973 and from 1978 to 1983 shared costs and results with the Associated Press (Sudman 1983). The entry into survey research by these media organizations represents a structural change, with certain clearly discernible consequences.

First, media use of poll results has increased. Public opinion surveys and polls made up a larger proportion of all focus social science research reported in newspapers in 1982 than in 1970—53 percent versus 46 percent. (No changes were apparent in the proportion of surveys reported in newsmagazines, nor in ancillary reports of public opinion surveys or polls in either newspapers or magazines.) Second, all the media that have their own polls have tended to feature their surveys prominently (and to give much less space to other poll results).

Finally, a more subtle use of poll findings has been evolving, in which these findings are incorporated into a story focused on a more general issue and largely based on more conventional reporting techniques. For example, a February 6, 1983, *New York Times* story by William Schmidt, headlined "Poll Shows Lessening of Fear That U.S. Is Lagging," interweaves paragraphs reporting CBS–*Times* national sample survey results with segments of interviews with public officials around the country. Photographs of two of these are featured with the article. Thus, the public opinion poll has here been used as counterpoint to the more traditional news story, which relies primarily on interviews with visible political and business leaders to comment on current policy issues.

In a sense, this change in the use to which poll results are put is indicative of the change that has taken place in the reporting of social science generally between 1970 and 1982—that is, an increasing tendency to bring information drawn from the social sciences to bear on stories about events in society at large. Table 9.2 documents this trend toward increasing use of ancillary social science references by all the media.

Changes in the Kinds
of Social Science Reported

In 1970 the most common news story focused on social science reported the results of a research study. In 1982 studies remained dominant in the *New York Times* and the *Washington Post,* but reports of data with no reference to a study had outstripped research reports in the *Wall Street Journal* and in the newsweeklies, and data were the most frequently mentioned social science element on television newscasts as well. Social scientists—interviewed, profiled, or in obituaries—were the third most frequently mentioned social science element in focus stories, though generally far behind the other two. (Social scientists mentioned in connection with a study are not included in this count.) The remaining social science elements we had identified—namely, discussions of methods, organizations, theory, and institutional aspects—were the focus of scattered attention only.

In stories with *ancillary* social science content, references to social scientists, with or without direct quotes, were far and away the most often cited social science element. This was true in both 1970 and 1982, and in newsmagazines as well as newspapers.

Changes in Visibility

We have seen that the number of stories with ancillary social science content increased from 1970 to 1982; the average number of social science elements mentioned per story also increased. But how visible were these changes? In order to answer this question, we consider changes in (1) where the story appeared, (2) how long it was, and how much of its content consisted of social science material, (3) where in the story the first mention of social science occurred, and (4) whether or not some visual element accompanied the story.

Placement

Whether or not a reader encounters social science in the mass media depends largely on where the item containing the social science reference is placed. If it appears on the newspaper's front page, or even on the first page of another section, it is much more visible than if it appears on an inside page. In the case of newsmagazines, cover stories have a greater likelihood of being noticed than other stories.

By the criterion of *front-page* placement, social science stories have been relatively visible, compared with the "average" news story, but no change in visibility has taken place over time.[6] Some 10.0 percent of focus

---

[6] It is difficult to know what the most appropriate comparison would be. Social science stories are more likely to make the front page than the "average" story—only about 5 percent of all stories appear on page 1, except in the *Wall Street Journal,* where numerous short items

social science stories appeared on the front page in 1982 compared with 9.7 percent during a comparable period in 1970; the figures are 12.1 and 11.6 percent for ancillary stories in 1982 and 1970, respectively (see Table 9.3, which shows figures for all three newspapers and all three news-magazines).

If the criterion is broadened to include placement on the *first page of other sections,* a considerable increase in the visibility of social science is apparent between 1970 and 1982: from 3 to 13 percent for focus stories and from 7 to 18 percent for stories with ancillary social science content. The increase in the number of separate sections making up two of the newspapers in our sample—that is, the *New York Times* and the *Wall Street Journal*—no doubt accounts for much, if not all, of this increase.

No such increase in the visibility of social science has occurred in newsmagazines. The percentage of focus social science stories featured on the cover, or receiving prominent mention on the table of contents page (a device not really equivalent to front-page placement), actually declined between 1970 and 1982, while the percentage of ancillary stories receiving such treatment showed a nonsignificant increase.

In both 1970 and 1982 stories focused on social science *data* were most likely to be featured on the front page of the newspaper or on the first page of another section. This was also true of newsmagazines in 1970, when almost a quarter of the stories about social science data were fea-tured as cover stories and another 39 percent received prominent men-tion. By 1982, although stories about social science data were still most likely to be featured on the cover, social science studies were more likely to receive prominent mention on the table of contents page.

What we have described as stories about social science data ordinarily report unemployment figures, interest rates, and other economic indi-cators without any reference to the social science research from which such data are derived. Thus, most people are likely to be unaware of them as involving social science theories, concepts, or methods. Not a single story about some social science element other than data was featured on the cover of a newsmagazine in our 1970 sample; exactly one such story

increase the percentage. Science stories probably constitute a more meaningful reference category, and here we are fortunate in having comparison data available for three newspa-pers—the *Los Angeles Times,* the *New York Times,* and the *St. Louis Post-Dispatch*—monitored for a synthetic two-week period in 1963 and again in 1973 (Nathe 1974).

By this comparison social science stories received relatively generous coverage—a finding borne out by our analysis of AAAS convention coverage (see chapter 4). Only 6.6 percent of science stories appeared on the front pages of these newspapers in 1963 and 5.7 percent in 1973. A scant 3.3 percent of science stories appeared on the front page of other sections in 1963; by 1973 this was true of 12.9 percent. In this study, incidentally, "science" was defined to include social science as well.

TABLE 9.3

Placement of Focus and Ancillary Social Science Stories,[a]
in Newspapers and Magazines, by Year

	1970	1982S[b]	1982T[b]
Focus			
Newspapers			
Front page	9.7%	10.0%	8.8%
Other first page	3.1	12.8	12.7
Prominent mention	0.8	6.1	4.9
Other	86.5	71.1	73.7
(N)	(259)	(329)	(577)
	$\chi^2 = 31.28; p < .01$[c]		
Magazines			
Cover story	7.7	10.5	4.8
Prominent mention	20.5	0.0	9.5
Other	71.8	89.5	85.7
(N)	(39)	(19)	(42)
	$\chi^2 = 4.53; p = .104$		
Ancillary			
Newspapers			
Front page	11.6	12.1	12.1
Other first page	7.0	18.1	18.0
Prominent mention	3.3	5.9	4.8
Other	78.1	63.9	65.2
(N)	(483)	(675)	(1176)
	$\chi^2 = 26.70; p < .01$		
Magazines			
Cover story	11.3	6.6	5.5
Prominent mention	9.9	18.0	20.4
Other	78.9	75.4	74.2
(N)	(71)	(92)	(165)
	$\chi^2 = 2.12; $ n.s.		

[a] Excluded from the category of focus stories in both years are letters and columns written by social scientists about non–social science topics.
[b] 1982S denotes the subsample of 1982 coverage which matches the 1970 sample period; 1982T denotes the total 1982 sample.
[c] All tests are for significance of difference between 1970 and 1982S. Chi-square values for the ancillary tests have been adjusted to reflect the reduction in effective sample size due to weighting. The effective size is .71 of the sample size shown.

TABLE 9.4

Placement of Focus Social Science Stories,[a]
by Topic and Year (Newspapers Only)

Topic and Placement	1970	1982S[b]	1982T[b]
Economy			
Front page	23.4%	12.3%	10.4%
Other first page	2.6	15.6	16.1
Prominent mention	2.6	8.4	6.5
Other	71.4	63.6	67.0
(N)	(77)	(154)	(279)
	$\chi^2 = 14.77; p < .01$[c]		
Foreign Economies			
Front page	0.0	2.1	1.2
Other first page	0.0	6.3	3.7
Prominent mention	0.0	6.3	3.7
Other	100.0	85.4	91.5
(N)	(2)	(48)	(82)
	(χ^2 cannot be computed)		
Government and Politics			
Front page	4.3	9.5	6.3
Other first page	4.3	7.1	7.8
Prominent mention	0.0	4.8	4.7
Other	91.5	78.6	81.3
(N)	(47)	(42)	(64)
	$\chi^2 = 3.91$; n.s.		
Foreign Governments			
Other	100.0	100.0	100.0
(N)	(12)	(14)	(29)
	$\chi^2 = 2.12$; n.s.		
Social Control			
Front page	2.2	11.1	10.8
Other first page	4.3	5.6	6.5
Prominent mention	0.0	3.7	2.2
Other	93.5	79.6	80.6
(N)	(46)	(54)	(93)
	$\chi^2 = 5.16$; n.s.		
Health			
Front page	7.4	8.7	12.8
Other first page	0.0	17.4	12.8
Prominent mention	0.0	8.7	6.4
Other	92.6	65.2	68.1
(N)	(27)	(23)	(47)
	$\chi^2 = 8.23; p < .05$		

TABLE 9.4 (Continued)

Topic and Placement	1970	1982S[b]	1982T[b]
Demographics			
Front page	9.5%	0.0%	—
Other first page	4.8	18.2	20.8%
Other	85.7	81.8	79.2
(N)	(21)	(11)	(24)
	$\chi^2 = 2.45$; n.s.		
Relationships and Style			
Front page	0.0	2.8	1.9
Other first page	4.2	8.3	5.7
Prominent mention	0.0	2.8	3.8
Other	95.8	86.1	88.7
(N)	(48)	(36)	(53)
	$\chi^2 = 3.48$; n.s.		

[a]Excluded from the category of focus stories in both years are letters and columns written by social scientists about non–social science topics.
[b]1982S denotes the subsample of 1982 coverage which matches the 1970 sample period; 1982T denotes the total 1982 sample.
[c]All tests are for significance of difference between 1970 and 1982S.

was featured on a newsmagazine cover in 1982. Appropriately enough, it was a survey—*U.S. News'* ninth annual survey of "1,548 opinion molders in 30 fields"—which, typically enough, provided readers with virtually no details about such matters as sample design, response rate, or dates on which the interviewing had been done (see chapter 11 for more on the reporting of social science research).

We also looked at the topics of focus social science stories to see whether some topics were more likely to receive prominent placement than others (Table 9.4). In 1970 social science stories about the economy were far and away most likely to appear on the front page. In 1982, although social science stories about the economy constituted an even larger proportion of all focus social science stories, fewer of them appeared on the front page, with more featured on the first page of another section.

Twenty-six percent of the focus social science stories on health appeared either on the front page or on the front page of another section in 1982, and, as can be seen from Table 9.4, this represents a significant increase in visibility from 1970.

Although the number of focus social science stories in newsmagazines is very small, in both 1970 and 1982 the only social science stories likely to be featured on the cover were those dealing with the economy.

Space

Regardless of medium and year, ancillary stories are significantly longer than focus social science stories; in fact, they are between two and three times as long. That is, stories about social science as such tend to be much shorter, on average, than stories about other topics into which some social science material has been incorporated. Neither focus nor ancillary stories, however, show any consistent changes in length over time (see Table 9.5).

TABLE 9.5

Amount of Space for Focus and Ancillary Social Science Stories,[a] by Media and Year

Media and Focus	Average Number of Inches		F-Value and Significance[c]
	1982S[b]	1970	
New York Times			
Focus	14.3(130)	17.3(138)	$F(year) = 18.61; p < .01$
Ancillary	22.9(297)	35.9(234)	$F(focus) = 33.02; p < .01$
Wall Street Journal			
Focus	9.8(88)	6.9(33)	$F(year) = 2.71; p = .10$
Ancillary	19.9(141)	17.8(56)	$F(focus) = 53.05; p < .01$
Washington Post			
Focus	12.9(111)	11.8(91)	$F(year) = 0.02;$ n.s.
Ancillary	23.7(238)	23.9(197)	$F(focus) = 57.14; p < .01$
Newsweek			
Focus	17.3(3)	14.0(6)	$F(year) = 0.30;$ n.s.
Ancillary	26.3(26)	30.4(22)	$F(focus) = 3.21; p < .10$
Time			
Focus	13.0(2)	8.9(13)	$F(year) = 2.02;$ n.s.
Ancillary	41.0(32)	29.2(29)	$F(focus) = 5.00; p < .05$
U.S. News & World Report			
Focus	11.4(14)	7.2(20)	$F(year) = .00;$ n.s.
Ancillary	28.3(34)	31.0(20)	$F(focus) = 32.10; p < .01$

NOTE: In these analyses the length of an item, in column inches, is the dependent variable, and year and focus/ancillary status are entered as independent variables. Because column width varies between media and even within the same medium from section to section and day to day, we used linear column inches as an indicator of visibility. Measurements for 1970 media were corrected for reduction due to microfilm readers, but some imprecision may have occurred as a result of variations between machines.
[a] Excluded from the category of focus stories in both years are letters and columns written by social scientists about non–social science topics.
[b] 1982S denotes the subsample of 1982 coverage which matches the 1970 sample period.
[c] Interactions are not significant except in the case of the *New York Times*.

Even though there had been no consistent change in length from 1970 to 1982, it seemed possible that the fraction of ancillary stories devoted to social science content might have increased over time. Table 9.6 indicates that in all three newspapers the proportion of stories consisting of a phrase or one or two sentences declined between 1970 and 1982, although the change was significant only for the *Times*. No changes could be discerned in newsmagazines. Even in 1982, however, half of all ancillary references consisted of no more than one or two sentences. These figures show very little variation from one medium to another.

Social Science Mention

Still another way in which the visibility of social science might have increased between 1970 and 1982 was by being mentioned earlier in the news story, since headlines and lead paragraphs are most likely to catch the reader's attention. The data do not bear out this supposition, however. There is no evidence that social science elements were featured any more prominently in ancillary news stories in 1982 than they had been in 1970.

Visuals

The final element we looked at in connection with change in the visibility of social science was the presence of some kind of illustration, since graphs, tables, or photographs, like front-page placement, could serve to draw attention to such items.

About a third (31 percent) of all social science items were accompanied by visual material in 1970; this proportion had increased to 39 percent in 1982. And while ancillary stories were more likely to be accompanied by illustrations than focus stories, both types of stories were more likely to be illustrated in 1982 than in 1970. By this criterion, then, the visibility of social science in the news had increased. The most common type of illustration, in both 1970 and 1982, was a photograph, with graphs running far behind in second place.

Changes in the Topics of Social Science Stories

The topic of each of the social science stories selected in 1970 and 1982 was coded into one of eight broad categories: U.S. economy; foreign economies and international trade; U.S. government and politics; foreign governments and international relations; social integration and social control;

health; demographics; and relationships and lifestyles. More detailed sub-categories were also coded; for example, under "U.S. Economy" were such headings as "government economic policies," "economic indicators," and "economic theories," with more specific subheadings under each of these—for example, "producer price index" and "GNP" under "economic indicators." "Social integration and social control" includes two broad classes of stories: those pertaining to religion and education, on the one hand, and those pertaining to crime and law enforcement, on the other.

Stories about the U.S. economy dominated social science news in both 1970 and 1982 in all media (see Table 9.7); the tendency was even more marked in 1982 than it had been in 1970. What is most striking in Table 9.7 is the general similarity of the distributions, both across different types of media and over time. As we show in more detail below, the relative frequency of social science stories about the economy increased between 1970 and 1982, but other categories showed very little change. In newspapers and newsmagazines, stories about the economy were followed in frequency by stories about government and politics, social integration and social control (in 1982 the order of these two categories was reversed), relationships and lifestyles, health, and, finally, a smattering of other topics.

Television news, for which we had no 1970 baseline, differs from the other media by its greater relative emphasis on public opinion polls, which made up more than a third of social science reporting on politics on TV. At the same time, television featured relatively more social science stories on international relations than the other media and devoted twice as many stories to economic indicators. Relatively fewer lifestyle and relationship stories involving social science were featured on television news-

TABLE 9.6

Percentage of Story Devoted to Social Science Content, by Media and Year

Media and Percentage[a]	1970	1982S[b]
New York Times		
1 66.1%	50.4%	50.9%
2 21.9	34.8	31.5
3 8.2	11.1	12.4
4 3.8	3.7	5.2
(N)	(233)	(297)
		$\chi^2 = 16.61; p < .01$[c]

TABLE 9.6 (*Continued*)

Media and Percentage[a]	1970	1982S[b]
Wall Street Journal		
1 76.3	63.7	60.8
2 16.4	24.6	24.6
3 3.6	8.9	12.5
4 3.6	2.8	2.0
(N)	(55)	(141)
	$\chi^2 = 2.62$; n.s.	
Washington Post		
1 61.5	52.8	56.0
2 25.6	33.3	30.7
3 9.2	9.5	9.4
4 3.6	4.4	4.0
(N)	(195)	(238)
	$\chi^2 = 4.25$; n.s.	
Newsweek		
1 72.7	69.2	61.3
2 13.6	26.9	32.3
3 13.6	3.8	4.3
4 0.0	0.0	2.2
(N)	(22)	(26)
	$\chi^2 = 1.74$; n.s.	
Time		
1 62.0	71.4	78.2
2 34.5	22.2	18.2
3 3.4	6.3	3.6
4 0.0	0.0	0.0
(N)	(29)	(32)
	$\chi^2 = 3.37$; n.s.	
U.S. News & World Report		
1 60.0	61.7	56.3
2 30.0	20.6	20.6
3 5.0	14.7	19.8
4 5.0	2.9	3.2
(N)	(20)	(34)
	$\chi^2 = 6.13$; n.s.	

[a] 1 = phrase or one or two sentences; 2 = more than a sentence but no more than 2 quarter; 3 = more than 2 quarter but less than half; 4 = more than half.

[b] 1982S denotes the subsample of 1982 coverage which matches the 1970 sample period.

[c] All tests are for significance of difference between 1970 and 1982S. Chi-square values for the ancillary tests have been adjusted to reflect the reduction in effective sample size due to weighting. The effective size is .71 of the sample size shown.

TABLE 9.7

Topics and Subtopics of Social Science Stories, by Media and Year, Focus and Ancillary Combined

	1970		1982		
	News-papers	News-magazines	News-papers	News-magazines	TV
U.S. Economy					
Government economic policies	6%	4%	10%	10%	5%
Economic indicators and conditions	11	18	14	15	28
Private sector–producers	6	6	7	12	2
Private sector–consumers	0	1	1	0	1
Economic theories	0	0	1	1	0
Miscellaneous economic	3	0	5	1	0
Poverty, welfare	2	0	1	1	0
(N)	(28%)	(29%)	(39%)	(40%)	(36%)
Foreign Economies and International Trade	2	3	8	2	1
(N)	(2%)	(3%)	(8%)	(2%)	(1%)
U.S. Government and Politics					
Politicians	3	2	2	7	9
Congressional and State legislative activities	1	0	1	0	0
Campaigns and elections	3	3	2	1	0
Public opinion	4	2	3	2	5
Mass movements and collective behavior	4	6	1	2	0
Race and ethnic relations	4	2	1	0	0
Miscellaneous political	3	3	2	0	0
	(22%)	(18%)	(12%)	(12%)	(14%)
Foreign Governments and International Relations	7	12	7	10	15
	(7%)	(12%)	(7%)	(10%)	(15%)

Social Integration and Social Control					
Religion	1%	1%	1%	1%	1%
Education	7	0	4	3	3
Crime	2	2	3	1	3
Law, law enforcement	2	4	2	1	5
Military	1	3	0	2	0
Culture (art, literature, etc.)	3	5	5	6	3
Science, social science	2	1	1	2	0
	(18%)	(16%)	(16%)	(16%)	(15%)
Health					
Health and medical care	1	3	2	0	1
Diseases and conditions	2	2	3	1	7
Moods, mental states	0	1	0	0	1
Mental illness, suicide	2	3	1	0	0
Addictions	1	1	1	2	2
Miscellaneous health	1	1	1	2	2
	(7%)	(11%)	(8%)	(5%)	(13%)
Demographics					
U.S.	0	0	1	1	1
Foreign	1	0	0	0	0
Migration	0	0	0	2	0
Demographic trends	0	1	0	0	0
Census	2	1	0	1	0
	(3%)	(2%)	(1%)	(4%)	(1%)
Miscellaneous	1	3	1	1	0
(N)	(1%)	(3%)	(1%)	(1%)	(0%)
Relationships and Lifestyles					
Relationships	9	9	5	5	2
Lifestyles	1	0	1	0	0
Hobbies and leisure activities	0	0	1	1	0
	(10%)	(9%)	(7%)	(6%)	(2%)
(N)	(802)	(117)	(2,397)	(218)	(86)

NOTE: Because of rounding errors, columns do not add exactly to 100%. Table 9.7 is based on the total weighted sample of social science stories.

casts than in the other media; on the other hand, stories about health were featured relatively more frequently there.

With some striking exceptions, distributions among the more detailed subcategories were likewise similar across types of media and over time. Among the exceptions, we note that the newsmagazines paid greater attention to economic indicators in 1970 than did the newspapers, whereas the newspapers devoted more attention to social science stories on education.

Data on topics are presented separately for focus and ancillary stories, and by individual media, in Table 9.8. As usual, data are shown for 1970, for the matching 1982 subsample, and for the full sample of 1982 stories. Because sample sizes are now much reduced, we confine subsequent discussion to the general topic only, ignoring the more elaborate subheadings shown in Table 9.7.

The first thing to notice is that the rank orderings of topics for focus and ancillary stories are rather similar, even though the relative frequencies may differ.[7] It is not intuitively obvious that this should be the case— that stories written about the substance of social science should show the same relative emphasis among broad topic areas as those written about events in the social world, where social science content is brought in only peripherally. What this similarity suggests is that the relative frequency with which both focus and ancillary social science stories appear in the media reflects editorial and reportorial judgments about news values: With some exceptions, what's new and interesting in general is also what's new and interesting in the social sciences. This is reminiscent of a finding by Johnson (1963), whose editors used substantially the same criteria for judging science news as nonscience readers did; they did not use the criteria of scientists, science writers, or science readers. It also accords with the comments made by those journalists we interviewed (see chapter 3).

Shifting our attention from comparisons between focus and ancillary stories to changes between 1970 and 1982, we note that statistically significant changes in the relative frequency with which different topics were featured occurred for both ancillary and focus stories, with the exception of the newsmagazines, where small numbers generally precluded findings that reached statistical significance. Two changes occurred with regularity across most media and across both focus and ancillary stories:

---

[7] For the *New York Times* and *Wall Street Journal* the probabilities associated with the Spearman rank-order correlation coefficients for 1970 focus/ancillary distributions are $p = .16$ and .17; the coefficient attains significance for the *Washington Post*. In 1982 the coefficients are significant for the *Times* and the *Post* but not for the *Journal*.

Social science reporting about economic issues increased between 1970 and 1982, and such reporting about political issues declined.

In part, this change in media emphasis may reflect changes in the world of events. The 1970 period which we monitored included the shootings at Kent State and the bombing of Cambodia, as well as other events of the Vietnam war and protests against it; these were coded as "political" events. No comparably traumatic political events occurred during the 1982 media-monitoring period.

One is tempted, however, to assert a change in media emphasis despite similarity in the underlying events; 1970, like 1982, was a period of inflation, high interest rates, high unemployment, and declining GNP. Indeed, looking only at the headlines—"When Is a Recession?" "Consumer Prices Up," "U.S. Sees New Dip in GNP," "Nixon's New Worries about Recession," "Employment Here Down," "U.S. Output Down," "Brother, Can You Spare a Job," "The Economy: Crisis of Confidence," "Rising Pessimism," "Jobless Rise Sharpest in 5 Years," "Warnings of a Recession Follow April's 4 Million Jobless Figure"[8]—it was sometimes difficult to place the year in which a story belonged. Nevertheless, despite this underlying similarity, the proportion of stories about economic issues which either focused on some aspect of social science or introduced ancillary references to social science increased dramatically from 1970 to 1982, perhaps reflecting both a greater tendency on the part of journalists to draw on economic facts and expertise in this area and the prevalence of more economic specialists among reporters. The change, that is, appears to reflect changes intrinsic to the media as an institution, rather than simply changes in the world of events.

Variations in Coverage of the Same Event

Some of the differences described in the first section of this chapter may arise because different social science stories are being reported in different media. In this section we attempt to control for this source of variation by restricting the comparisons to "identical" events. Because of the paucity

---

[8]Headlines from, respectively, *New York Times,* March 23, p. 59; *Wall Street Journal,* March 24, p. 1; *Washington Post,* March 27, p. 1; *Time,* March 30, p. 81; *Times,* April 13, p. 34; *Times,* April 17, p. 1; *Times,* April 20, p. 83; *Time,* June 1, p. 64; *Times,* May 28, p. 51; *Washington Post,* May 8, p. 1; *Times,* May 9, p. 33—all from 1970.

Among newspapers, the increased economic coverage comes largely as a result of increases in stories about government policies and about economic indicators. Newsmagazines also carried more stories about government economic policies in 1982, but fewer indicator stories; the overall increase for newsmagazines reflects small increases in most other categories.

TABLE 9.8

Topic of Focus and Ancillary Social Science Stories,[a] by Media and Year

Media and Topic	Focus			Ancillary		
	1970	1982S[b]	1982T[b]	1970	1982S[b]	1982T[b]
New York Times						
U.S. economy	21.9%	42.6%	45.2%	35.9%	37.8%	40.3%
Foreign economies	1.5	2.3	3.0	3.6	3.3	7.2
U.S. government and politics	13.1	14.0	9.1	22.7	11.9	10.3
Foreign governments	5.1	1.6	2.6	10.5	9.0	9.2
Social integration	13.9	13.2	12.2	15.5	12.9	10.7
Social control	4.4	4.7	6.1	2.3	8.1	7.1
Health	11.7	10.1	10.4	3.6	10.5	9.3
Demographics	5.8	3.1	3.9	0.5	2.2	1.6
Relationships and lifestyles	22.6	8.5	7.4	5.5	4.3	4.4
(N)	(137)	(129)	(230)	(220)	(290)	(530)
	$\chi^2 = 21.67; p < .01^c$			$\chi^2 = 20.16; p < .05$		
Wall Street Journal						
U.S. economy	81.8	42.0	42.3	46.3	51.2	59.4
Foreign economies	0.0	35.2	35.6	9.3	9.6	10.5
U.S. government and politics	12.1	4.5	6.0	20.4	6.4	6.1
Foreign governments	0.0	0.0	—	0.0	11.0	8.3
Social integration	0.0	3.4	2.7	9.3	14.2	8.9
Social control	0.0	1.1	0.7	7.4	0.7	0.8
Health	0.0	3.4	4.0	3.7	6.8	5.5
Demographics	3.0	3.4	4.0	3.7	0.0	0.0
Relationships and lifestyles	3.0	6.8	4.7	0.0	0.0	0.4
(N)	(33)	(88)	(149)	(54)	(141)	(247)
	$\chi^2 = 24.12; p < .01$			$\chi^2 = 19.12; p < .01$		

Washington Post

U.S. economy	14.9%	35.5%	37.1%	25.1%	30.6%	33.5%
Foreign economies	—	4.5	4.1	0.5	3.2	5.1
U.S. government and politics	20.7	16.4	14.7	28.8	16.3	14.8
Foreign governments	3.4	1.8	2.0	6.3	7.2	8.9
Social integration	8.0	14.5	12.2	19.9	17.8	14.3
Social control	10.3	4.5	5.6	5.8	8.7	7.9
Health	11.5	5.5	7.6	7.3	7.0	5.6
Demographics	13.8	2.7	3.6	2.6	1.7	1.9
Relationships and lifestyles	17.2	14.5	13.2	3.7	7.4	8.0
(N)	(87)	(110)	(197)	(191)	(236)	(386)
	$\chi^2 = 26.98; p < .01^c$			$\chi^2 = 12.04$; n.s.		

Newsweek, Time, and U.S. News & World Report

U.S. economy	35.9	47.4	28.6	23.9	43.6	42.8
Foreign economies	5.1	—	—	3.0	2.2	3.1
U.S. government and politics	15.3	15.8	9.5	17.9	18.4	14.5
Foreign governments	2.6	—	—	19.4	10.6	13.8
Social integration	2.6	15.8	14.3	10.4	8.9	11.1
Social control	5.1	5.3	7.1	9.0	4.5	3.1
Health	12.8	5.3	19.0	10.4	6.1	4.0
Demographics	5.1	—	4.8	0.0	3.4	4.0
Relationships and lifestyles	15.3	10.5	16.7	6.0	2.2	3.7
(N)	(39)	(19)	(42)	(67)	(90)	(163)
	$\chi^2 = 7.03$; n.s.			$\chi^2 = 8.66$; n.s.		

[a]Excluded from the category of focus stories in both years are letters and columns written by social scientists about non–social science topics.
[b]1982S denotes the subsample of 1982 coverage which matches the 1970 sample period; 1982T denotes the total 1982 sample.
[c]All tests are for significance of difference between 1970 and 1982S. Chi-square values for the ancillary tests have been adjusted to reflect the reduction in effective sample size due to weighting. The effective sample size is .71 of the sample size shown.

of social science on television, comparisons are restricted almost entirely to the print media.

The decision about whether or not an underlying event was "the same" or "different" was not always easy to make. For example, are two news stories based on the same poll (for example, by Gallup), but emphasizing different questions, based on the "same" or "different" events? Our decision was to treat them as different. Or are two news stories, one which focuses on the announced drop in GNP and another which mentions GNP as one of several aspects of the economy, to be considered as based on the "same" or "different" events? Again, our decision was to treat them as different. Finally, are two stories, both about the drop in Reagan's popularity, but based on different polls, based on the "same" or "different" events? Once again, we opted for treating them as based on different events. All of these decisions are arguable, but they affected only a minority of the stories analyzed here. For the most part, decisions about whether an event was the "same" or "different" in different news accounts were reasonably clear-cut.

The events covered by more than one medium tended to fall into two broad categories. In the first were routine stories about regularly recurring events, such as the release of the weekly money supply figures, or the monthly unemployment figures, or the monthly survey of consumer confidence by the Conference Board. As these examples illustrate, many of these stories were about economic indicators, often though not always reported without information about the studies from which they were derived. (The Conference Board survey is a good illustration of an indicator which is still being reported in the context of the survey from which the data are obtained, though one can imagine a time in the future when the media will simply report that consumer confidence is up by two points over the month before, without mentioning the origin of the data.) Gallup poll results, to which a number of the media subscribe, also tended to be reported by several of them. So, too, did findings from the 1980 census, which can also be conceived of as a "regularly recurring event," though on a much elongated scale. Reports of these events in the media tended to rely on press releases, or on wire service reports based on these releases, but there were variations in this respect from one medium to another. One newspaper, for example, might use the wire service write-up of a Conference Board survey, while another might assign a reporter to cover it in greater detail.

The second category of events covered by more than one medium were "important" events, those which editors and reporters at several of the media perceived as newsworthy and to which several of them assigned reporters. A National Academy of Sciences report on ability tests, for example, fell into this category, as did the release of a Surgeon General's report on the relation between nutrition and cancer.

Events covered by only one of the media in the sample, by contrast, tended to be those of special interest to only one city, or those resulting from what might be called "enterprise" reporting—a feature on the causes of crime, for example, or on the sequelae of divorce for young children. The idea for these stories might originate in a press release or an article in one of the specialized journals intermediate between scientists and the lay public, such as *Psychology Today* or *Human Behavior*. But the appearance of the story in a particular mass medium is likely to have resulted from an idiosyncratic concatenation of circumstances, such as the interest and skill of a particular reporter and/or editor and the availability of space.

We carefully examined a number of the stories about the "same" event which appeared in several of the media in our sample in order to identify and, if possible, categorize the nature of the differences in the way they were handled.

Some of the variations we discovered in this way are patterned and easily accounted for. For example, on May 5, 1982, the *New York Times* ran a 12-inch bylined story about a survey sponsored by the Federation of Jewish Philanthropies to determine the size of New York's Jewish population. The *Boston Globe* gave the story 2¼ inches, picked up from an AP release, in a column headed "U.S./World News Briefs." The same difference between hometown and out-of-town interest can be seen in coverage of a New York City police department study of homicides: 20½ inches in a story by Barbara Basler in the *New York Times* of February 9, 1982, and 3¾ inches in a February 10 *Washington Post* roundup of news around the country.

Sometimes, indeed, there was little variation to account for. For example, most of the newspapers in our sample regularly covered the Conference Board's monthly survey of consumer confidence, giving the story roughly similar amounts of space and attention, with the *Wall Street Journal* perhaps the least attentive of the four. Or, again, both the *New York Times* and the *Boston Globe* on February 25, 1982, printed virtually identical accounts of Nobelist James Tobin's remarks at a financial conference sponsored by the Conference Board. The story was apparently based on an Associated Press write-up, slightly modified by the *Times* (which did not acknowledge the source).

Ordinarily, however, there were variations in the way individual media covered the same event, but these tended to be variations on a theme and for the most part were neither patterned nor predictable. For example, the *Washington Post,* the *Wall Street Journal,* and the *New York Times* all covered a National Association of Purchasing Managers survey on February 8, 1982. Although all three stories were similar in length, the *Times* story, by Linda Chavez, gave prominent attention to a new economic indicator developed by Ted Torda, describing in some detail its construction and properties. The *Journal* also mentioned the new index, but in much less detail. Although the two newspapers reported similar facts, the *Times* headlined its story "Survey Finds Economy Still Weak," whereas the *Journal*'s head was "Buying Agents See Some Gains in the Economy." The gains, also noted by the *Times* in its lead paragraph, consisted of a slowing in the rate of decline. The *Post,* under the head "Confidence in Economy Improves," gave two sentences to the Purchasing Managers' survey in the context of a story about the Conference Board's monthly survey of consumer confidence.

To take another example, the *Times, Globe,* and *Journal* all ran stories of roughly similar length on an NBC poll in which a majority of those surveyed agreed that the network newscasts should be expanded to an hour (from half an hour). All three also mentioned the different results obtained in an earlier poll and linked the differences to the differing interests of those sponsoring the two surveys and to differences in question wording. But while the *Times* focused on the institutional conflicts involved and headlined its story "One-Hour Newscast Backed in Poll," the *Globe*'s Kenneth R. Clark, under the headline, "Similar Surveys Breed Dissimilar Answers," started off with, "Some sage, deep in wisdom, once observed that there are three kinds of lies: 'lies, damned lies, and statistics,'" and emphasized the self-serving nature of the "truth" revealed by the two surveys. The *Journal* mentioned the conflicting earlier survey in its subhead but, like the *Times,* tended to emphasize the issues underlying the discrepant results.

Still another example is the relatively brief coverage which the *Times, Post,* and *Globe* all gave to a National Institute of Justice study of the effects of helping crime victims on the helpers. The March 22, 1982, *Globe* story, in its entirety, read as follows:

VICTIMS' HELPERS SUFFER—STUDY

Associated Press

WASHINGTON—Eighty percent of friends, relatives, neighbors and others who help crime victims often suffer their own hidden costs, including increased fear, suspicion and insecurity, according to a federally funded report released yesterday.

"For some supporters, this meant feeling nervous or frightened; in others, increased suspicion of people; and in others, feeling less safe at home or on the street," the report said.

The findings were contained in a Justice Department report,
"Victims and Helpers: Reactions to Crime."

Both the *Times* account (based on AP) and the *Post* account (based on UPI) gave a few additional details (*Post:* "Victims experienced a decrease in positive feelings such as joy and contentment, and an increase in nega- tive . . . states such as depression and guilt. . . . The twenty-six-month study by the Victims Services Agency for the National Institute of Justice cost $261,815 and surveyed crime victims in three New York City neighbor- hoods: the Fordham section of the Bronx, Flushing in Queens, and Park Slope in Brooklyn").

The *Globe, Journal, Times,* and *Post* all gave prominent display on June 17, 1982, to by-lined stories reporting on a National Academy of Sciences study, commissioned by the National Cancer Institute, of the relation of diet and nutrition to cancer. In addition, both NBC and CBS gave the story prominent attention.

One interesting variation in the way different media covered this story had to do with how prominently criticism of the report, by such groups as the American Meat Institute and the National Cattleman's Association, was featured. The *Journal* reported such criticisms about one third of the way into the story, under the subhead "Conclusions Attacked," devoting about 12 percent of the total space to them. The *Globe* did not report any criticism until about half way into the story, but also devoted about the same proportion of space to it. The *Times* did not report the Meat Insti- tute's comments until the last quarter of its story, and then gave them no more than 6 percent of the total space. The *Post,* while reporting the comments somewhat earlier, also gave them relatively little space. Neither of the TV accounts mentioned the Meat Institute criticisms, nor did the *Times* "Week in Review" summary. Only the *Times,* in both of its stories, pointed out that earlier "contradictory" findings pertained to heart disease rather than cancer, and the "Week in Review" story further attempted to reconcile the discrepancies by noting, "The nutrition board [which had said there was no need to reduce fat intake] was weighted with biochem- ists who look for direct evidence of cause and effect. Panel members [who evaluated the cancer-diet link] included epidemiologists and public health experts, who rely more on statistical correlations to reach conclusions." For those members of the audience who had read the earlier newspaper accounts, this effort to reconcile conflicting findings was crucial, but only the *Times* made the attempt.

Still another of the events covered by several media in the sample was the release of a National Academy of Sciences study of health care. The February 9, 1982, *Wall Street Journal* story, in its entirety, read as follows:

Racial patterns in health care show that blacks and other minorities often need care more than whites, but generally get less and of a lower quality, a National Academy of Sciences report said. The study cited "striking" differences in dental and nursing home care, and cited strong evidence of racial bias.

A *Washington Post* story of the same day, based on UPI, ran to 8 inches and gave several additional findings, but did not provide readers with the title of the report nor where it might be obtained. Only the *New York Times* account, likewise based on UPI, included the title of the report.

On February 25, 1982, the *Times, Post,* and *Journal* all reported on a University of Michigan study of drug use by teenagers. While the *Journal* devoted only an inch on page 1 to the story, the *Times* and *Post* stories were much longer (33 inches) and similar in the amount of detail provided. Only the *Times,* however, mentioned that the information had "been obtained under a special dispensation from the Justice Department, so that no Federal, state, or local police authorities may obtain personal information on the students from the researchers," and noted that the study "is considered one of the most reliable indicators of drug abuse trends, otherwise notoriously hard to measure." Only the *Times,* too, gave the exact title of the report and information about where it might be obtained.

One of the most interesting social science stories covered during the period of our study was a Census Bureau report on the implications of different ways of defining poverty. All four newspapers reported the Census Bureau study—the *New York Times* in three different stories—as did *Newsweek* and *U.S. News & World Report.* Inclusion of a 4 × 3 matrix in the Sunday (April 18, 1982) *Times,* illustrating how the three different methods, applied to different household budget items, such as food and housing costs and medical care, changed the number of families defined as living in poverty, undoubtedly did the most to clarify the implications of the different methods outlined in the Census Bureau report. The *Wall Street Journal* devoted most of its space to speculating on possible uses to which the Reagan Administration might put the findings (the *Journal* seemed to take it for granted that some version of the alternative methods, all of which included some in-kind benefits as part of family income, should be substituted for the existing method, which counted cash income only), and to reporting on the negative reactions of "social services" groups to the report. While *U.S. News* provided a concise summary of the report's basic findings, *Newsweek* devoted relatively more space to exploring their implications and the problems associated with them. (The follow-up to this study two years later illustrates another aspect of social science reporting on which we have already commented: the failure of such reporting to cumulate. On April 23, 1984, Robert Pear—one of the original reporters—reported on the front page of the *Times,* "U.S. Weighing Change in Poverty Programs." The story, which detailed Administration plans for convening a panel of economic experts to suggest ways of measuring the value of noncash benefits, made no reference to the Census Bureau study carried out two years earlier.)

Although it is tempting to multiply examples of multiple coverage, the point made at the beginning of this section still applies: These comparisons do not, for the most part, permit us to generalize about how any one medium characteristically covers a social science story. True, if an event occurs in New York, the *Times* in all likelihood will give it more play than the *Post,* and the *Journal,* having a more specialized set of interests, may well give it less. But aside from this pattern—true in general, and not only for social science—the only distinction that seems to emerge is the *Times'* practice of identifying a published source for social science research. While other media do this from time to time, the *Times* does it most consistently.

Perhaps the most obvious explanation for the absence of startling differences among the media we analyzed is the fact that they are more alike than different; that (with the exception of the *Globe*) all are "national" media, following a style and an emphasis that differentiate them from local television stations, small-town newspapers, and magazines aimed at specific audiences.

Two other generalizations, to some extent contradictory, emerge from our analysis of these multiples. First, evidently the "facts" of a story do not entirely constrain the journalist's presentation or interpretation. The *Journal* can emphasize the fact that the glass is half full, the *Times* that it is half empty. The *Post* can highlight the research underlying the diet-cancer study, the *Times,* its recommendations.[9]

Second, the form first given to an event—as, for example, in a press release or wire service story—often limits the amount and kind of detail

---

[9] For a contrary view, see Polsby (1967). Polsby analyzed coverage by the "prestige" press of a poll of attitudes toward the Vietnam war sponsored by Stanford University professors. Polsby asserts that the "prestige" press made little use of the authors' careful report and analysis. He believes that this was because the report contained many more findings than could be accommodated in a news story, and also because the poll's political implications made the authors' interpretations unacceptable to some reporters.

Nevertheless, although Polsby emphasizes differences among the media, his analysis shows two main strands (leaving aside a highly critical column by Evans and Novak, which was distributed to newspapers nationwide). One followed the *Washington Post* and the Washington *Star* in reporting elements emphasized by the Stanford group's own report and press release; the other followed Tom Wicker of the *New York Times,* whose analysis of the data emphasized interpretations at variance with those in the Stanford report.

that subsequently appears in the media. Because reporters may not have time to gather additional information, the original source of a story—and in the case of social science research this may well be a university or government agency public relations department—is thus in a position to influence not only the basic factual details but sometimes even the emphasis in subsequent media accounts. For example, a detailed analysis by Lynne Sussman (1983) of press coverage of a 1982 Department of Defense Study of American youth, designed to shed light on the characteristics of the all-volunteer armed forces, underscores the importance both of the primary source and of the initial media report in shaping subsequent media accounts.

Perhaps the best illustration of how a press release, and the original press briefing, structured the initial coverage of a social science study is the saga of the "Coleman Report" (1966). As Grant and Murray (1985:5) point out; "The Johnson civil rights advocates distorted [the Report] by exaggerating alleged differences between black and white schools, when the real news was that there were fewer differences than anyone had thought." And Haskins (1985:82) notes: "Aides to Education Commissioner Howe wrote a press release that, if not inaccurate, was certainly misleading. Evidently they did so with full confidence that the Washington press corps would rely on the press release and not the text of the Coleman Report itself." In fact, as Grant and Murray point out, "Most of the nation's mass press was misled by the summary that had been issued in July and found the full report impenetrable when it arrived six weeks later" (Grant and Murray 1985:16; see also Hunt 1986, chap. 2). Eventually, the record was set straight, but only after articles by Coleman, Jencks, and Nichols had appeared in the specialized press (Grant and Murray 1985:16).

All this does not imply that press releases determine which social science is selected for coverage. Only 3 of 90 press releases in the "incoming communications study" (see chapter 6) resulted in traceable stories. Clearly, other factors determine which of many studies that come into reporters' ken will actually catch their attention. But once the decision to cover the study is made, press releases figure in a large proportion of the social science stories written. Forty-seven percent of the social science "study" stories analyzed in Part I originated with the social scientist's initiative; and for most of these, reporters "made do with the press release or study report, a conversation or two with the researcher, a quick reading of available material, and their own good sense" (see chapter 7). Note that these stories were sampled from the major social science stories written each week; for the average story, press releases were in all likelihood even more important.

Interestingly enough, a similar conclusion about the importance of the scientist source for the quality of reporting was reached by Freimuth, Greenberg, DeWitt, and Romano (1984:72) in an analysis of the quality of newspaper reporting on cancer. Noting that newspapers generally omit detailed information in cancer stories—such as cancer incidence rates, prevention, and treatment—the authors point out that:

> . . . scientific liaisons working closely with . . . news gatekeepers might substantially affect coverage of cancer throughout the United States. The vast majority of cancer stories concerned news of fast-breaking events. . . . While the press liaisons who supply information about cancer may not be able to influence news editors' definitions of what constitutes hard news, they may be able to influence the manner in which cancer news is reported. Their own understanding of the implications of cancer news can be translated for use by the media in the press releases and statements they disseminate.

A recent study by the Twentieth Century Fund (Nelkin 1984) on the reporting of new technologies and their risks has similarly located primary responsibility for the quality of press coverage with the news organizations' sources, not the media themselves. And although news organizations could diminish their dependence on information sources by training reporters in complex scientific issues, such training is not generally available to reporters at the present time, nor do we see it as being readily or widely available in the foreseeable future.

Summary

Contrary to our expectations, there was no more coverage of social science qua social science in the news media in 1982 than there had been in 1970, at least in the three "national" newspapers and the three newsmagazines for which we carried out a systematic comparison. In the newspapers, but not the newsmagazines, we did observe an increase in ancillary references to social science in the context of other reporting. And if the aim is to provide behavioral science insights for the better understanding of news events, such ancillary references may serve the purpose as well as—perhaps even better than—the reporting of social science as such.

By two criteria—placement on the first pages of sections other than the front page and the use of accompanying illustrations—the visibility of both focus and ancillary social science items increased from 1970 to 1982. None of the other indicators of visibility we examined—first-page placement, length of story, fraction of story devoted to social science content, or where in the story the reference to social science first appeared—showed any consistent significant change. And even those changes in visibility that did occur were limited to the newspapers in the sample. However, it is possible that these changes in the visibility of social science reporting account for the impression that the amount of such reporting has increased.

Our examination of social science reporting on different topics suggested that general news values, rather than social science values, governed the distribution of such reporting. First, there were marked resemblances among the various media in their coverage of the various topics, with television showing the greatest divergence from the other two. Second, such resemblances also existed for the topics of focus and ancillary stories in each medium during the same year. We interpreted these convergences as indicating that what's new and interesting in general is also what's new and interesting in the social sciences—a conclusion that may be obvious once stated, but is not necessarily what social scientists have in mind when they yearn for greater coverage by the media.

We expected to find patterned variations in social science reporting between different kinds of media—newspapers, newsmagazines, and television. Specifically, we expected to find more reporting of social science, as well as more detailed reporting, in print than on television. And, because of the more leisurely tempo of the newsmagazines, we expected to find greater adherence to scholarly conventions there than in the daily papers.

As we had expected, the print media carried many more social science items than television, even on a per-issue (or per-broadcast) basis. The television audience is of course much larger, and so those items that are aired reach a wider public. But the time constraints of the evening newscasts, as well as their focus on events of national interest, militate against the inclusion of much social science content.

The newspapers in our sample, rather than the newsmagazines, carried the greatest number of social science items, not only absolutely (which is of course to be expected), but also per page. And the newspaper accounts were, on the average, also longer. Thus, coverage of social science depends on available space, not only in an absolute but in a relative sense. Newspapers, with more editorial space, can more readily afford the luxury of including the occasional social science story.

Because of the brevity accorded most social science news on the TV evening newscasts, we expected television to be least informative about details of research methods and so on, but to our surprise the differences between television and the print media were, for the most part, neither large nor consistent. Nor were there large or consistent differences in this respect between newspapers and newsmagazines.

In short, although there is much less social science on television than in newsmagazines, and less in newsmagazines than in the newspapers of our sample, the differences among them, so far as the quality of reporting is concerned, turned out to be less than we had expected (see also chapter 11).

Furthermore, despite Roshco's belief that the conventions of weekly newsmagazine coverage would be more hospitable to social science reporting than those of newspapers—because the newsmagazine is less time-bound than the daily paper and more receptive to discussions and analyses of values and opinions—the newsmagazines in our sample were, if anything, less receptive to social science reporting in 1982 than they had been in 1970.

In order to try to extract some general principles that governed the way the different media in our sample reported social science, we analyzed a series of "events" covered by more than one of them. What emerged from this comparison is the conclusion that variations among the media in our sample are, ordinarily, variations on a theme, the basic details of which are often dictated by the source—perhaps a wire service story based on a press release—which underlies the several media accounts. But the conclusion is largely restricted to the print media, since we had too few television stories to permit a comparison.

Although this dependence on a source shows up most clearly when there are several different accounts of the same underlying event, the likelihood is that much social science reporting is highly reliant on a single source. And local or regional media, which generally command fewer resources than those enjoyed by the national media we studied, are likely to be even more dependent on press releases or wire service accounts.

It follows that social scientists may often be in a position to influence the reporting of social science research by the way they structure releases to the press. The care social scientists themselves exercise—or fail to exercise—in their communication with journalists may well set the standards for how social science will be reported by the press to the general public. At the least, it is likely to set the limits within which much social science reporting takes place.

10

Social Scientists as Sources

ALL REPORTERS, FROM THE CUB REPORTER TO THE SEASONED VETERAN, MUST GO TO others, to the designated actors, for their material. Roshco (1975), following Lippmann and James, has observed:

> [T]he mass-media reporter is prototypically an observer, describing the issues others frame, the problems they raise, the solutions they offer, the actions they take, the conflicts in which they engage. Thus, the nature of news as a form of knowledge makes the reporter dependent upon news sources for most of the knowledge he will transpose into media content.

Sports reporters may be allowed on the playing field, but they don't engage in the game any more than other reporters engage in the topic they're reporting. Journalists may, in Tuchman's phrase, make news, but they are not the newsmakers. This reliance on sources, and the difference between expert and journalistic knowledge, is captured succinctly in Jeremy Tunstall's characterization of the specialist-reporter: "An effective specialist is largely defined as a person who is on personal terms with important persons in the relevant field" (1971:160). It is not, in other words, possession of his own knowledge about a subject that defines the specialty reporter, but rather knowledge about and familiarity with those expert sources who can provide the necessary acquaintance with the subject.

In *The Visible Scientists* (1977) Rae Goodell examines a few "media star" scientists, and in "The Science Writing Inner Club" (1980) Sharon

Dunwoody examines a few star science reporters, both of whom have, in their separate ways, tended to dominate science news. Our data suggest, by contrast, that most news organizations do not define social science as a beat, that most journalists who report on social science are not specialists in that subject, and that neither one clique of social scientists nor one clique of journalists dominates the reporting of social science news in the national media. Editors are even less likely to have a particular responsibility for or sustained experience with social science news. On the whole, then, and with some striking exceptions—for example, Abe Raskin in his day and Leonard Silk in ours—those doing and those overseeing the reporting of social science are not likely to be personally knowledgeable about social scientist sources. We know that reporters seek, and editors expect, credible sources: how well, given their intermittent attention to the social science arena, do they accomplish this goal?[1]

This chapter examines the relation between eminence in social science and visibility in the media in order to shed light on two broader questions: First, is the public's interest in the social sciences well served by the sources cited by journalists—that is, do the media really tap the "experts" in their field? Second, is there a bias toward eminent social scientists, who are asked to comment on everything and whose work is more likely to be covered than equally important work by younger, less eminent scientists? The first part of the chapter looks at the characteristics of social scientists mentioned in the media we monitored—their fields, institutional affiliations, and gender, for example—and at whether or not the distribution of these characteristics has changed over time. We also examine the functions which quotes from social scientists serve in news accounts. In the second part of the chapter we look at individual scientists who were cited in the media, asking in particular whether those who achieve a high degree of media visibility are also those who are recognized as authorities by other social scientists.

Characteristics of Social Scientists in the News

At least one social scientist was mentioned in 49 percent of the social science stories falling into our sample in 1970 and in 43 percent of those

---

[1] One clue comes from our interviews with social scientists. Asked whether the person selected by the journalist to comment on the social scientist's study was an appropriate source, 69 percent (of thirteen) said "yes," 15 percent qualified their answer, and 15 percent said, in effect, "not very."

selected in 1982—a total of 831 social scientists in 1970 and 2,470 in 1982, when the sampling period was approximately twice as long. Most of them—about 80 percent—were quoted, either directly or indirectly, in the media account. In each case we noted whether the social scientists were the subject of the news story, or whether they were mentioned in an ancillary role only. The latter were, of course, much more frequent; social scientists as subjects appeared in only 7 percent of the media items in 1970 and in 8 percent of those in 1982. In what follows, we look separately at these two categories of mention, restricting the analysis to the first-mentioned social scientist in both categories. In both 1970 and 1982 two thirds of the news stories mentioned only one social scientist.

Social Scientists as Subjects of News Items

In both 1970 and 1982 most social scientists who were the subjects of a media story, and whose institutional affiliation was known, were university-based (Table 10.1). (For approximately 14 percent we could not discover the institutional affiliation either from the media account or from standard reference works.) In both years more social scientist subjects came from economics than from any other single social science field— 41.5 percent in 1970 and 50 percent in 1982. In 1982 psychiatrists, sociologists, and psychologists were next in frequency, with approximately 15, 10, and 9 percent of mentions.

Although the largest single category of 1982 stories in which a social scientist was the subject consisted of interviews with economists[2] about some aspect of Reagan's economic policies, several other contexts for featuring social scientists could be distinguished. One category consisted of noteworthy government officials: for example, Janet L. Norwood, who was appointed to the Bureau of Labor Statistics, and Robert C. Wood, former HUD Secretary and Boston school superintendent, who was named to a task force on the role of the federal government in the schools. Another category consisted of social scientists featured on newspaper human relations or lifestyle pages—for example, a psychologist who had written books about father-son relationships, a social anthropologist who had written about childbirth, a psychologist who treats both people and pets, a debate among psychoanalysts and psychiatrists about patient-analyst relationships. A third category was polling; two of the stories falling into

---

[2]The question of why some economists rather than others is difficult to answer. Some appear to have been selected because of their current or past positions as governmental advisers, others because of positions they had taken in their writings. Some, however (Henry Kaufman, Alan Sinai) appear to be sought out regardless of the particular economic issue or their own position with respect to it.

TABLE 10.1

Institutional Affiliation of First-Named Social Scientist
as Subject of Story, by Year

Institutional Affiliation	1970	1982S[a]	1982T[a]
University	63.2%	50.0%	39.0%
Government	15.8	20.8	14.6
Other Research Organization	5.3	8.3	9.8
Other	15.8	20.8	36.6
(N)	(38)	(24)	(41)
	$\chi^2 = 1.08$; $df = 3$; n.s.		

[a] 1982S denotes the subsample of 1982 coverage which matches the 1970 sample period; 1982T denotes the total 1982 sample.

our sample featured a speech by, and an interview with, pollsters Caddell and Wirthlin, respectively. The remaining social scientists appear to have been selected because their work was linked to other topics in the news or because they themselves were controversial: a political scientist who had designed a war game; a psychiatrist interviewed about forensic psychiatry in the courtroom; a sociologist-priest who had written a best seller.

In both 1970 and 1982 most social scientists who were the subject of a news story (more than 90 percent in almost every social science field) were men.[3]

Social Scientists in an Ancillary Role

Like other news stories with ancillary social science content, the number of stories with ancillary references to social scientists increased from 1970 to 1982, as did the number of social scientists per story.

In 1970 the majority of these social scientists whose institutional affiliation was known belonged to a university, but by 1982 this proportion had dropped to one third, largely at the expense of social scientists from "other" and "other research" organizations (Table 10.2). In turn, this change is related to the increasing number of references to economists,

---

[3] Men also predominated among social scientists who died during the period of our study and whose obituaries appear in our files: 80 percent or more, depending on the field.

In only two or three of the 1982 obituaries which we examined in detail were the achievements of the person *as a social scientist* the reason for the obituary, most notably in the case of Helen Lynd. The remaining obituaries appear to have been included because of the person's position—in government or as a university president, for example—rather than because of his or her status as a social scientist.

TABLE 10.2

Institutional Affiliation of First-Named Social Scientist
in Ancillary Role, by Year

Institutional Affiliation	1970	1982S[a]	1982T[a]
University	54.5%	33.6%	34.8%
Government	21.0	14.0	13.8
Other Research Organization	3.9	17.1	18.5
Other	20.6	35.3	32.9
(N)	(310)	(408)	(709)
	$\chi^2 = 44.82; df = 3; p < .01$		

[a] 1982S denotes the subsample of 1982 coverage which matches the 1970 sample period; 1982T denotes the total 1982 sample.

who are often based in business corporations and economic research firms. In 1970 just one third of the social scientists mentioned were economists; by 1982 that proportion had increased to almost three fifths.

Like those social scientists who were the subject of a news item, most social scientists in an ancillary role were men: 86 percent in 1970 and 87 percent in 1982.

The Functions of Quotes from Social Scientists

In order to understand how journalists used what social scientists said, we developed a typology of the "functions" which quotes served in the story, somewhat akin to the typology developed by Garfield (1977–78) for scholarly citations (see chapter 11, p. 244). We discovered that most such quotes could be classified without too much difficulty into one of three mutually exclusive main categories.

(1) The quote is an integral part of the story, with the reporter telling part of it through social scientist sources instead of in his or her own words. Such quotes might be used to provide information either about an event or about research. For example, in a story headed "New Insights into Alcoholism" (*Time,* April 25, 1983, p. 88), Jane O'Reilly defines alcoholism by quoting Harvard psychiatrist George Vaillant: " 'You are an alcoholic,' says Vaillant, 'when you're not always in control of when you begin drinking and when you stop drinking.' " It is a technique used

especially often in economics reporting, which has become mainly a process of soliciting opinions from economists—" 'he said, she said' journalism," as *New York Times* economics columnist Leonard Silk puts it. "The profusion of published comments from such experts as Otto Eckstein, Lester Thurow, Michael Evans, and Henry Kaufman," writes Chris Welles, former director of the Bagehot Fellowship program in economics and business journalism at Columbia University, "might lead one to conclude that they spend their entire day on the phone with the press."

(2)   The quote is not an integral part of the story, in the sense that a crucial part of the narrative would be missing if the quote were omitted, but is used by the reporter to provide evaluation, interpretation, or, sometimes, balance. For example, in the same story just quoted, O'Reilly states, "Other professionals agree with Vaillant's glum assessment. 'We don't do anything adequately,' admits Dr. Robert Milman, director of the Alcohol and Drug Abuse Service at Payne Whitney Psychiatric Clinic in New York City." Again, an evaluative or interpretive quote may be used to illuminate either an event in the real world or a piece of research—either the social scientist's own or that of another. This appeared to be the most frequent usage of comments from social scientist sources.

Since he is often in no position to evaluate it himself, the journalist must, in Garfield's words, "avoid responsibility" and "lean heavily on the work of others," for both validation and criticism of the social science he is reporting. An interesting question—unanswerable in the present context—is whether the journalistic norm that dictates balance in the search for commentary may at times give criticism more weight than it deserves, in terms of either the actual distribution or the quality of divergent opinions among social scientists themselves.

(3)   The quote is used in order to enhance the journalist's credibility or to provide legitimacy or authority to his account or, one sometimes suspects, to repay a social scientist source. This usage was judged to be relatively infrequent in our sample of stories.

Regardless of the function served by a particular comment from a social scientist, the intent of introducing such a quote at all, we reasoned, is to impart some sort of expertise to the story. Accordingly, we coded—not for each individual comment, but for all those attributed to any one social scientist used in an ancillary role in a news story—whether or not in the opinion of the coder it reflected the social scientist's knowledge, or whether the quote was used only to provide an *appearance* of expertise. Although the judgment required appears to be a fairly subjective one, reliability of coding—as measured by the coefficient kappa—was an acceptable .749 for this item.

A quote may have been coded as *not* reflecting expert knowledge for any of a variety of reasons. The quote may be arguably incorrect, as in the case of an Argentine sociologist quoted as having said, "The formation of great nations is incompatible with the climatic conditions of the tropics." Or it may reflect expertise, but not necessarily in the area of the social scientist's training, as in the case of an economist commenting on President Reagan's chances of getting his "new federalism" through Congress. But the overwhelming majority of quotes in both years was coded as reflecting expert knowledge.

Visibility and Eminence

In order to investigate the relationship between two status hierarchies—visibility in the mass media and eminence in social science—we drew a sample of all social scientists mentioned in either 1970 or 1982.[4] The distribution of media citations for this (weighted) sample, by year, is shown in Table 10.3, separately for economists and others. As can be seen from the table, most social scientists—though a somewhat smaller proportion among economists than others in both years—received one media mention only. At the other extreme—those receiving six or more media citations during the brief monitoring period—there are only a handful of social scientists, but there is a suggestion that economists are more likely

---

[4]For both 1970 and 1982 we listed the first three social scientists mentioned in every news story classified as a social science story. The social scientist might be the subject of the story, an ancillary source referred to in the story, the author of a column or book review, or the author of a book being reviewed. (Ordinarily, of course, only one of these contexts applied, and fewer than three social scientists were cited in any one context.) In 3,105 (unweighted) stories, we counted 1,152 *different* social scientists—306 in 799 stories in 1970, and 846 in 2,306 stories in 1982. (The number of different scientists mentioned is not equivalent to the number of mentions of a social scientist, since some were mentioned more than once.) Of these, 844 had been mentioned once and 308 more than once.

Subsequent analyses are based on a sample consisting of all social scientists mentioned more than once, plus a subsample of those mentioned only once, weighted to reflect these differential probabilities of selection. The sample consists of 623 names and the analysis is based on a weighted N of 366, which reflects the design effect introduced by sampling different strata with different probabilities.

Two other points should be made in connection with this analysis of scientist sources. First, we compared four weeks in 1970 with seven weeks in 1982, instead of selecting a matching 1982 subsample, as we had done for other analyses. For this reason, we make no direct comparisons between the two years but only compare standardized rates (for example, the percentage of scientists receiving one mention only), which are less likely to be affected by the different lengths of the sampling periods.

Second, for this analysis we did not weight stories that were included only because they mentioned an economist in an ancillary context. Had we done so, the number of economists would have been slightly larger and so, in all likelihood, would have been the number of those mentioned more than once. The number of other social scientists, however, would not have been affected.

TABLE 10.3

Percentage of Economists and Other Social Scientists Receiving One
Media Mention or More During 1970 and 1982 Monitoring Periods

Number of Media Citations	1970			1982		
	Economists	Other Social Scientists	Total[a]	Economists	Other Social Scientists	Total[a]
1	78.3%	84.1%	84.5%	76.4%	89.0%	84.0%
2	13.0	8.7	9.3	10.4	6.5	7.4
3	0.0	2.9	2.1	3.8	1.3	2.2
4	4.3	2.9	3.1	3.8	0.6	1.9
5	0.0	0.0	0.0	1.9	0.6	1.1
6 or More	4.3	1.4	2.1	3.8	1.9	3.0
(N)	(23)	(69)	(97)	(106)	(154)	(269)

[a] Includes social scientists whose field was not known; hence, total column is greater than sum of other two columns.

than other social scientists to receive more than six media citations. Thus, Table 10.3 indicates that while most news about social scientists is not news about media stars, multiple references to the same person do occur. A little later, we consider just what these multiple citations mean.

As our measure of eminence, we used the number of citations to the social scientist's work in the year preceding the media citations—that is, 1969 and 1981, respectively—as documented in the *Social Science Citation Index* (SSCI).[5] Then, in order to probe how media attention to social scientists conforms with or deviates from recognition by their peers, we compared the number of their science citations with the frequency of their media citations.

A great deal of research has been done on the properties of the Science Citation Index (and its companion Social Science Citation Index) and on the correlates of eminence as measured by citations, in particular by the Coles (for example, Cole and Cole 1973, esp. pp. 21–36). This research also indicates that the number of citations in any one year correlates highly with lifetime citations. Accordingly, we felt that this measure afforded us a generally accepted indicator of a social scientist's standing among his peers.

Obviously, journalists do not consult the science citation records in deciding which scientists to contact and to cite in their news stories. But the comparison of media citations and science citations gives us an oppor-

[5] We thank Karen Ginsberg for carrying out this task.

tunity to explore the extent to which news values and science values converge to shape news about social scientists.

Most social scientists, of course, are not cited in the news media at all. We began by asking whether those who are cited there are more likely also to be cited by their peers than the average social scientist included in the Social Science Citation Index. For 1970 and 1982 media-cited scientists combined, the average number of social science citations is 27.23 (with 6 outliers, with a total of more than 4,500 citations, excluded). The average number of citations received by social scientists with *any* scholarly citations (that is, those included in SSCI) was 3.34 in 1969 and 4.28 in 1981.[6] Thus, those social scientists cited in the media are clearly much more eminent among their peers than the total group included in the Social Science Citation Index. And the latter group, of course, excludes an unknown number of social scientists who have no scholarly citations at all.

In an effort to elaborate this finding, we correlated the two sets of mentions—media citations, on the one hand, and social science citations, on the other. Because both variables were highly skewed, with most scientists receiving only one citation or very few citations, we employed two data transformations. One collapsed all media citations of six or more and also collapsed the continuous SSCI variable into a fifteen-category variable (see Table 10.5, note b); the other used the logarithms of both variables. Pearson correlation coefficients run on both transformations yielded essentially the same results; only those based on the categorical version are shown in Table 10.4, by year and social science field.

For 1970 the correlation between media citations and scholarly citations, among those with any media citations, was about .24—lower for economists and higher for other social scientists. In 1982 the correlation for economists was about what it had been in 1970, but it was considerably lower than it had been for other social scientists. (All coefficients, except those for 1970 economists, where N = 21, are significantly different from zero.) Although still statistically significant, the 1982 correlation of .13 between media attention and scientific recognition means that the latter accounted for only about 1 percent of the variance in the former.

Number of citations in the scientific literature is a social fact with which we would expect few journalists to be acquainted, but the prestige of the university department with which a social scientist is associated is an alternative, more visible symbol of authority. For those social scientists affiliated with universities we therefore examined the correlation between

---

[6]Of the 623 scientists in our sample of media-cited scientists 226 received no scholarly citations at all. The average number of such citations, for those with any, was 43.46 (again excluding the outliers).

TABLE 10.4

Pearson Correlations Between Media Citations and Social Science
Citations,[a] by Year and Social Science Field

| | Social Science Field | |
Year	Economics	Other Social Science
1970	0.17 ($p = .237$) (N = 21)	0.29 ($p < .01$) (N = 68)
1982	0.18 ($p < .05$) (N = 105)	0.13 ($p = .05$) (N = 152)

[a] Social scientists whose only media mention consisted of an obituary have been omitted from this table.

TABLE 10.5

Means and Standard Deviations for Table 10.4

| | Social Science Field | |
	Economics	Other Social Science
1970		
Media Citations[a]		
Mean	1.46	1.30
Standard deviation	1.11	.87
	(N = 21)	(N = 68)
Social Science Citations[b]		
Mean	4.45	5.84
Standard deviation	5.21	5.13
	(N = 21)	(N = 68)
1982		
Media Citations[a]		
Mean	1.60	1.25
Standard deviation	1.30	.88
	(N = 105)	(N = 152)
Social Science Citations[b]		
Mean	3.30	5.32
Standard deviation	4.76	5.25
	(N = 105)	(N = 152)

[a] Categories are as follows: 1, 2, 3, 4, 5, 6 or more.
[b] Categories are as follows: 0 = 0, 1 = 1, 2 = 2, 3 = 3, 4 = 4, 5 = 5, 6–10 = 6, 11–15 = 7, 16–20 = 8, 21–30 = 9, 31–40 = 10, 41–50 = 11, 51–70 = 12, 71–120 = 13, 121–200 = 14, 201–999 = 15.

the number of media citations and the prestige rating of the university department, when this was available from Jones, Lindzey, and Coggeshall (1982). Such ratings were available for only 79 scientists in the total weighted sample and for only 54 of the 1982 sample (both totals exclude social scientists whose only media citations involved obituaries). To our surprise, these correlations were lower than those between social science citations and media citations: .29 for economists and .09 for other social scientists in 1970; and .12 for economists and .05 for others in 1982. None of these coefficients is significantly different from zero. Thus, if anything, the social scientist's personal prestige is a better predictor of media mentions than institutional prestige.

In an effort to clarify these findings further, we decided to look more closely at those social scientists with many media citations. We identified all those who had been cited five or more times in our 1982 sample of stories, and three or more times in 1970,[7] and looked at the stories in which they appeared. As a result, it became apparent that media mentions can be accumulated in a variety of ways.

We identified four principal routes through which media mentions of an individual scientist can multiply: (1) a delimited news event reported in several of the media (properly speaking, this is not a case of multiple mention at all); (2) a continuing story reported serially in one or several of the media; (3) a recurrent standard news event for which the individual scientist is official director or spokesperson and which was reported recurrently in one or several of the media during the period of study; (4) and implication of the social scientist in several news events, each reported in one or several of our media.

In the first category fall reports of just-released study findings or a newly published book, with several media simultaneously picking up the same story and citing the same researcher or author. Ongoing reports of trials, with repeated quotations from psychiatrists or other social scientist witnesses, fall into the second category. Monthly news reports based on routinely released economic data from government (for example, Bureau of Labor Statistics, Department of Commerce) or private agencies (for example, the Conference Board), with commentary from economist spokespersons in those agencies, fall into the third category, as do recurring poll stories with interpretations from the pollsters directing those surveys. The scientists in these three categories are cited as a direct result of their social location in relation to a particular news event. It is the news event which dictates who will be cited, and not the characteristics of the

---

[7] Four percent of the weighted sample met this criterion in 1982 and 7 percent in 1970.

scientist. Scientific expertise, as recognized by social science citation counts, plays no part in the selection.

In the fourth category we begin to see the phenomenon wherein known, quotable experts are turned to again and again by the media; the scientists are often (especially in business stories) not integral to the story, but reporters solicit their views to enliven their copy. In the main, scientists in this category are media staples rather than media stars, but at the far end this category does encompass the "visible (social) scientists," as well as allusions to such classic figures as Marx and Freud.

If one is interested primarily in the relation between scientific prestige and media attention, it can be argued that a different sampling plan—one that samples social scientists directly—would be more appropriate than the one we used, which identified social scientists as a result of their appearance in a specified set of media during a specified period of time. Dunwoody and Scott (1982), for example, found that two thirds of their Ohio sample of 111 scientists and social scientists at two universities had had some contact with journalists, and in a subsequent study Dunwoody and Ryan (1984) found that a similar proportion of a national sample of scientists and social scientists had had contact with one or more journalists during the preceding year. Both Boltanski and Maldidier (1970; cited in Dunwoody and Ryan 1984) and Dunwoody and Scott (1982) found that higher-ranking scientists were more likely to be involved in media interactions than lower-ranking scientists. However, Dunwoody and Scott found *no* relation between productivity, as measured by number of publications in refereed journals, and number of contacts with journalists.

In our own study more than a hundred social scientists, identified because they or their research had appeared in our media sample in 1982, were interviewed (see chapter 2). About one third were selected for interview because they had been quoted in the news story and two thirds because a study they had been working on had been cited in the media.[8]

Of those who had been interviewed by us because they were *quoted* in the media, every single social scientist claimed to have been mentioned in news stories before, and 56.5 percent claimed to have appeared more than twenty times. Among those social scientists whose studies had been reported on, media citation was less frequent but still substantial; 15.2 percent claimed to have been interviewed by a journalist more than twenty times before.

There is a suggestion, therefore, that social scientist media stars do exist and that they are to be found more often among the "quoted" scien-

---

[8]In keeping with our findings concerning the reporting of social science research (see chapter 11), a large proportion of the latter were not identified in the news story at all, but had to be tracked down by calls to the sponsoring institution.

tists than among those whose research is being reported on. This surmise is borne out by two subsequent questions, which asked about the subject of the earlier media citations and where they had appeared.

Among the quoted scientists, 85 percent had been interviewed about the same subject as the current story or about a related subject in the same general area. But 13.6 percent had been interviewed before on a different subject or about a mixture of same and different subjects. (The rest gave assorted other replies.) Almost all previous media appearances of this group—97.4 percent—had been in the national news media.

Among social scientists interviewed because of their research, the pertinent figures are somewhat smaller. Only 9.8 percent had been interviewed about a different subject or about a mixture of subjects (whereas 90.4 percent had been interviewed before about the identical subject or one in the same general area), and only 75 percent had appeared before in any media.

We therefore repeated our science citation analysis for those social scientists whom we had interviewed, using as the number of media citations their self-reported prior contacts with journalists. The number of social science citations (for the year preceding our study) for the 127 interviewed social scientists ranged from 0 (for 25 of them) to 542 (for Paul Samuelson). Excluding the outlier (Samuelson) results in a modest but statistically significant correlation of .22, somewhat higher than the similar correlation between number of social science citations and number of media citations during a specified five-month period. Thus, it appears that a small but significant relationship does exist between eminence in the scholarly and in the public realms, between recognition by journalists and recognition by one's peers.

However, we cannot use this finding as evidence that the *most* appropriate social science experts are being sought out by journalists. In a study of the role of editors in social science reporting, Endreny (1985) identified four main categories of editor/producer responses to the question of how they evaluated the credibility and competence of their scientist-sources: (1) formal position, (2) reputation, (3) nature of research findings, and (4) reporter. The largest number of responses fell into the first two categories, and the smallest number fell into the third.

For news editors reputation assumes a kind of independent primacy. They do not examine the extent to which that reputation derives from specific theoretical or research expertise that permits the scientist to speak with authority on the particular matter at hand. Certainly journalists seek out scientists who are renowned in an appropriate subject area, but they often define subject area broadly and loosely. Indeed, more editors mention formal position and institutional affiliation than reputation, and these are even more indirect than reputation as indicators of a source's substantive expertise. Endreny's research suggests that journalists are much more likely to seek out those in certified positions, rather than those with certified knowledge—hoping for, but not necessarily probing, a fit between the two. Position and/or affiliation is taken as a sign of reputation; reputation, in turn, is taken as a sign of knowledge.

An event that forcefully illustrates this point occurred during the revision of this chapter.

The author of a book on career women's personal lives was extensively quoted in the *Washington Post* (April 11, 1986) as a research psychologist with expert knowledge about young people's sexual attitudes. Before the *Post* story, he had appeared on the CBS morning news (March 5, 1986) and on "Good Morning America" (March 19, 1986); he was also interviewed on National Public Radio (April 7, 1986) and on the Phil Donahue show (April 1, 1986). The "findings" from his books were disseminated widely. *U.S. News & World Report,* getting ready to do a story on sexually transmitted diseases, and aware of the *Post* story, asked its New York office to interview the researcher. At the end of the interview, the journalist asked some routine background questions.

The answers caused some uneasiness; the journalist checked a few other facts and became even more suspicious; within a few weeks, he was investigating the research on which two trade nonfiction books—well reviewed, though not in the scholarly press—had been based.

The investigation—in which the journalist enlisted the aid of several social scientists—raised questions about both the man's credentials and the research itself. In the meantime, however, in the space of a few weeks, the "researcher" had become an "expert" whose views had gained wide currency in several prestigious national media, and whose claims to authority were being legitimated by the reporters who sought him out. He was an expert in the *Washington Post* because he had been an expert for CBS, and an expert for NPR because he had been featured in other media. But no social scientists appear to have been asked to evaluate the research on which these claims were originally based.[9]

Summary

In this chapter we have tried to answer several interrelated questions. Who are the social scientists who are cited in the national media? What are their

---

[9] The story, by Dan Collins, finally broke in the *Daily News* of July 19, 1987, p. 4, under the headline, "'Whiz' Stories Hard to Figure; Big Writer's Numbers Don't Add Up," and was subsequently picked up by print media around the country.

characteristics? Are there social scientists to whom journalists go often, and for comment on a variety of topics? Whether or not such media stars exist, to what extent is frequency of citation in the media correlated with eminence among the social scientist's peers, as measured by the number of citations in the Social Science Citation Index?

One or more social scientists were mentioned in almost half the stories falling into our sample in both 1970 and 1982. Most of these were university-based, and in both years more of them came from economics than from any other single social science field. The relatively few social scientists who were featured as the subject of a news story were most likely to be either economists interviewed about some aspect of Reagan's economic policies or psychologists and psychiatrists featured on the "lifestyle" pages of newspapers. Among social scientists mentioned in an ancillary context, the period from 1970 to 1982 saw a marked increase in economists and in social scientists based outside the university. Overwhelmingly, the social scientists cited in the media, whether as subjects or in an ancillary context, were men.

We distinguished various uses to which quotations from social scientists might be put by reporters. One usage, especially common in economics reporting, is to tell the news story primarily through comments from social scientist sources—a style described by Leonard Silk as "he said–she said" journalism. A second usage—the most common in our experience—was to ask the social scientist to provide evaluation or interpretation, either of the event underlying the news story or of the research being featured. Finally, and relatively infrequently, quotations from social scientist sources appear to have been used to enhance the journalist's credibility or lend authority to his account. Overwhelmingly, we judged that the comments reflected expert knowledge on the part of the social scientists being quoted, though we did not attempt to evaluate their accuracy.

As a result of our analysis of citation frequency, we concluded that there are some "media stars" among social scientists. Even during the short period in which we monitored the media, some social scientists received more than six media mentions. However, the pattern can be seen even more clearly from our interviews with social scientists whose work was being reported in the media or whose comments were being solicited. Almost all of these social scientists had been interviewed by journalists before, and more than half of those who were asked to comment for the media on events or on the research of others claimed to have been interviewed more than twenty times before.

Furthermore, those scientists cited frequently in the media tend also to be cited frequently by their social science peers, though again this tendency is somewhat more pronounced in the group we interviewed than in the random sample of social scientists cited in the press. Among the latter, multiple mentions (during the limited period in which we monitored the media) can occur for many reasons, some having nothing to do with the scientist's eminence in his or her social science field—for example, occupying a position which features in a recurrent news story. (Of course, such reasons may also account for multiple media contacts in the interviewed sample.)

Nevertheless, as a group, social scientists cited in the media are clearly more eminent than the average social scientist. The average number of social science citations, for all those cited at all, was 3.34 in 1969 and 4.28 in 1981. Among social scientists cited in the media in 1970 or 1982, the number was 27.23—more than six times as large.

The cited social scientists are, on average, more eminent. Are they therefore better qualified to comment on the event or research on which their views are sought? That is a question more difficult to answer. In all likelihood, most of the time the social scientist asked to comment is not the *most* appropriate source, though he or she may well be *appropriate*. (Journal and grant proposal referees may be no more appropriate than media sources, but we have no evidence on this point—only the experience of one of us as the editor of a scholarly journal.) Sometimes, as we have seen, the person may be totally inappropriate. Reporters tend to seek out sources used by other media. Once expertise seems to have been validated by such a media appearance, other reporters may be lulled into a false sense of security, and continue to use the source without independent checks. The system could be improved if reporters used social scientists as sources of referral to other, more appropriate social scientists, and if the latter were willing to function in that role. Understandably, time constraints may not always permit the series of phone calls such a referral system would require.

The Quality of Social Science Reporting

11

ROBERT DARNTON'S RICHLY EVOCATIVE "WRITING NEWS AND TELLING STORIES" (1975) develops the thesis that while "the context of work shapes the content of news . . . stories also take form under the influence of inherited techniques of storytelling," and he concludes, "as [the reporter] passes through his formative phases he familiarizes himself with news, both as a commodity that is manufactured in the newsroom and as a way of seeing the world that somehow reached the *New York Times* from Mother Goose." Other analysts of why news is the way it is have sought to explain it by reference to a cultural action perspective which points out that a news story is, in part, a *story*—that is, a distinct and rather stereotyped form, governed by literary conventions as well as organizational necessities.

Both of these perspectives argue that news is, in part, a contrivance which, regardless of substance, must be given the form of "a good story," a "good read." The essential aim of science, on the other hand, is the production of new knowledge and its subsequent sharing with the community of one's peers. The details which the scientist regards as essential to this communication may well be deemed inessential by the journalist and perhaps detrimental to his obligation to write a good story. In other chapters we consider in some detail the mechanisms by which social science research finds its way into the mass media. Here, we emphasize again that media needs and interests, rather than those of the social sciences, are crucial and that a process of negotiation between reporters and their scientist sources, and of competition and negotiation between editors and reporters, or among editors, producers, and other news executives, is involved (see especially Epstein 1973; Gans 1979; Sigal 1973; Tuchman 1978b; Winsten 1985).

To the extent that reporters of science are becoming better educated and more specialized, they may show greater appreciation for the values of science; but, as Dunwoody and Stocking (1985) and Winsten (1985) have aptly noted, the science reporter's abstract respect for such values may be sorely tested under the real-world pressures of the workplace. Moreover, anecdotes (Darnton 1975) as well as systematic study (Johnson 1963) indicate that even when the science reporter's values display considerable congruence with the values of the domain of science that is his beat, editors reveal primary concern with the storytelling, readability dimensions of the news account. And though the importance of the topic may also count, it is importance in a general sense, and not importance within some social science discipline. Writing in the February 1979 *Newsletter* of the National Association of Science Writers (vol. 27, no. 1, p. 2), Joel Shurkin, then a science writer for the *Philadelphia Inquirer,* made a similar point about science reporting when he wrote about the recently concluded AAAS meeting: "It is undeniably true that the stories filed were second-rate in terms of cosmic importance. . . . [M]ost of our customers and editors have forgotten that we have done the climate story every year for the last four years. They still like it."

In the remainder of this chapter we do three things. First, we examine some characteristics of the social science research reported in the media. Such research was the most frequent reason for selecting stories focused on social science in 1982 and the second most frequent reason (after mention of social scientists) for selecting stories that mentioned social science in an ancillary context. Second, we contrast in some detail the presentation of social science research in the media with the norms for its presentation in scholarly journals. The implicit question addressed by the comparison is this: If the public had access only, or primarily, to the mass media for information about current social science research, what would they be likely to see? How does social science in the media differ from social science as it is meant to be portrayed in the scholarly literature, a portrait presumably closer to the "real thing"? Finally, we look at some instances of the reporting of social science that we consider problematic, and ask what the consequences of such reporting are likely to be for the public and for social science as an institution.

The focus of the chapter is obviously selective. Earlier in this book (see chapter 3), we noted that the social scientists we interviewed tended to be satisfied with the coverage of their research. Such reactions have generally been found by other studies as well (Tankard and Ryan 1974; Ryan 1979; Dunwoody and Scott 1982). Here, instead, we emphasize some of what we consider to be problematic in the coverage of social science research, instead of highlighting its positive aspects or attempting a more balanced view. Like other social science research, ours offers a partial perspective, and should be understood as such.

This chapter, like chapter 9, examines changes over time. The changes here have to do with the quality of social science reporting— "quality" being defined for the most part narrowly, as adherence to the norms for communicating scientific research. The perspective on quality is that of social science, not journalism or literary style. Where a significant change since 1970 has taken place, that fact is noted in the text; the absence of a reference indicates the absence of change.

The most obvious aspects of quality neglected by this definition are the accuracy of the reporting and the significance and competence of the research singled out for attention by the press. So far as accuracy is concerned, we rely on the judgments of the interviewed social scientists, who tended to be satisfied with this aspect of coverage as with others. But we would like to know whether the research reported on for the general public is important, and whether or not it is well done, yielding valid and reliable information. We would also like to know whether it is better or worse, more or less important, than research that goes unreported.

Such judgments are notoriously difficult to make, especially in the short run. Accordingly, we say very little about the quality of the social science reported in the media, recognizing this as a shortcoming in our own work. We do, however, examine in some detail how the editors/producers in the media we studied go about assessing the quality of the social science studies they report on.

Some Characteristics of Social Science Research Reported in the Media

In 1982[1] we coded 853 stories containing a reference to social science studies; 421 of these studies were coded as surveys or polls of opinions or

---

[1] The analyses in this chapter are based on the first study coded for each story; 79.4 percent of stories mentioned only one study. Some research reported in the media was undoubtedly overlooked. For example, we probably missed many economic forecasting studies done by business forecasting firms, when the media presented only the forecasts without reference to a study. On the other hand, some studies were picked up as social science studies only because they had been done by a social scientist, even if they did not qualify on the basis of subject matter.

attitudes.[2] In 193, or a little less than half of the 421, the survey was the focus of the news story; in the rest the reference to a survey was subsidiary to the story's main theme. One half of all the focus studies reported by newspapers in 1982 were coded as opinion or attitude surveys; this was true of 36 percent of those reported on television and of 17 percent of those reported by newsmagazines. The proportions of surveys were even higher for studies mentioned in an ancillary role: 49 percent of such studies in newspapers, 59 percent of those in newsmagazines, and 71 percent of those on television. None of these proportions represents a substantial change from 1970: In 1970 as in 1982 opinion surveys were the dominant type of study referred to by the national news media in their coverage of social science research.[3]

Although these were surveys of opinion, and ordinarily of opinion about public rather than private life, they were not, with rare exceptions, election polls. We deliberately selected 1982 and 1970 as our comparison years in order to avoid inflating the count of social science studies with the flood of public opinion polls that characterize reporting in an election year.

Some flavor of the range of opinion research reported in the media in 1982 can be gleaned from the following partial list of specific survey topics: presidential preferences, presidential approval, political parties; drugs and drug usage; confidence in and evaluations of the economy; social security; welfare and poverty; drinking age, punishment for drunk drivers; unemployment; satisfaction with life and work; threat of nuclear war, nuclear weapons, arms control and the proposed nuclear freeze; the Middle East; the Soviet Union; civil liberties; terrorism; the environmental movement, environmental protection and regulation; residential segregation and bias. If a topic is newsworthy, the news media are likely, at some time, to report survey results pertaining to it. Much more rarely do they report surveys that have no clear link with currently salient events—for example, surveys of satisfaction with life and work.

In what follows we describe some characteristics of the social science research reported in the national media in 1982. Because opinion and

---

[2]By opinion and attitude surveys we meant to include what is generally regarded as public opinion research; more specialized studies—for example, evaluation studies and studies of audience shares—were excluded from this category even if they used survey methods, provided we recognized them as such. Although some studies may have been incorrectly classified as a result, the error was probably not large. The most likely errors we made were to classify as opinion or attitude surveys some studies that dealt primarily or exclusively with reports of behavior rather than attitudes, but we cannot estimate the magnitude of this confusion.

[3]"Other studies" consisted of epidemiological research, evaluation research, experiments, secondary analysis, economic studies, audience or market research, and "other."

attitude surveys constituted such a large proportion of all research, their characteristics are discussed separately from those of "other studies," which comprise a heterogeneous category. Where they occurred, changes since 1970 are also mentioned.

Compared with other types of social science research in the news, the following is true of the surveys reported in the media in 1982:

1. *Surveys were much less likely to originate at a university and much more likely to originate with the media.* The proportion of media surveys has increased substantially since 1970, at the expense of those originating with government and other research organizations. About 20 percent of surveys reported in newspapers in 1982, and an even higher percentage of those reported in newsmagazines or on television, were surveys initiated and, in most cases, carried out by the media (Table 11.1).[4] Thus, increasingly, the surveys the public is exposed to in the media are carried out to serve the imperatives of news organizations.

Other social science studies reported in the media are much more likely to reflect the interests of academic social scientists. About 20 percent of such studies, compared with 9 percent of surveys, originated at a university in 1982, and only about 2 percent of such studies were reported as originating with the media. In newspapers, but not newsmagazines, the role of the university declined between 1970 and 1982 and that of government increased.

2. *Surveys were more likely to identify the sponsor of the research.* This statement is to some extent misleading: Television and newsmagazines were much more likely to identify sponsors of surveys than of other studies, but this was because they were often talking about their *own* surveys. Newspapers were no more likely to identify survey sponsors than those of other studies—in both cases, only about one quarter of the time (see Tables 11.3 and 11.4).[5]

3. *Surveys were more likely to be about some aspect of government and politics.* The modal public opinion story in 1982 was about government or politics (Table 11.2). By way of contrast, about 50 percent of all studies other than opinion surveys which were reported in the media were rather evenly divided between economics and health, with another 20 percent or so falling into the area we labeled social integration and social control, which consists, on the one hand, of stories devoted to

---

[4] In contrast, Paletz et al. (1980) found that 40 percent of the television polls in 1973, 1975, and 1977 were done by Gallup or Harris; and Gallup, Harris, and other established polling organizations conducted 65 percent of those reported in the *Times!*

[5] Paletz et al. (1980) report that sponsors were identified in 25 percent of the *Times* poll stories, and in even fewer of those on television.

TABLE 11.1

Institutional Origin, by Type of Study, Type of Media, and Whether Story Is Focus or Ancillary (1982)

Institutional Origin	Focus			Ancillary		
	News-papers	News-magazines	TV	News-papers	News-magazines	TV
Surveys						
University	11.7%	—	—	7.0%	6.3%	—
Government	17.7	—	37.5%	8.6	6.3	—
Other Research Organization	21.5	50.0%	—	28.5	25.0	30.0%
Media-Initiated Poll, Self-Executed	20.4	25.0	62.5	15.6	21.9	40.0
Media-Initiated Poll, Other-Executed	1.1	25.0	—	2.7	6.3	—
Other	19.3	—	—	16.1	12.5	—
Don't Know	8.3	—	—	21.5	21.9	30.0
(N)	(181)	(4)	(8)	(186)	(32)	(10)
Other Studies						
University	21.7	20.0	21.4	22.9	13.6	—
Government	26.7	25.0	35.7	21.9	9.1	25.0
Other Research Organization	14.4	20.0	7.1	16.7	31.8	—
Media-Initiated Study, Self-Executed	1.7	5.0	—	2.1	—	—
Media-Initiated Study, Other-Executed	—	—	—	—	—	—
Other	21.7	10.0	28.6	14.6	13.6	50.0
Don't Know	13.9	20.0	7.1	21.9	31.8	25.0
(N)	(180)	(20)	(14)	(192)	(22)	(4)

TABLE 11.2

Topic, by Type of Study, Type of Media, and Whether Story Is Focus or Ancillary (1982)

Topic	Focus			Ancillary		
	News-papers	News-magazines	TV	News-papers	News-magazines	TV
Surveys						
U.S. Economy	27.6%	—	—	17.2%	21.9%	10.0%
Foreign Economies	3.3	—	—	0.5	—	—
U.S. Government and Politics	40.3	75.0%	62.5%	36.6	37.5	—
Foreign Governments and International Relations	2.2	—	—	22.0	21.9	70.0
Social Integration and Social Control	13.3	—	12.5	11.3	9.4	10.0
Health	3.9	25.0	25.0	7.0	—	10.0
Demographics	1.7	—	—	1.1	3.1	—
Relationships and Lifestyles	7.7	—	—	3.8	6.3	—
Miscellaneous	—	—	—	0.5	—	—
(N)	(181)	(4)	(8)	(186)	(32)	(10)
Other Studies						
U.S. Economy	26.7	20.0	7.1	28.6	50.0	50.0
Foreign Economies	5.6	—	—	5.2	4.5	—
U.S. Government and Politics	5.6	—	—	2.6	—	—
Foreign Governments and International Relations	1.7	—	—	4.2	—	—
Social Integration and Social Control	19.4	25.0	28.6	27.1	13.6	50.0
Health	28.9	30.0	57.1	20.8	4.5	—
Demographics	6.7	15.0	—	5.2	13.6	—
Relationships and Lifestyles	5.0	10.0	7.1	6.3	13.6	—
Miscellaneous	0.6	—	—	—	—	—
(N)	(180)	(20)	(14)	(192)	(22)	(4)

TABLE 11.3

Details of Reporting, by Type of Media and Whether Story Is Focus or Ancillary (1982)

| | Surveys | | | | | |
| | Focus | | | Ancillary | | |
Detail	News-papers	News-magazines	TV	News-papers	News-magazines	TV
Sponsor named:						
Yes	32.6%	75.0%	75.0%	21.0%	25.0%	40.0%
Mention of Data:						
Yes	93.4	100.0	100.0	88.2	96.9	90.0
Interpretation or Analysis:						
Yes	30.9	25.0	0.0	18.3	15.6	10.0
Information about Subgroups:						
Yes	39.8	100.0	62.5	16.7	12.5	10.0
Information about Change over Time:						
Yes	40.9	50.0	50.0	19.9	25.0	10.0
Reference to a Published Source:						
Yes	29.8	25.0	0.0	12.4	12.5	10.0
No	64.6	25.0	37.5	83.3	84.4	80.0
Does not apply; media poll	5.5	50.0	62.5	4.3	3.1	10.0
Number of Investigators:						
Unknown	83.4	75.0	100.0	91.4	93.8	100.0
Information about Method:						
Yes, detail	46.4	50.0	50.0	11.8	9.4	0.0
Yes, name only	48.1	50.0	37.5	82.3	84.4	100.0
No	5.5	0.0	12.5	5.9	6.3	0.0
Mention of Discrepant Findings:						
Yes	3.9	25.0	12.5	2.2	3.1	0.0
Mention of Supporting Findings:						
Yes	11.6	0.0	0.0	6.5	18.8	0.0
(N)	(181)	(4)	(8)	(186)	(32)	(10)

TABLE 11.4

Details of Reporting, by Type of Media and Whether Story Is Focus or Ancillary (1982)

| | Other Studies | | | | | |
| Detail | Focus | | | Ancillary | | |
	News-papers	News-magazines	TV	News-papers	News-magazines	TV
Sponsor Named:						
Yes	30.0%	25.0%	7.1%	20.9%	9.1%	25.0%
Mention of Data:						
Yes	87.8	60.0	50.0	75.5	68.2	25.0
Interpretation or Analysis:						
Yes	46.1	50.0	42.9	20.8	13.6	25.0
Information about Subgroups:						
Yes	45.6	40.0	42.9	22.4	18.2	—
Information about Change over Time:						
Yes	40.0	20.0	14.3	15.6	27.3	—
Reference to a Published Source:						
Yes	50.6	60.0	57.1	26.0	22.7	25.0
No	48.3	35.0	42.9	74.0	77.3	75.0
Does not apply; media poll	1.1	5.0	—	—	—	—
Number of Investigators:						
Unknown	60.6	50.0	71.4	73.4	68.2	100.0
Information about Method:						
Yes, detail	15.0	10.0	—	4.2	—	25.0
Yes, name only	21.7	25.0	21.4	17.2	18.2	—
No	63.3	65.0	78.6	78.6	81.8	75.0
Mention of Discrepant Findings:						
Yes	13.3	0.0	21.4	6.8	0.0	0.0
Mention of Supporting Findings:						
Yes	18.9	10.0	0.0	9.4	31.8	0.0
(N)	(180)	(20)	(14)	(192)	(22)	(4)

religion, education, and other activities relevant to socialization, and, on the other, to stories about law enforcement and crime. Compared with 1970 proportionately more focus opinion surveys as well as other studies were devoted to economic issues in 1982, with a corresponding decline in surveys related to demographic trends and in "other studies" related to political issues. There was little change with respect to other topics.

4. *Surveys were much more likely to include some mention of data.* More than 90 percent of all opinion surveys reported in the media included some mention of data in 1982—a proportion substantially higher than that for other types of studies (see Tables 11.3 and 11.4), especially those reported in newsmagazines and on television. Newspapers, but not newsmagazines, were more likely to include data in social science stories in 1982 than in 1970.

5. *Surveys were much less likely to include any interpretation or analysis of the findings.* Only 31 percent of focus newspaper stories about surveys, 25 percent of those in newsmagazines, and none of those reported on television included such interpretation or analysis in 1982 compared with 46 percent of focus stories about studies other than surveys, regardless of where they appeared. (There was much less difference between ancillary reports of surveys and ancillary reports of other studies: 17.5 percent of the former and 20 percent of the latter included some interpretation or analysis of the findings in 1982.) Newspapers, but not newsmagazines, were more likely to include some interpretation or analysis in focus social science stories in 1982 than in 1970.

Most opinion surveys reported in the media, like most other kinds of studies reported there, originated in the United States in both 1970 and 1982. The single exception was the category of ancillary surveys reported on TV—71 percent of these, consisting for the most part of foreign public opinion polls, originated *outside* the United States in 1982.

What conclusions can we draw from the portrait presented so far? Most obvious but perhaps most important is the fact that the agenda for social science reported in the media is set by the *public* agenda, not by that of social science—a finding that emerges clearly from the interview study as well. This hardly comes as news to the people in charge of public relations for science and social science organizations. In deciding what symposia to schedule for press conferences, for example, AAAS staff take into account what subjects are currently in the news (see chapter 5).

The link to topics in the news is especially evident in the case of survey research. As a result, the findings reported tend to be relatively ephemeral. As we have seen, the media have become more frequent originators of surveys. And to the extent that they report on their own research, media needs—for speedy as well as topically relevant results—

increasingly shape the content as well as the methodology of the surveys reported.

Furthermore, while social scientists have learned to pay less attention to simple marginals in favor of much more complex analyses (Schuman and Kalton 1985), so far marginals remain the staple of media reporting. And although in 1982 between 36 and 45 percent of all stories about social science studies, including surveys, provided information about subgroups or about changes over time, this information was generally presented without analysis or interpretation.

Social Science Research for Two Audiences

As we have seen, social science research reported in the media tends to be a distinctive subset of all research—namely, that related to currently newsworthy topics. But the most significant difference between social science research as written for the general public and for other social scientists has to do with the way research findings are presented. In newspapers, newsmagazines, and on television, findings resulting from one piece of research, done in a particular time and place, with a distinct sample and a specified research instrument, are often presented as if they were universal truths, holding for all people everywhere.

"Single parents report that their children are becoming more independent and responsible as a result of the increased roles they have to play in the management of the household," writes Elin McCoy in the *New York Times* of May 6, 1982. Only later do we learn that this sweeping conclusion is based on studies of twenty families in Massachusetts and sixty in California.

In what follows we identify several media practices that contribute to this image of social science and contrast them with the norms governing the reporting of social science research in scholarly journals.

1. *Reference to a published source.* When an article in a scholarly journal presents findings from prior research, the source of those findings is expected to be clearly indicated, either in a footnote or in a list of references. (That the finding may not always be accurately reported, even in scholarly journals, is another matter; see Garfield 1977–78. But at least, the reader can go back to the original source to verify the accuracy of the report.)

In media reports of research, on the other hand, a published source for research results is indicated less than half the time (see Tables 11.3 and 11.4), even when the research is the focus of the story, and less than a quarter of the time when the reference to research occurs in an ancillary context.[6]

Media reports of surveys cited a published source less than 30 percent of the time in focus newspaper stories and a little more than 10 percent of the time in ancillary stories in all media. Reports of studies other than surveys were somewhat more punctilious in citing a published source. Between 50 and 60 percent of all focus stories about studies other than surveys referred to a published source in 1982, and about 25 percent of all ancillary stories did so, as well. Newsmagazines were more likely to cite a published source in 1982 than in 1970; there was no significant change for newspapers.

We are not the first to have noted the relative absence of references to a published source in the popular media. Garfield (1977–78:217–18), for example, writes:

> Outside of the formal journal literature, of course, articles without references abound. Most newspapers and magazines—even those that purport to cover scientific and technical news—are almost completely void of references. This omission not only throws doubt on the reporter's authority and credibility, but can also be extremely frustrating to those readers with a real interest in the subject. Their curiosity is aroused but cannot be satiated. It seems like links to the primary literature sometimes are deliberately eliminated to add to the mystique of the reporter's sources. Some newspapers and magazines—notably the New York Times and Science News—usually supply at least one reference in text for major articles. It usually consists of a statement such as "in the latest issue of the New England Journal of Medicine." But this amounts to little more than a token effort. . . .
>
> What newspaper and magazine editors—as well as many scientists and journal editors—don't realize is that citations are a form of communication. . . . [I]n order to communicate effectively and intelligently about scientific and technical subjects, explicit citations are essential.

Dunwoody (1984) has made a related point. Noting that the media constitute primary sources of scientific and technical information for non-scientists, she urges the media to provide the kind of information—namely, references—that will enable the reader to pick up "where the news stories leave off."

---

[6]More than half (52 percent) of these citations are to a project report, 22 percent to a journal article, and 11 percent to a book.

We also asked whether or not it was possible to locate the published source of the research from the information given in the news story. There were no significant differences in this respect among media, between focus and ancillary stories, or over time: In about 80 percent of the cases where a source was mentioned the information given in the news story was adequate for locating it, though it took precisely the form Garfield described.

2. *Identification of the researcher.* Citation of scientists responsible for prior relevant research is, of course, prescribed behavior when writing for a scholarly journal (for example, Garfield 1977–78; Kaplan 1965). Merton (1973[1957]) locates the roots of this requirement in the norm of science which enjoins originality on its practitioners. "On every side the scientist is reminded that it is his role to advance knowledge and his happiest fulfillment of that role, to advance knowledge greatly. . . . Recognition for originality becomes socially validated testimony that one has successfully lived up to the most exacting requirements of one's role as a scientist" (p. 293). And to recognize priority, as by citing another's work, is to acknowledge the scientist's right in his or her intellectual property. To this function of citation we might add another: the linking of findings with a person. Merton points out that "scientific knowledge is impersonal in the sense that its claim to truth must be assessed entirely apart from its source." But "house effects" in survey research have been documented (Turner and Krauss 1978; Smith 1982), and person effects may also exist: Some*one* else might have found some*thing* else.

However, identification of the scientists who carried out the research being reported is far from accepted practice in the media (see Borman 1978, where this was the most frequently cited omission). In about three quarters of the studies coded it was impossible to tell how many people had been responsible for the research, though one or more social scientists may have been named in connection with the project; if anything, this tendency had increased since 1970. "Black Americans are four times more likely than whites to suffer severe kidney disease. . . , a study from Alabama said today," announced a UPI dispatch in the *Washington Post* of May 27, 1982, identifying the investigators only as "researchers at the University of Alabama at Birmingham and the Birmingham Veterans Administration Medical Center."

The author is likely to be unknown to a mass audience; the institution under whose auspices the study was done is much more likely to be familiar. Hence, media references to institutional auspices are used to both locate and legitimate the research being reported. For example, consider this item, reprinted in its entirety from page 1 of the *Wall Street Journal,* March 23, 1982: "Unemployed workers' children are more likely to get ill and for longer periods than the offspring of those still working, a University of North Carolina study suggests. The youngsters seem most vulnerable at the time of a layoff. Afterwards, the risk drops."

However, failure to identify the researcher is much more common in the reporting of opinion and attitude surveys than in the reporting of other kinds of social science research (see Tables 11.3 and 11.4). In 1982 the percentage of stories in which the number of social scientists carrying out a study was *unknown* was 87.5 percent for newspaper reports of surveys, 92 percent for newsmagazine reports, and 100 percent for reports of surveys on television. By way of contrast, the figures for other kinds of social science research were considerably lower though still not trivial: 67 percent for newspaper stories, 59.5 percent for newsmagazine stories, and 78 percent for television stories.

In part, of course, the tendency not to identify an individual as the researcher responsible for an opinion or attitude survey reflects the reality of how many surveys are conceived and carried out. Such surveys are large, collective enterprises; they are done by "Gallup," "Harris," or "Yankelovich," rather than by individual researchers employed by these organizations (Paletz et al. [1980] refer to these organizations as "conductors"). Although one individual may ultimately be responsible for a particular survey, the collective attribution fairly reflects the complexity of its creation.

Other surveys, however, are done by survey organizations for individual investigators; they reflect an individual, not a bureaucratic, sensibility. After all, the *Midtown Manhattan Study* (Srole et al. 1962), *The Academic Mind* (Lazarsfeld and Thielens 1958), and *The Civic Culture* (Almond and Verba 1963) were all studies done by means of survey research. In such cases an individual researcher can be identified in the media account. Unfortunately, we were unable to distinguish those surveys which were appropriately identified only by an organization's name from those in which an individual could have been identified as well. But it does seem to be true that, especially in the case of surveys, the news media substitute organizational for individual identification. Whereas most stories left the identity of the researcher in doubt, fewer than 10 percent of focus stories failed to identify the type of institution in which a survey originated.

3. *Discussion of the methods used.* Very few social science stories in the media discuss the methods used in any detail—only 18 percent of the studies we analyzed in 1982—and only 30 (of 853) contained any evaluation of those methods. Newspapers were more likely to provide such details than either of the other media, but even among those newspaper stories we have classified as "focus" social science, only 31 percent gave any detail about methods in 1982. For studies mentioned in an ancillary

role only, the figure drops below 8 percent. Very little change occurred between 1970 and 1982 in this respect.

Surveys of public opinion were considerably *more* likely than other types of social science studies to provide some information about the method used (see Tables 11.3 and 11.4). Just about half of the focus surveys in our sample provided some detail about methods; all but a handful of the rest at least named the method used, though an unknown number of these "surveys" were, in fact, instances of what is referred to later in this chapter as pseudo research. Among surveys reported in an ancillary context, only about 10 percent provided any methodological detail, but, again, virtually all the rest named the method used.[7]

By contrast, only 14 percent of stories about studies other than surveys provided any details about the methods used, even when the study was the focus of the news story. An additional 22 percent named the method (for example, experiment, secondary analysis), whereas the rest provided no information whatever. Among studies other than surveys which were reported in an ancillary context, almost 80 percent provided no methodological information at all.

Media reports of surveys thus provide more information than other studies about the method used. But how adequate is the information provided?

Paletz et al. (1980:505) found that 67 percent of their *New York Times* articles reported sample size and 43 percent gave the dates of the survey; the figures for the NBC and CBS evening news programs were lower. But aside from sample size and survey dates, information was minimal. In 95 percent of the TV stories and 70 percent of those in the *Times,* for example, none of the polling questions was quoted in its entirety, though words or phrases from some of the questions were often quoted. Sampling error was given in only 7 percent of the stories in the *Times.*

We did not record the precise details provided by media stories about surveys. But we did stipulate that mention of *any two* of the following would qualify a survey as providing "details" about methods: sample size, interviewing dates, wording of any question, and response rate. Thus, we know that at least 50 percent of the focus surveys and 90 percent of the ancillary surveys failed to provide even two bits of information about how the survey was done. Interestingly enough, surveys reported on television

---

[7]To some extent, this finding may be an artifact. Studies labeled as surveys were easily classified as opinion or attitude surveys; some surveys not so labeled may have been misclassified into another category, where they would have contributed to the "no information about methods" category. However, we believe that such instances of misclassification, if they occurred, were rare.

were no less likely to provide details, according to this crude classification system, than those reported in newspapers.

As we have seen, the lack of attention to methodological detail does not necessarily result from lack of reporter knowledge or interest. In over half the contacts between the journalists and social scientists we interviewed, research methods were reportedly discussed. But these discussions are not reflected in the news story as it appears, and methodological soundness rarely seems to be an explicit journalistic criterion for selecting a study.[8] We consider some reasons for this in the section on pseudo science later in this chapter.

As it turns out, the media differ less in this respect from scholarly journals than might have been supposed. Noting that concern about the reporting of survey procedures has focused mainly on the mass media, Presser (1985) asks whether such details are ordinarily included in scholarly articles drawing on survey data. He points out that there is evidence that this has not always been the case, quoting a 1967 National Research Council Committee's report and an analysis of sociology articles by Alwin and Stephens (1979). His own analysis of articles based on survey data which have appeared in the leading journals of four social science disciplines indicates that the problem persists and that there has been little improvement with the passage of time. Even restricting the analysis to those articles reporting data the authors themselves had collected or that had been collected by other individuals (that is, excluding data collected by large survey organizations, for which extensive documentation is ordinarily available but is not necessarily presented in detail in any given article) reveals that *fewer than half* of them reported on each of the following: sampling method, response rate, the wording of any question, year of the survey, or interviewer characteristics. "These reporting levels," writes Presser, "are not markedly better than those of the much criticized mass media, despite the considerably greater space available in journals."

4. *Placing research findings in context.* In an article for a scholarly journal it is considered customary to put one's findings in context: to provide an indication of whether they are in accord with, or depart from, the findings of related research (Wilson 1952; Kaplan 1965). We have, unfortunately, no data on how regularly this norm is followed. We do

---

[8]Most of the literature that comes closest to touching on this does so only inferentially, by way of case studies, or indirectly (accuracy studies, dimensions of judgment). Furthermore, most of these references pertain to natural science, and even the more explicit ones address *inclusion* of methodological information in an article rather than evaluation of it.

Some anecdotal references are Weigel and Pappas (1981, esp. p. 485) and Tankard and Showalter (1977). Indirect references come from Tichenor et al. (1970), Johnson (1963), Tankard and Ryan (1974), and Ryan (1979). One indirect reference leading to a contrary conclusion is Rich (1981), who suggests high attention to technique.

know, however, that the proportion of media stories providing such a context is very small. In 1982 between 0 and 15 percent of focus stories about social science research (depending on the medium) provided supporting information and between 0 and 24 percent of ancillary stories did so; the figures were about the same for discrepant information.

Focus stories in newspapers significantly more often provided supporting information in 1982 than they had in 1970, and this was also true of ancillary stories in newsmagazines. There were no changes over time in the tendency to provide discrepant information.

When we examined these practices separately for opinion surveys and other social science studies, we found that they were somewhat more common in the reporting of other studies than in the reporting of surveys (see Tables 11.3 and 11.4). In newspaper reports, for example, 13 percent of focus stories about studies other than surveys included some discussion of discrepant findings compared with 4 percent of stories about surveys; and 19 percent of stories about other studies included supporting findings compared with 12 percent of stories about surveys. The same trends, though on a reduced scale, were apparent for surveys and other studies reported in an ancillary context.

Although these figures do not reflect the extent to which other social scientists are quoted as agreeing or disagreeing with the findings reported, they do accurately reflect the extent to which quotations from such expert sources refer explicitly to corroborating or discrepant research results. That is, they reflect the presence or absence of information, but not that of opinion.

The evidence above comes from an analysis of social science studies reported in a variety of media over a period of several months. However, the same conclusion was reached when we examined coverage of a specific event—the 1982 AAAS meetings. Overwhelmingly, reporters covering those meetings concentrated on the day's news, ignoring conflicting or supporting views from other sources even when these were directly relevant to the session being reported on.

Among the relatively few news stories that provided a context for research findings during our monitoring period, and did so superbly, was one by Harold M. Schmeck, Jr., in the *New York Times* of June 18, 1982, on a four-year study demonstrating a reduced risk of ovarian cancer among women who used birth control pills. "'Our figures agree with those of earlier studies that estimated a reduction of about 40 percent to 50 percent in the risk of ovarian cancer among oral contraceptive users,'" Schmeck quotes the researchers as saying, "However, a study done by epidemiologists of the New York State Health Department and reported earlier this week at a meeting in Cincinnati did not show a protective effect of oral contraceptives against ovarian cancer, according to Dr. Solley, who said he had no explanation for the discrepancy."

So far, we have identified several media practices that, alone or, especially, in combination, contribute to what we have referred to as the image of a disembodied, timelessly true social science. The number of news stories lacking one or more of the qualifications that would help to put the research in context is not trivial. Just about 50 percent of the newspaper and newsmagazine stories focused on a social science study in 1982 were lacking all, or all but one, of the elements we coded as helping to put social science in perspective. In 1970 this was true of 55 percent of the newspaper and newsmagazine stories. Note that these are minimal requirements: for example, the method used must only be named, not discussed in any detail. As we have seen, very few changes had taken place with respect to any of these practices since 1970.

However, it would be misleading to imply that all media reports of social science research contribute to this impression. On the contrary, there are reports of research that, in the space of a few column inches, clearly convey complex and subtle information.[9]

For example, an AP story run in the *New York Times* of October 12, 1980, under the headline "Study Shows London Executions May Have Affected Murder Rate," manages in 10¾ column inches to tell readers the conclusion of the study (highly publicized executions of convicted killers in London from 1858 to 1921 deterred other murders, but for no longer than two weeks), the name and institutional affiliation of the researcher (David Phillips, of the University of California at San Diego), a published source (the current issue of the *American Journal of Sociology*), the possible limitations of the findings ("Dr. David Phillips . . . cautioned that the London findings might not necessarily apply to contemporary America"), the methods used (tracing statistics through local coroners' offices to develop weekly murder rates, rather than the monthly or yearly figures used by other researchers, and restricting the study to executions that received extensive newspaper coverage), apparently discrepant research done by others, and an explanation for the discrepancy, as well as an interpretation of the significance of the findings ("Dr. Phillips noted that political conservatives believed a deterrent effect existed while liberals generally did not. He called both sides' views accurate").

We estimate that no more than 7 percent of the studies in 1982 focus stories included all five of the elements mentioned above. A disproportionate number of these, however, are what might be called "core" social

---

[9]In a study of magazine science writing, Borman (1978) found that omission of relevant information was often related to brevity, but that "a few short articles . . . demonstrated that accuracy and brevity could be combined."

science stories, that is, dealing with concerns central to social science as a discipline, rather than evaluations of social programs, polls of public opinion, and the like.[10]

In 1982 we identified 105 *New York Times* stories that were classified as featuring a social science study. Of these, at most eleven could be construed as "core." Two dealt with the consequences of divorce for children, one with children's fears, one with delinquency, one with the relation between television and crime, one with suicide, one with differences in educational achievement between blacks and whites, one with student concerns about the future, two with alternative definitions of poverty and some implications of these differences, and one with flirting as social interaction. (No two of these stories, incidentally, were written by the same reporter, and only two appeared in the Science Times.)

When we compared these eleven stories with all focus social science studies reported in our sample of newspapers in 1982, we found very sizable differences so far as the inclusion of key elements was concerned. For the most part these differences were in the direction of much greater specificity for the "core" social science stories, which were also considerably longer than the average 1982 *New York Times* focus social science story. For example, the number of investigators was much more likely to be indicated in such stories (82 versus 28 percent) and at least one of them was almost always named; published sources were much more likely to be referred to (73 versus 42 percent); an interpretation of the findings was much more often offered (73 versus 39 percent); and discrepant as well as supporting findings from other research were more likely to be included (27 versus 9 percent and 46 versus 15 percent, respectively). These studies were also much more likely to be done under university auspices than the general run of studies (64 versus 17 percent). Only with respect to methods was there little difference: in 27 percent of core studies, compared with 31 percent of all studies, the method was described in some detail, and the number of stories in which no information about methods was provided at all was actually greater for the "core" studies than for the average story about social science research (55 versus 34 percent). All of these findings are in line with the differences between attitude surveys and other studies already described; at most, two of the "core" studies could be described as attitude surveys.

---

[10]We are grateful to Robert K. Merton and Harriet Zuckerman for suggesting this line of analysis. The selection of core studies was done independently, by Eleanor Singer and Phyllis Endreny, without regard to how they were reported. The *New York Times* was selected because we assumed, on the basis of impressions formed during the study, that social science reporting would be most comprehensive there.

Social Research in an Ancillary Role

So far, we have been concerned almost exclusively with social science research reported in what we have called focus stories—that is, those in which the social science study is at the center of attention. In this section we look, very briefly, at social science research in an ancillary role—research brought in by the reporter in the context of a news story focused on a related topic. The most obvious, but by no means the only, example is the mention of a poll result in a story focused on some candidate's political campaign.

Such mentions of social science research perform a variety of functions in a news story. Garfield (1977–78:216–17) has cited a number of reasons for reference citations in a scholarly work: ". . . to help trace the development of the present contribution, provide background reading, criticize or dispute previous work, authenticate data and identify methodology." He goes on to say:

> *Citations are also used as a social device for validating priority claims. . . . Citations may represent an author's attempt to enhance his own reputation by associating his work with greater works, or to avoid responsibility by leaning heavily on the work of others. Citations can also be intended to curry favor with influential colleagues or referees, to honor a mentor or friend, or to convey the impression of exhaustive knowledge.[11]*

With the exception of establishing priority, all of these citation functions, suitably adapted from one institutional sphere to another, can be identified in social science reporting in the mass media, though we did not attempt to quantify the frequency with which they occurred. Reporters cite research to convey additional (background) information, to support conclusions they have reached or reported, to support challenges to those conclusions, to enhance credibility or claims to validity, and to acknowledge or pay debts to sources.

As we have noted in chapter 9, it is the ancillary use of social science which has increased dramatically in most media since 1970, and this is true of social science research cited in an ancillary context, as well. But with rare exceptions reporting of elements needed to put such research in context has *not* increased. Ancillary references to social science are even

---

[11] Cole (1975:207ff.) identifies ten major functions of citations to Merton's "Social Structure and Anomie," the following four of which account for 71 percent of the citations: as part of the relevant literature, as legitimations of the citer's own work, in interpreting the results of the citer's study, and in formulating a research problem.

less likely than focus stories to cite a published source, to provide information about methods, or to supply supporting or discrepant information, and there has been little change in this respect between 1970 and 1982. Thus, the image of a social science "without caveats" is even more prevalent in those stories we have labeled ancillary than in those that are focused on social science.

Some Problems in the Reporting of Social Science Research

So far, we have discussed the quality of social science reporting in terms of its adherence to, or departure from, norms for scientific communication in general. In this section we briefly discuss two other problematic aspects of social science coverage in the press: the reporting of "pseudo" science and the reporting of conflict and contradiction between research findings or between social scientists.

Social Science and Pseudo Science

An unknown proportion of "studies" reported in the popular media consists of activities that most social scientists would agree do not constitute "research" at all: "surveys" of a magazine's readers, based on responses by self-selected subscribers; phone-ins to 900 (or 800) numbers sponsored by television networks; or interviews with convenience samples. Even though the number of "respondents" to such "surveys" can sometimes reach several hundred thousand, the method of phone-ins or write-ins violates all the rules of sampling on which legitimate surveys are based.

Although the two procedures may, by accident, yield the same or similar results, there is no way of knowing when that will happen. For example, after the speech in which a U.S. ambassador all but urged the removal of the UN from the United States, ABC conducted both a 900 number phone-in and a regularly conducted telephone survey. Whereas 67 percent in the phone-in (with more than 100,000 telephone calls) said the UN should leave the United States, 66 percent in the poll said the UN should stay. And when the "Don't know's" were eliminated, the 66 percent who said stay rose to 72 percent. "We had the spectacle of two ABC polls asking essentially the same question on the same day showing more than diametrically opposed results." Roper (1983) pointed out:

> What is the effect of this on the public? . . . And what sociologically useful purpose does ABC perform by putting two so-called polls on

the air which show diametrically opposite results? Journalists cor-
rectly make the point that the public has a right to know. By provid-
ing diametrically opposite polling results, is ABC fulfilling the right
to know? Or is ABC merely convincing people that you can prove
anything you want with a poll?

In our count of social science content in the media, such instances of pseudo social science as instant polls, write-ins, and the like have been included. We have done this both because we assume that is how they are perceived by the general public and because it is often impossible, given the paucity of information about methods, to know when a news story reports the results of a legitimate survey and when it represents the write-up of a piece of pseudo research.

Call-ins often make dramatic copy. But what is interesting to readers and viewers is not necessarily either good science or important science. Weiss notes (chapter 5) that Dunwoody (1982), who analyzed press cover-age of the 1977 and 1979 AAAS meetings, suggests two reasons why science reporters, who claim to dislike social research and find it difficult to evaluate, nevertheless gave it good play. One is that many social science stories have obvious reader relevance. The second is that social science is easier to understand than other scientific research and, as Weiss puts it, reporters with a deadline may be drawn to papers they can easily under-stand. But neither of these criteria is necessarily designed to assure the quality or scientific importance of the social science reported.

In her study Endreny (1985) investigated how thirty-three editors in our national media judged the validity of social science research. Most typically, she found, they proceed with a loose, common-sense notion of validity which asks, "Do the results make sense?"

Editors tended to translate the concept of validity so that it fit under the rubric of objectivity. Asked, "How do you go about assessing the valid-ity of a study such as this?" they frequently answered with explicit or implicit regard to balance and fairness or outside experts. These strategies may be, as Gans discusses more generally, "efficient" surrogates for the scientific assessment of validity, but they certainly are not equivalent.

While editors often address validity by looking for "balanced" (and) "expert" presentations that satisfy the profession's insistent regard for "objectivity," there is another significant and highly consequential way in which they address validity—that is, by deliberate dismissal of its urgency in specific instances. If they believe a study's findings to "make sense," to be "uncontroversial" or not central to the news story, the scientific validity of the research becomes either unproblematic or irrelevant. The obvious consequence is that even the imperfect surrogate probes into validity may be arbitrarily suspended so long as the editor "feels comfortable" about the study, or, conversely, accepts its imperfections because it is newsworthy.

The responses to the "validity" question were coded into five categories. The categories, constructed to capture both journalistic and scientific approaches to validity, were defined as (1) intrinsic research elements—such as sample, questions, other methodological or conceptual issues; (2) extrinsic research elements—such as researcher affiliations, background, reputation; (3) expert corroborations—such as "interview other experts," "fit in with what other experts are saying"; (4) circumstantial—such as "make sense," "ask common-sense questions," "go to the people"; and (5) trust the reporter.

Approximately one fifth of the editors interviewed referred to intrinsic research elements, but most of those references were either elliptical or perfunctory. Editors not only do not regard themselves as personally responsible for examining a study's methodology, but, furthermore, do not look for any detailed assessment of the methodology from others.

Sometimes, in fact, the news process enfeebles concern for method, even when allusion to methodology is present. One editor commented how, in reporting the results of a sex "survey" based on magazine readers, "we did try to point out the limits and biases." Those limits and biases were so obvious that almost no social scientist would take the "study" seriously, and certainly no scholarly journal would publish the results. Yet, for the newspaper editor, the source and subject of the study had such compelling newsworthiness as not only to outweigh all methodological deficiencies but, further, to earn front-page placement on an inner section. And the brief allusion to "limits and biases" in the copy is all but lost in the long article.

Of all thirty-three editors, only one expressed personal responsibility and competence for the direct methodological assessment of social science studies. He is one of the few editors with an advanced degree in a core social science, and the only one with a continuing—though not exclusive—responsibility for social science news. How, in general, would this editor assess the validity of a study? "I would read it," said he, matter-of-factly, adding, "Since I'm familiar with experimental design and statistics, I would look at the sample design, size and statistical applications of the study."

Slightly over one third of the editors identified extrinsic qualities of the researcher(s) as grounds for validation of the research. Research conducted by a qualified researcher or research institute is, ipso facto, quality research and, thereby, apparently valid. Typical of responses falling into this category were these: "In general, we look for institutional ties . . ."; "I had quite a few questions for the reporter (especially because this was to be on page one) on what the outfit was, who funded the study, what is the firm's track record"; and "I rely mainly on the reputation of the researcher. . . . Credentials are the important consideration."

An alternative route for assessing validity was through direct or indirect consultation with other experts in the field. Although this route may appear to parallel that of peer review, it is often very different. For example, experts may be asked to comment on another identified scientist's research without actually having seen the research. Indeed, to the extent that, in quest of balance, journalists deliberately seek out those known to be in the "opposing camp," this method may exaggerate the importance of discrepant points of view.

A response category far more commonly elicited was "trust in reporters." One editor sought to make a distinction between the editor's ability to make news judgments and his dependence on the reporter for validity judgments. However, in the course of his response, the editor merely reiterated the dominance of the journalistic reconceptualization of validity. The editor began his answer by noting that generally the first question asked of the reporter was, "What is the opposition?"; and later he described the advantage of the reporter as, "He is more used to tracking a field, so he can assess more readily what is new." Thus, the specific questions the editor is likely to ask to check on the quality of a study are, "How is this new?" and "What is the opposition?"

As noted earlier, most reporters "doing" social science stories are not science or social science specialists. Therefore, if the editor's demands for validation are minimal and imprecise, reporters are not likely to be more rigorous and systematic on their own. Basically, what the editors seem to mean when they say they rely on the reporter's judgment is that, at least when the study being reported on is a substantial part of the news story, they rely on the reporter to have determined that this is a "respectable" study—in many ways a far more social than scientific judgment.

While the editors rarely assumed either personal responsibility or competence for the methodological validation of reported research, several expressed no qualms about making a personal determination as to when validity was problematic. Basically, the editor finds the results either "reasonable" enough so as not to raise questions or surprising and controversial enough so as to require closer scrutiny. Thus, a television producer reported that he relied on the opinions of the reporter and field producer. "We'll consult other experts, if it's really controversial, but we don't generally do extensive checks." And another editor explained he had no reason to doubt the particular study and "since no findings were that sensitive, they didn't require as much checking as a more sensitive study." After echoing others in saying that he wasn't overly concerned about assessing the validity of certain studies, because none "really dealt with things that are controversial," a third editor recognized that "there's a tendency to bring news judgment rather than scientific evaluation" to such cases.

Indeed, we know that even when an editor finds a study so controversial as to require further scrutiny, that scrutiny is likely to take the traditional news mode of seeking comments from other experts; that is, to look for balanced opinions rather than intrinsic validity. In addition to those editors who implicitly translated assessment of validity into achievement of balance, several responded explicitly to the question on validity by reference to balance, for example, "We want to make sure we talk to enough people who have different views, so we are balanced and fair." Validity gets at the merits of research and its results; balance gets at the diversity— or, perhaps, the extremes—of opinions. Even when balance intersects with validity, in that the differing viewpoints are based on the experts' careful evaluation of the validity of another's research, it is the simple expression of the oppositional claims, apart from their substantive or methodological grounds, which are likely to be transmitted to the public. As Weigel and Pappas (1981) have written in their study of the reporting on the Coleman "White Flight Thesis": ". . . if criticism did emerge it was unlikely to convey a sense of the methodological and interpretive issues that concerned many of Coleman's colleagues. . . . The reader learned only that other credentialed experts disagreed with Coleman, but remained uninformed about the reasons prompting such disagreement" (p. 485).

"When the Masters All Fall Out . . ."

Most social scientists probably agree that phone-ins do not constitute legitimate social science research, and, at the other end of the scale, there are undoubtedly studies that all, or most, social scientists would agree had been competently done and resulted in valid information. In between lie those studies—probably the most numerous category—which are subject to divergent evaluations by social scientists themselves and which find their way into the popular press either through prior publication in a scholarly journal, through press releases issued at professional meetings or by the researcher's institution, or perhaps through some of the specialized journals devoted to the dissemination of science information (*Psychology Today, Human Behavior, Scientific American,* and the like).

In the reporting of such research, conflict and contradiction appear to be inevitable. This is so for several reasons:

1. Most social science research findings are partial and contingent, but the thrust within journalism is toward less qualification and more

dramatic assertion. Winsten (1985) has described the competition for recognition among reporters and science editors at leading news organizations and has described, as well, the pressure reporters feel to alter stories in order to make them more interesting—to exaggerate the existence of conflict, to overstate consensus, to "come as close as we can within the boundaries of truth to a dramatic, compelling statement. A weak statement will go no place" (Winsten 1985:9). But "dramatic, compelling" assertions are also easier to falsify; and new, apparently contradictory research findings may be more likely to find their way into the press, as well.

2. Sometimes social scientists engage in advocacy research or testify in court as expert witnesses. In those circumstances, to quote Jencks, "[Y]ou are dealing with an adversary process. On virtually every major issue, you are going to have social scientists on both sides."[12]

During the 1982 period when we were monitoring social science coverage in the media, the country was treated to the spectacle of a parade of eminent psychiatrists testifying for both the prosecution and the defense in the widely publicized trial of John Hinckley for the attempted assassination of President Reagan. And on December 11, 1983, the *Times* began a story on the Shoreham nuclear power plant as follows:

> *The Long Island Lighting Company generated a bevy of experts last week—sociologists, pollsters, attorneys—to argue that the utility could safely evacuate people living near its Shoreham nuclear reactor. . . . A sociologist testifying on Lilco's behalf said emergency workers would fulfill their responsibilities in the event of a serious reactor accident. Sociologists consulting for Suffolk maintained, however, that workers would experience "role conflict" and forsake their duties to take care of their own families first.*

3. In addition to these reasons for the appearance of conflict and contradiction in the reporting of social science research, there is the fact that conflict is news. In the *New York Times* of April 30, 1982 (p. A30), Nicholas Wade scathingly commented on a story in the May 1982 issue of *Psychology Today,* in which "'eleven of the best minds in the field' describe what each considers to be 'the most significant work in psychology over the last decade and a half.'" Under the headline, "Smart Apes or Dumb?" Wade rhetorically asks, "Can psychology be taken seriously as a science if even its leading practitioners cannot agree on its recent advances?" Although a more dispassionate reading of the *Psychology Today* article tells a somewhat different story, Wade deliberately chose to emphasize areas of disagreement among social scientists.

---

[12] Quoted in Fred M. Hechinger, *New York Times,* April 7, 1981.

We do not want to be misunderstood as blaming the press for bad reporting when it features disagreements among social scientists. Rather, we see in the combination of several ingredients—the partial knowledge achieved by the social sciences, the push toward "strong" assertions by reporters and editors, the often conflicting perspectives social scientists bring to their work, the apparently common-sense nature of much social science content, and the news value of conflict and dissensus—the potential for increasing public skepticism about the validity and utility of the social sciences:

> *"When the masters all fall out,*
> *What can the student do but doubt?"*

The Special Case of the Polls

In our monitoring of the reporting of social science, "poll" stories, explicitly identified as such, made up 36 percent of the 521 stories which contained any mention of a social science study in 1982 and identified the research method used; surveys or polls of public opinion together made up 82 percent. Turner and Martin (1985) estimated that over 200 million copies of newspapers containing poll results reached the American public in a one-month period (July 1–30) in 1980. According to A. E. Gollin (personal communication), representatives of over 100 newspapers indicated, at a meeting of the Newspaper Research Council in 1982, that they conducted their own polls, and the number is still growing. In presenting the results of these polls the media tend to be meticulous in reporting sample size and sampling error, and not much else. "Survey researchers," wrote political scientist Anthony Broh in a letter to the *New York Times* of October 30, 1980,

> *recognize the influence of . . . methodological differences on poll*
> *results. Along with sampling error, the differences in polling meth-*
> *ods can easily create 7 or 8 percent variations in candidate popu-*
> *larity from one poll to the next. The media, however, interpret poll*
> *results with little sensitivity to the different methods among polling*
> *agencies.*

Thus, the polls—the most ubiquitous example of social science in the media—illustrate dramatically some of the problems with social science reporting identified in the preceding section. In the nature of the case discrepant poll results are often obtained and widely disseminated. But in the way they are reported there is little understanding or explanation of the reasons for these variations.

In 1967 Philip Meyer, then a Nieman Fellow at Harvard and a member of the Washington Bureau of Knight Newspapers, published an article titled "Social Science—A New Beat?" In it he pointed to the transformation of social science from an armchair to an empirical science with "immediate practical application," and he urged journalists to develop the critical sophistication needed to separate the wheat from the chaff. "Social science," he said, "has not yet shaken down to the point where it is easy to identify the fringe operators. There is no equivalent of a local medical society to put the finger on a quack pollster." "Many newspapers," he went on to point out,

> *blandly report the outcomes of polls as if all polls were alike. . . .*
> *Earlier this year, [Harris and Gallup] produced opposite results*
> *on the relative popularity of Richard Nixon and George Romney*
> *among Republican voters. Papers which subscribed to both polls*
> *shrugged their editorial shoulders and ran the conflicting reports*
> *side by side without comment, in the time-honored tradition of "let-*
> *ting the reader decide." If the highly educated staff of a metropoli-*
> *tan newspaper cannot interpret such a discrepancy, how can the*
> *poor reader be expected to do it?*

There are some indications that this situation is beginning to change, albeit slowly. During the entire sampling period of 1982, not a single methodological social science story appeared on the front page of any newspaper, and less than a handful of such stories appeared anywhere in the media. But on August 15, 1984, the *New York Times* ran a front-page story by Robert Reinhold which examined at length the methodological variations that might have accounted for the discrepant presidential poll results then being reported. On the following day the *Wall Street Journal* featured, on page 2, a similar analysis by political scientist Carl Everett Ladd, executive director of the Roper Center for Public Opinion Research. And in reporting the results of the *Times*-CBS polls, the *Times* now regularly includes a boxed statement indicating that sampling error is only one part of total survey error.

Summary

We began this examination of how social research is reported in the media by asking: If the public had access only, or primarily, to the mass media for information about current social research, what would they be likely to see? How does social science in the media differ from social science as portrayed in the scholarly journals, and what are the consequences of this difference likely to be, for the public and for social science as an institution?

In 1981 an article appeared in the *Journal of the Market Research*

Society (23:209–19) titled "Analyzing Data: or Telling Stories?" In a way that is an apt description for the disparate functions of the social scientist and the journalist. The scientist aims to get closer to the truth and to tell others about it. The journalist aims to tell an interesting story, and, it is hoped, a true one. These aims are not antithetical, but they differ in the priorities they assign to the elements involved.

These differences in priorities have consequences both for the kind of social research that gets reported in the mass media and for the way it is reported, as well. *General* criteria of newsworthiness, not those specific to the realm of social science, govern *what* social science is reported in the media. And journalistic tradition, rather than social science norms, governs *how* such research is reported. Those qualifications so dear to the heart of social scientists—that these findings hold for this sample, in this place, and, especially, under these conditions—are almost universally ignored.

But few facts established by social scientists attain universal validity. As a result, mass media audiences not infrequently encounter research findings that appear to contradict earlier research. And because conflict, rather than consensus, is "news," journalists may be tempted to highlight such disagreements among social scientists.

Further, the media do not attempt to distinguish "good" research from "bad"; they are concerned less with the scientific value of the information communicated than with its entertainment value (see also Rokeach 1968; Broh 1980; Wheeler 1980; Noelle-Neumann 1980). The most blatant example is the recent attention given by the media to phone-ins, write-ins, and electronic "polls," but other examples could readily be cited.

Related to the shortcomings just decribed is the media's failure to provide a context of relevant findings for those from a particular study, and the general paucity of analysis and interpretation, especially of survey results. Others (for example, Broh 1980; Crespi 1980; Noelle-Neumann 1980; Paletz et al. 1980) have commented on this shortcoming as well.

Furthermore, because media coverage has long been considered desirable by university press offices and is coming to be considered as a "good" by social science organizations as well, there is a tendency to adapt press releases to media values, and to feature what is obviously interesting instead of making accessible research findings that may be more difficult to communicate to a mass audience. But to the extent that rewards from other social spheres follow attention by journalists, the values of social science may well be distorted by this process. If funding follows newsworthiness and reader interest—and our social scientist and journalist respondents tell us that it sometimes does—the cause of social science is not necessarily well served.

12

Some Implications of the Findings

THE GOOD NEWS FROM THIS STUDY IS THAT MOST SOCIAL SCIENTISTS WERE SATISFIED with the coverage they received in the national media. And, further, social science in the media is easier to read, and often more interesting, than the social science research reported in scholarly journals. The bad news is that this readability is often achieved at a price and that individual satisfaction is no guarantee of collective quality.

In this concluding chapter we talk briefly about four problems in the reporting of social science, as well as about the roots of these problems and some proposed remedies.

1. Social science findings are partial and contingent. But in the mass media, these contingencies are too often ignored.

We identified several media practices that, alone or, especially, in combination would help to put social science research in context: reference to a published source; identification of the researcher; discussion of the methods used; and reporting of supporting or discrepant findings from other research. The number of news stories lacking these qualifiers is not trivial. In 1982 just about half of the newspaper and newsmagazine stories about a social science study were lacking *all,* or all but one, of the elements we coded as helping to put social science in perspective. Less than 10 percent of the stories we analyzed reported discrepant social science findings, and only 14 percent reported supporting findings. About

75 percent left the identity of the researchers in doubt, and 54 percent did not include a reference to a published source for the study. Only 18 percent of the stories included some details about the methods used; and only 30 stories (out of 853 involving a social science study) included some evaluation of those methods. All of these omissions contribute to the image of a disembodied social science whose findings are timelessly true, applying to all people everywhere. And we know that isn't what social science is about.

Research findings depend on where, and especially on how, the research was done. For example, the psychologists Robert Rosenthal and Ralph Rosnow suggested, in *The Volunteer Subject* (1975), that a whole body of social psychological "knowledge" may be limited to the compliant college sophomores who served as subjects in much of the research on which that so-called knowledge is based. And sociologists take for granted that changes in the wording of questions asked on a survey will result in different distributions of responses.

In fairness, it should be said that news stories about studies other than surveys included more of these details than stories about surveys did, and *major* social science stories were especially likely to do so. On the other hand—and counter to our expectations—newspapers and newsmagazines were no more likely to present such details than television, in spite of TV's greater constraints on time. So far as we could tell, there had been virtually no change in these reporting practices between 1970 and 1982.

2. Second, and related to this first point, is the media's handling of social science findings that appear to be at odds with one another. Because of the partial and contingent nature of results, two studies may report conflicting findings or come to different conclusions on the basis of the same findings. How the media deal with such inevitable instances of conflict is important.

We found a tendency to deal with them in one of two ways. Either the findings were presented as discrete, disconnected bits, with no reference to the conflicting research; this was the more common practice. Or else discrepant findings were cited, but with no effort to reconcile the discrepancy. Occasionally, conflict was highlighted; but this reporting of conflict rarely addressed the *reasons* for disagreement among social scientists. Such highlighting of conflict thus serves news values, but not science values.

3. An unknown proportion of so-called studies reported in the news media do not constitute legitimate research at all: for example, so-called surveys of a magazine's readers, based on responses by self-selected subscribers; or phone-ins to telephone numbers sponsored by television networks; or interviews with so-called convenience samples—that is, peo-

ple stopped at locations convenient to the reporter. The presentation of such pseudo research in the media ordinarily does not differ at all from the presentation of bona fide studies. The implication is that all research is of equal value, all results equally plausible (or implausible). To quote Leo Bogart quoting a TV newscaster presenting the results of a phone-in: "These results are probably wrong, but we thought you'd like to have them anyway."

4. The social science research reported in the media is often chosen for its obvious reader relevance or dramatic value. But what is interesting to readers and viewers is not necessarily either good science, in the sense of providing valid or reliable knowledge, or important science, in the sense of making a significant contribution to knowledge about social life. As we saw earlier, during the period of our study the lead articles in the leading social science journals were without exception overlooked by the press. At the same time there were two stories on the same small study of divorced families in Marin County, California, a report on a study of mother love based on dubious findings, and a report on studies of flirting behavior, based on methods that are never described.

What are some reasons for these weaknesses in social science reporting?

Most immediately, the reasons lie in the constraints on reporting for the mass media. Journalists operate under limitations of time and space for the preparation and presentation of stories which social scientists are not subject to. Even more important, journalists cannot take the interest of their audience for granted. But to capture the attention of an audience with other things on its mind takes strong, dramatic assertions—fewer qualifications, rather than more. Thus, the forces playing on reporters and editors as they go about their business run counter to those making for more accurate reporting of social science research.

Sometimes social scientists—or the public relations officers in universities, government agencies, or professional organizations—may themselves contribute to this result. In writing releases for the press, they may adopt a journalistic style in order to capture reporters' attention and, thereby, get a national audience for their work.

Compounding the problems above, and especially important in the reporting of pseudo research or research of poor quality, are two other facts. One, which emerged clearly from our interviews, is that much social science research is not defined as such by reporters or editors. And if a story about, say, attitudes toward nuclear power, or satisfaction with the conditions of work, or differences in sex roles, is not seen as involving social science research, then social science criteria for evaluating and reporting such research will not come into play.

The second fact is reporters' unfamiliarity with research methods.

While social science techniques are becoming increasingly sophisticated, the training of reporters is neither designed nor intended to keep pace with them. As a result, reporters are dependent on the evaluations provided by other social scientists. And these may not always be easy to come by, nor may reporters have time to seek them out. Or they may rely on such indirect indicators of quality as the social scientist's affiliation or reputation.

Underlying these problems in the reporting of social science are the reward structures in both science and journalism. The social scientists interviewed by Weiss clearly felt that they reap a variety of professional rewards as a result of media exposure. And the curious reversal of values by which *Footnotes,* an official American Sociological Association publication, honors in each issue those social scientists who have recently been featured in the mass media seems to bear them out.

The risk, it seems to us, lies in the possibility that social science will be distorted by being evaluated, and rewarded, according to news values rather than those intrinsic to the field. For journalists, too, seek recognition, in the form of visibility and attention to the stories they write. And the chances for such attention, as Winsten and others have pointed out, are better when the fit between the story and news values is good.

Can anything be done to remedy these problems? Here are three modest proposals, only two of which pertain to journalists:

1. Provide training for reporters in the methods of social research—training designed to help them sort the wheat from the chaff (see also Wheeler 1980; Whiloit and Weaver 1980; and MacDonald 1978; all cited in Gollin 1980). Although some social scientists have expressed skepticism about the value of this approach, others have tried to put it into practice. Social scientists from the University of Michigan Survey Research Center, for example, teach regular seminars in survey methods for editors and reporters of the *Detroit Free Press.* And the Russell Sage Foundation, mindful of the highly complex skills needed in the reporting of risks, has supported the work of Victor Cohn, a veteran science reporter for the *Washington Post,* in developing a primer for reporters on the statistical methods used by scientists.

If reporters are trained to ask the hard questions, researchers will increasingly have to answer them. As a result, the reporting of research findings may become more critical and more selective.

Should all reporters learn such skills? Probably, because they are relevant to *all* research, not just that done in the social sciences.

2. Although training for reporters can reduce their dependence on experts, it will not eliminate it. Therefore, reporters should, as a matter of routine, develop a file of social scientists who can serve as resources in

evaluating the quality of different kinds of research and who are willing to do so on fairly short notice, much as referees do for journal editors. Universities and social science professional associations might well help put together such rosters of resource scientists.

Interestingly enough, such a recommendation, if followed, would put social science reporting in a position science reporting has already moved away from. According to Logan (1985),

> *Science reporters today correct misinformation and reveal information the scientific community prefers to conceal . . . [they] also frequently discuss science in terms of its impact on economics, government or public policy and analyze clashes between scientific research and social values. . . . Both approaches were rare 15 years ago, when science reporters concentrated more on translating the research findings of prominent scientists than the social impact of science and scientific controversy.*

Thus, some science reporters are attempting to sort the wheat from the chaff (often to the dismay of scientists), while social science reporting is still in a much earlier, pre-authority phase.

3. Just as journalists must be trained to ask better questions, so social scientists must be trained to provide better, more useful, and more detailed information to the press. Furthermore, some of the discretion has to be taken out of this process. The American Association for Public Opinion Research, for example, *requires* that certain information must be made available when the results of a survey are released. Along with the findings, the social scientist must disclose relevant information about how those findings were obtained: among other things, who sponsored the research, who carried it out, when, on what kind of sample, how the interviews were done, and the exact wording of all questions. The journalist does not have to *use* the information, but the Code of Ethics says he or she has to *get* it.

There is no good reason why the ethics codes of other professional organizations in the social sciences should not be changed to include a similar requirement. That would do a lot to raise the consciousness of both social scientists and journalists about the connection between research methods and research findings.

Unless the reporting of social science can be improved by selecting better research, and by reporting it with greater attention to its validity as well as its limitations, neither the public nor social science as an institution will be well served. Journalism, however, will not necessarily suffer, nor will individual social scientists in the short run. And therein lies the dilemma.

As it stands, *social scientists* tell dramatic stories to *reporters* because that is what *editors* want to deliver to the media *audience*. We believe it is important to develop incentives to change this sequence—to try to wean the public from an appetite for simple, dramatic social science news to an appreciation for a more complex view of social reality. But the changes have to begin within the institutions of social science and of journalism. And they have to be brought about in the way most such changes are: by changing the structure of sanctions and rewards.

Whether it can be done is doubtful. But it is certainly worth a try, because doing so would benefit public discourse, not only about social science, but also about social life.

Methodological Appendix

THE STUDY OF SOCIAL SCIENCE IN THE MEDIA CONSISTED OF TWO MAIN PARTS—content analysis of social science reporting in 1970 and 1982 and interviews with some of the reporters and social scientists whose work was quoted or cited in the media in 1982—in addition to several smaller studies. In this appendix we describe in detail the procedures used in the content analysis.

A Definition of Social Science

Social science is a term used widely and imprecisely. There is no single, concise definition of social science; in particular, there is no uniform designation of the fields of study that constitute the social sciences. Different social science organizations (for example, the Social Science Research Council), enterprises (for example, the Encyclopedia of the Social Sciences), and professionals have different conceptions of social science and different rules of judgment.

Our first research task thus became the construction of a working definition of social science. We began with a general notion that sought to give equal weight to the social and the science components: by social science, we meant to encompass the systematic study of human behavior and society. But what did that mean in specifics?

In order to translate our broad conception of social science into practical guidelines for its identification in the media, we decided on a basic approach that defined social science in terms of a specified number of academic disciplines. Some of these are unequivocal constituents of a broader area known as "social science"—that is, anthropology, criminology, demography, economics, political science/government, polling, psychology, and sociology. But many others did not fall so readily into place—that is, area studies, behavioral medicine, education, epidemiology, history, market research, policy analysis/public administration, psychiatry, and urban planning.

The problems posed by these latter fields all represented, in essence, questions about the extent to which they met social *and scientific* criteria. We wanted educational research, but not stories of PTA meetings; systematic analyses of policy decisions, but not articles about the administration of the City Department of Health and Human Resources; studies of the relationship between lifestyle and heart disease, but not development of cancer; psychiatric theories of mental illness, but not random clinical impressions. History, in particular, was problematic: Did it belong with the humanities or the social sciences? Ultimately, we dealt with history as we did with the other problematic fields, including each to the extent it aimed at generalizable knowledge. For area studies, history, and psychiatry, we required "social science orientation"; for education, policy analysis, public administration, and urban planning, we included only references to research or to academic practitioners as social science items.

Selection Rules

Once we had identified the disciplines that established the boundaries of social science, we proceeded to identify the elements or events that would signal reference to social science in a media story. Seven such elements were ultimately identified: mention of (1) a social scientist, (2) a social science research, (3) social science data, (4) a social science organization, (5) social science methods, (6) social science theory, and/or (7) institutional features of social science.

If we encountered any of these seven elements in connection with any of the fields we had defined as "social science fields," the media item in which the reference occurred was "selected" for our pool of social science items. As we have already noted, this was true regardless of whether the social science content was the *focus* of the item or constituted an *ancillary* element only.

The selection rules for each of the seven elements appear below. In each case, the rules are organized according to whether the element is *specified* (that is, named) or *unspecified;* for each of these categories the general rule (that is, *include* or *exclude*) is stated first, followed by listed exceptions.

1. *Social Scientists*

SPECIFIED

Generally In

Include letters, writings by social scientists on any social issue; also include obituaries.

Include graduate students in any of the designated social science fields (so long as they meet any conditions noted on the list of fields).

Include appointments to social science organizations designated as social science entities. (See rules on organizations.)

Exceptions

Exclude items about personal life or if social scientist is cited in other than professional role (for example, story on Alfred Kahn's nightclub act or story on a political scientist who is a crime victim).

Exclude appointments to or resignations from government positions (that is, political appointments).

Exclude news about chief government economists, that is, Chief of the Council of Economic Advisors (Dr. M. Weidenbaum) and Chairman of the Federal Reserve Board (Paul Volker). This exclusion is based on the assumption that news about these people is political, rather than social science, news. This exclusion is countermanded in cases where the official offers substantive economic analysis.

UNSPECIFIED

Generally Out

Exclude, for example, unnamed social researchers. Exclude also casual occupational titles such as "analysts" or "specialists."

Exceptions

Include if mentioned in conjunction with social science study, organization, data, methods, theory and/or institutional features (that is, qualifies on other criteria #2-7).

2. *Social Science Research*

SPECIFIED

Generally In

Include market research conducted with social science methods.

Exceptions

Exclude polls if they give *only* "horserace" findings, for example, "Joe Blow is 6 points ahead of Jane Doe in the latest poll."

UNSPECIFIED

Generally Out

Exclude, for example, casual references to "polls," "surveys," and so on. Also, exclude when findings given are only "horserace" results from polls.

Exceptions

Include nonspecific network references to a (probable) social science study. Here, because of the rigid time limits on network news stories, we make the presumption in favor of social science. (Subsequent coding of the story will capture the vagueness of the reference.)

In other cases, include unspecified study only if accompanied by social science data, or by other social science elements.

3. Social Science Data

SPECIFIED

Generally In

Include all data clearly derived from social science studies, for example, findings from surveys of public opinion. Also include most market research, which is derived from social science methods.

Include qualitative data—for example, from field studies.

Include, in addition, all mentions of data compiled for a specified list of social and economic indicators (see Table A.1). Only the listed indicators are to be taken, and indicators are to be taken only when they represent state, or national (U.S. or other nations) figures, or figures for the three metropolitan regions covered by the newspapers we're monitoring—New York City, Washington, D.C., and Boston.

Include national and state school enrollment figures.

Exceptions

Exclude voting data, unless further analyzed (for example, by ethnic groups).

Exclude population figures for countries other than the United States.

Exclude most attendance figures, local "police blotter" reports, and accident counts.

TABLE A.1

Social and Economic Indicators

	Source
SOCIAL INDICATORS	
Vital Statistics	
Birth rates	NCHS
Fertility rates	NCHS
Births to unwed mothers	NCHS
Death rates	NCHS
Deaths and injuries from motor vehicle accidents	NCHS
Infant mortality rates	NCHS
Marriage rates	NCHS
Divorce rates	NCHS
Annulment rates	NCHS
Health-Related Statistics	
Physician visits	NCHS
Dentist visits	NCHS
Hospital stays	NCHS
Expenditures for health care	SSA
Incidence of acute conditions	NCHS
Prevalence of chronic conditions	NCHS
Housing/Household Data	
Household composition data	Census
Children by presence of parents	Census
Living arrangements of older people	Census
Rent and value of housing units	Census
Perception of quality of neighborhoods	Census
Perception of neighborhood services	Census
Educational Statistics	
Teacher/pupil ratios in public/private schools (national and state data only)	NCES
Expenditures for education (state and national)	NCES
School and college enrollment (state and national)	Census
Educational attainment	Census
National assessment of educational progress	NIE, NCES
Employment Data	
Employment (by age, race, sex, industry)	BLS, Census
Unemployment (by age, and so on)	BLS, Census
Work stoppages and days idle	BLS
Part time/full time	BLS

TABLE A.1 (*Continued*)

	Source
Income and Earnings	
Average weekly earnings, by industry and occupation	BLS
Per capita personal income	BEA
Income distributions (by race and other characteristics)	Census
Persons below poverty level	Census
Statistics of income	IRS
Social Welfare	
Public and private expenditures for social welfare (unemployment, social security, disability, AFDC)	SSA
Public assistance recipients and average payments, by program	SSA
OASDI benefits, and recipients	SSA
SSI benefits, and recipients	SSA
Other financial and caseload statistics	SSA
Crimes	
Crimes reported to FBI (UCR)	FBI
Crimes reported by households	Census, Justice
Persons arrested, by age (*not* local precinct data)	FBI
Census Data	
Population shifts	Census
Population breakdowns	Census
ECONOMIC INDICATORS	
Prices and Expenditures	
Consumer Price Index	BLS
Producer Price Index	BLS
Family budgets	BLS
Personal consumptions expenditures	BEA, BLS
Production	
GNP	Commerce
Index of leading indicators	Commerce
Money Supply and Credit	
Consumer installment credit	FRB
Money supply (M-1, M-2)	

Note: BLS = Bureau of Labor Statistics
NCHS = National Center for Health Statistics
NCES = National Center for Educational Statistics
NIE = National Institute of Education
BEA = Bureau of Economic Analysis
IRS = Internal Revenue Service
SSA = Social Security Administration
FBI = Federal Bureau of Investigation
FRB = Federal Reserve Board

4. Social Science Organizations

SPECIFIED

Generally In

Include as a social science organization if

a) its primary activity is social science, or
b) it primarily employs social scientists

Include unfamiliar organizations whose name includes one of the specified social science fields and the word "Research," for example, Institute of Economic Research, Bureau of Social Science Research.

Federal government agencies are generally not considered social science organizations, with the following exceptions:

Bureau of Labor Statistics
Census Bureau
National Center for Educational Statistics
National Center for Health Sciences Research
National Center for Health Statistics
National Institute of Education
National Institute of Justice (and Juvenile Justice)
National Institute of Mental Health

Include under this category organizations which serve as resources specifically for social science research, for example, the Roper Center.

Exceptions

Exclude stories about appointments to government organizations (with the exception of the eight national research agencies enumerated above).

Exclude references to research organizations which are not engaged exclusively in social science research, for example, Rand, National Science Foundation (unless the mention is specifically focused on that organization's social science activities).

Exclude economic consulting firms, forecasting firms, and market research organizations unless they are accompanied by reference to a social science study.

UNSPECIFIED

Generally In

Include organizations explicitly characterized as being social science organizations (for example, "social science organizations have their eyes on the research funds") or as belonging specifically to one or more of the social science fields (for example, "representatives of the sociological and psychological associations have been conferring . . .").

5. *Social Science Methods*

SPECIFIED

Generally In

Include such commonly accepted methods of collecting social science data as the following:

  a) Sample surveys
  b) Polling
  c) Observation (systematic)
  d) Participant observation
  e) Field experiments
  f) Laboratory experiments
  g) Psychological testing (or aptitude, and so on)

Include such methods of data analysis as the following:

  a) Regression analysis
  b) Content analysis

Exceptions

Many of the methods above (e.g., field or lab experiments, or regression analysis) as well as others (e.g., path analysis) may be used in non-social science as well as in social science research. Thus, attention must be paid to the general context in which the method is being discussed/cited. Consult supervisor, if presence/absence of social science referent is unclear.

6. *Social Science Theory*

SPECIFIED

Generally In

Include any explicit reference to social science "theory."

Include reference to "model" *if* there is a clear connotation of systematic theory.

Include references to certain widely accepted theoretical systems without explicit mention of "theory" or "model"—for example, Freudianism, Keynesian economics, Marxism.

Exceptions

Exclude references to "theory" which represent unequivocally careless syntax meaning "notion," "personal view," and so on.

UNSPECIFIED

Generally Out

Exclude, for example, a sentence such as "Theories differ on the subject" with no elaboration.

7. *Institutional Features of Social Science*

SPECIFIED

> *Generally In*
>
>> Include, for example, funding, enrollment, research ethics, job/career possibilities, legislation in regard to social science generally, or to any of the fields listed.

UNSPECIFIED

> *Generally Out* (but consult supervisor)

Although these selection rules often proved relatively straightforward, in a surprisingly large number of cases ambiguities of interpretation had to be resolved. Thus, the selection rules and the content coding form, which ran to thirty-six pages, had to be supplemented by more than twenty pages of question-by-question specification and clarification. Here, we discuss only the most important issues that arose during the selection and coding process, and how we resolved them. As we have stressed, all of these decisions are in some respects arbitrary, and to the extent that other researchers adopt different rules, their definition of the amount and content of "social science in the media" will differ as well.

The Identification of Social Scientists

Mention of a social scientist was one element that qualified a story for selection into our sample. But how was a social scientist to be recognized by coders?

One way, of course, was explicit media identification: "Speaking at a meeting of the AAAS last night, sociologist Carol Weiss said. . . ." But suppose the media did *not* identify the speaker as a sociologist, but referred to her only as "Dr. Weiss." To rely on coder knowledge in such a situation was to invite idiosyncratic variation in selection criteria; to refuse to use coder knowledge when it was available seemed a waste of valuable resources. Accordingly, we compromised: We permitted "private knowledge" to determine the identification of most social scientists not identified by the media, but required positive identification (through use of official sources such as *Who's Who* and *American Men of Science*) of authors of columns and of nonfiction book reviews.

As the preceding paragraph suggests, we placed considerable weight on the media's explicit identification of persons and organizations as social science related. Where the media labeled an individual as a professional social scientist, or as a non–social scientist, we generally accepted the label. But where there was a question about someone's status, we made formal academic credentials a criterion. Although, for example, George Gilder has written a well-known book and frequent columns on the economy and is probably thought of as an economist by many *Wall Street Journal* readers, he has no advanced training in economics, and therefore mention of him or writing by him was not classified by us as social science content.

Like other people, social scientists occupy multiple statuses, and this fact required the elaboration of a series of rules about what to do when some of these other statuses are referred to in addition to, or instead of, the social science status. Thus, for example, an anthropologist appointed president of a college was no longer classified, by us, as a social scientist. A story only about some aspect of the personal life of a social scientist, for example, a professor of political science mugged on the subway, would also have been excluded. One of the thorniest dilemmas involved the chief government economists, that is, Chief of the Council of Economic Advisors and Chairman of the Federal Reserve Board. While the incumbents of those positions are acting as economists, they are also acting as major political appointees. With some exceptions, we excluded mentions of the CEA chief and the FRB chairman as more political than social scientific.

The Identification of Social Science Research

We made no attempt to distinguish "good" social science research from "bad" social science research. All research reported as done by a professional social scientist (that is, someone identified as belonging to one of our specified fields) or described as using social science methods was included, since we reasoned that all such studies would be perceived as social science by the media audience.

We also attempted to define a category of social science research done by journalists rather than social scientists. Only five stories were classified as falling in this category, however. (Stories about media polls were characterized as regular social science stories, since the actual polling operation was carried out by social scientists.)

The Identification of Social Science Data

What are "numbers" to the media are (sometimes) social or economic indicators to social scientists. Furthermore, these indicators are collected by social science methods, even though these have become so routinized that references to the studies or methods by which the indicators are obtained are rare. For both of these reasons—origin in social science studies and use by social scientists—we wanted to include some social and economic indicators as social science data whose mention in a media item would qualify that item for selection. The question was, which ones?

We consulted with a number of people with considerable experience in the use and even the development of social/economic indicators: Kenneth Prewitt, president of the Social Science Research Council; Harold Watts, Professor of Economics, Columbia University; E. D. Goldfield, of the Committee on National Statistics of the National Research Council; and Richard C. Rockwell, of the SSRC's Center for the Coordination of Research on Social Indicators. Our final list of indicators (see Table A.1) is based on the lists proposed by Goldfield and Rockwell. For the most part, they are produced by federal agencies; appear monthly, quarterly, or at least annually; and have a direct import for monitoring social and economic change.

Selection and Coding Procedures

The content analysis was done over a four-and-a-half month period in 1982 and a ten-week period in 1970. We sampled one week in three, selecting every social science story that appeared in the ten media during that week. Thus, we sampled social science reporting for seven weeks in 1982 and for four weeks in 1970. Television was not monitored in 1970; nor, because we relied on the microfilm holdings of Columbia University, was the *Boston Globe*. The sample weeks in 1982 were those of February 8–14, March 1–7, March 22–28, April 12–18, May 3–9, May 24–30, and June 14–20. In 1970 the weeks were March 23–29, April 13–19, May 4–10, and May 25–31, by design drawn from the middle of the 1982 period.

Two categories of story were encountered frequently enough and, at the same time, were so trivial in terms of social science content that we decided to subsample them instead of selecting and coding every occurrence. These were stories whose only social science content consisted of ancillary references to social indicator data (for example, the unemployment rate), ancillary references to economists employed by private business organizations (for example, banks, brokerage houses, and manufacturing concerns), or ancillary references to both indicator data and private economists. In 1982 such references were selected and coded during the first and fifth coding weeks only; in 1970 during the third coding week. In subsequent analyses these stories were weighted to what would have been obtained had we selected and counted them during all sample weeks—by a factor of 3.5 in 1982 and by a factor of 4 in 1970. We also calculated the resulting effective sample size (always smaller than the original, unweighted sample) and either adjusted chi-square values accordingly or adopted more conservative significance levels.

"Social science items" could come from any part of the newspaper, newsmagazine, or newscast except for advertisements or television listings. (We also ignored wedding announcements and death notices unaccompanied by obituaries.) News, sports, business, obituaries, book reviews, editorials, columns, letters to the editor, guest columns, cartoons, and comics all were potentially included. This meant that every item appearing in one of the sampled issues or newscasts had to be read or watched in its entirety before the preliminary screening decision—that is, was this a social science item or not—could be made. At the beginning of the study we watched every TV evening newscast on all three networks and selected social science items from the live broadcasts. Subsequently, we arranged to receive transcripts of the newscasts and selected and coded items from the transcript rather than the broadcast.

Our selection, coding, and editing procedures were designed to assure completeness and accuracy. The procedures were as follows:

1. Each issue of a newspaper or newsmagazine and each TV transcript was read in its entirety by a coder, who noted the headline (or other identifier) of each social science item on a "Selection Sheet" on which the name of the medium, the date, and the page number were also recorded.

2. For the first two weeks every issue was then read independently by a second coder; discrepancies between readers were resolved by Phyllis Endreny or Eleanor Singer.

3. Thereafter, only selected sections of newspapers, newsmagazines, and TV transcripts were read by two coders; the remaining pages were read by a single coder only.

4. After all social science items from a given issue of a medium had been listed, each item was given a case number and coded on a standardized form developed for that purpose. (Items were also listed, by medium, date, and case number, in a running log of social science stories.) Ambiguities were resolved in discussions with other coders and, ultimately, by Phyllis Endreny or Eleanor Singer.

5. Once an item had been coded, the coding form was edited by another coder for completeness, to ensure that every question that should have been answered was answered, and for consistency. Every third coding form was also edited for accuracy—that is, checked against the original media story.

6. The reliability of both the selection and the coding procedures was assessed by means of kappa, a statistic that measures the agreement among a number of n coders after adjusting for chance agreement—that is, after adjusting for the number of coding categories associated with each item and for the marginal frequencies with which each category was selected (Fleiss 1981).

It is, thus, a much more stringent test of intercoder consensus than is ordinarily employed, measuring reliability rather than simple agreement. For this reason values of .21–.40 are considered fair, .41–.60 moderate, .61–.80 substantial, and anything over .81 almost perfect (Landis and Koch 1977).

Coding reliability was assessed twice during the study—first in March, after about two weeks of coding experience, and again in June, after about four months. For each test we selected ten different social science stories, computing kappas for ten "core" items as well as a series of contingent items. Nine coders participated in the first test and seven in the second.

The "core" items consisted of basic information applicable to every story—for example, type of item, whether the social science content was focus or ancillary, what the main element in the story was, the amount of space taken up. For the March test a second series of eleven questions was drawn from the section on studies; for example, the number of studies mentioned, institutional origin, whether or not there was a reference to a published source.

In June reliability was again measured for both of these series of questions; in addition, reliability was assessed for another series of ten questions, pertaining to social scientists.

The average kappas, as well as the range, are shown below for all of the questions at both points in time.

	Core Items		Study Items		Scientist Items	
	March	June	March	June	March	June
Average kappa	.661	.774	.324	.517	—	.579
Range	.401–.863	.583–.956	.085–.495	.029–.783	—	.039–.869

Several things warrant comment about these data. First, coefficients are uniformly higher in June than they had been in March, both because we used the outcomes of the March test for additional training (and for the elimination of the weakest coder) and because the coders had had several additional weeks of coding experience.

Second, coefficients are higher for the "core" items, which had to be coded for every story, than for the questions on studies and social scientists, which had to be coded only some of the time. This result is to be expected both because coders received more practice on the "core items" and because the discriminations were easier to make.

Third, some of the coefficients for studies and scientists were very low. This was true in particular of some questions pertaining to social scientists, with coefficients of less than .10; and of one question ("Any discrepant findings from other research?") pertaining to studies, with a coefficient close to zero. Apparently, the discriminations called for by these questions were too difficult to produce reliable coding, and accordingly we made little or no use of these items in the analysis. For all other items, kappas fell into the acceptable range.

Finally, since all coding forms were edited for consistency and completeness, and one in three was checked for accuracy as well, the quality of coding was undoubtedly better than indicated by these coefficients.

The analysis just reported pertained to the coding of studies once they had been selected. We also, however, assessed the reliability of *selecting* a given story in the first place. Measured here was the consensus among coders in applying the selection rules reproduced above. For 214 items selected from the *New York Times, Wall Street Journal,* and *Washington Post* reliability as measured by kappa was .817. On 90.6 percent of all items (most of which were, of course, non–social science items), all eight coders were in agreement; but this was true of only 43 percent of those items that had been chosen by anyone. However, agreement by fewer than seven coders occurred in only 15 of the 214 items. Of these 15, 4 should not have been chosen and would probably have been weeded out; 5 are maybe's (a "study" of unknown origin, a satiric discussion of economic theory, 2 ambiguous references to theory, and a professor of ambiguous social science status); one is a tiny item in the *Journal* and the other a fleeting reference to an economist in a long article. Four, however, are references to polls that should have been seen; some of these would probably have been caught on double-reading.

In sum, the reliability of selecting social science items, as measured by kappa, was acceptably high. And again, since sections of all media were read by two coders, with discrepancies resolved by a coding supervisor, the selection accuracy was undoubtedly somewhat higher than indicated by the reliability coefficient.

Bibliography

Adler, Renata. "Annals of Law: Two Trials—I." *New Yorker,* June 16, 1986, pp. 42–96.

Adoni, Hanna, and Akiba A. Cohen. "Television News and the Social Construction of Economic Reality." *Journal of Communication* 28 (1978):61–70.

Almond, Gabriel, and Sidney Verba. *Civic Culture.* Princeton, NJ: Princeton University Press, 1963.

Alt, Mick, and Malcolm Brighton. "Analyzing Data: Or Telling Stories?" *Journal of the Market Research Society* 23 (1983):209–19.

Altheide, D. L., and R. P. Snow. *Media Logic.* Beverly Hills, CA: Sage, 1979.

Alwin, Duane, and S. Stephens. "Use of Sample Surveys in the Social Sciences." Paper presented at the 145th national meeting of the American Association for the Advancement of Science, Houston, January 3–8, 1979.

American Psychological Association. *Media Guide.* Washington, DC: American Psychological Association, 1984.

American Society of Newspaper Editors. *Relating to Readers in the '80's.* Survey conducted by Clark, Martire, and Bartolomeo, May 1984.

Atkin, Charles K., and James Gaudino. "The Impact of Polling on the Mass Media." *Annals of the American Academy of Political and Social Science,* 1984, pp. 119–28.

Barber, Bernard. "Toward a New View of the Sociology of Knowledge." In L. A. Coser, ed. *The Idea of Social Structure: Papers in Honor of Robert K. Merton.* New York: Harcourt Brace Jovanovich, 1975.

Barton, Allen H. "Consensus and Conflict among American Leaders." *Public Opinion Quarterly* 38 (1974–75):507–30.

———, and Wayne Parsons. "Measuring Belief System Structure." *Public Opinion Quarterly* 41 (1977):159–80.

Berke, Iris Polk. "Evaluation Into Policy: Bilingual Education, 1978." Doctoral dissertation, Stanford University, June 1980.

Berry, Fred C., Jr. "A Study of Accuracy in Local Dailies." *Journalism Quarterly* 44 (1967):482–90.

Bishop, Walton B. "Analysis of News Coverage for the 148th Annual Meeting of the AAAS." College of Journalism, University of Maryland, 1982.

Bogart, Leo. *Press and Public.* Hillsdale, NJ: Lawrence Erlbaum Associates, 1981.

Boltanski, Luc, and P. Maldidier. "Carrière Scientifique, Morale Scientifique, et Vulgarisation." *Social Science Information* 9 (1970):99–118.

Borman, S. C. "Communication Accuracy in Magazine Science Reporting." *Journalism Quarterly* 55 (1978):345–46.

Boruch, Robert F., and Laura C. Leviton. "Contributions of Evaluation to Education Programs and Policy." *Evaluation Review* 7, no. 5 (1983):563–98.

Bowen, D. C.; R. Perloff; and J. Jacoby. "Improving Manuscript Evaluation Procedures." *American Psychologist* 27 (1972):221–25.

Breed, Warren. "Social Control in the Newsroom." *Social Forces* 33 (1955):326–35.

Broberg, K. "Scientists' Stopping Behavior as Indicators of Writer's Skill." *Journalism Quarterly* 50 (1973):763–67.

Broh, C. Anthony. "Horse-Race Journalism: Reporting the Polls in the 1976 Presidential Election." *Public Opinion Quarterly* 44, no. 4 (1980):514–29.

Caplan, Nathan. "A Minimal Set of Conditions Necessary for the Utilization of Social Science Knowledge in Policy Formulation at the National Level." In Carol H. Weiss, ed. *Using Social Research in Public Policy Making.* Lexington, MA: Lexington Books, 1977.

Cater, Douglass. *The Fourth Branch of Government.* New York: Vintage, 1959.

———, and S. Strickland. *TV Violence and the Child: The Evolution and Fate of the Surgeon General's Report.* New York: Russell Sage Foundation, 1975.

Chemical and Engineering News, "Experts Impressed with Media Reports," vol. 64 (February 3, 1986):17.

Cole, Bruce J. "Trends in Science and Conflict Coverage in Four Metropolitan Newspapers." *Journalism Quarterly* 52 (1975):465–71.

Cole, Jonathan R. "Health Risks in the Media: Some Food for Thought." In Hubert J. O'Gorman, ed. *Festschrift for Herbert H. Hyman,* Middletown, CT: Wesleyan University Press, forthcoming.

Cole, Stephen. "The Growth of Scientific Knowledge." In Lewis A. Coser, ed. *The Idea of Social Structure.* New York: Harcourt Brace Jovanovich, 1975.

———, and Jonathan R. Cole. *Social Stratification in Science.* Chicago: University of Chicago Press, 1973.

———, and Gary A. Simon. "Chance and Consensus in Peer Review." *Science* 214 (1981):881–86.

Coleman, James S., et al. *Equality of Educational Opportunity.* Washington, DC: U.S. Government Printing Office, 1966.

Communications Institute. "The Reporting of Human Behavior: A Study of Bridge-Building between Behavioral Sciences and Journalism." New York: Communications Institute, 1970.

Crawford, E. T., and A. D. Biderman, eds. *Social Scientists and International Affairs.* New York: Wiley, 1969.

Crespi, Irving. "Polls as Journalism." *Public Opinion Quarterly* 44 (1980):462–76.

Danielson, Wayne A., and John B. Adams. "Completeness of Press Coverage of the 1960 Campaign." *Journalism Quarterly* 38 (1961):441–52.

Darnton, Robert. "Writing News and Telling Stories." *Daedalus* 104, no. 2 (Spring 1975):175–94.

Derthick, Martha, and P. J. Quirk. *The Politics of Deregulation.* Washington, DC: Brookings Institution, 1985.

Deshpande, Rohit, and Gerald Zaltman. "Patterns of Research Use in Private and

Public Sectors." *Knowledge: Creation, Diffusion, Utilization* 4, no. 4 (1983):561–75.

Dubas, Orest, and Lisa Martel. *Science, Mass Media and the Public.* Media Impact, vol. 2. Ottawa: Information Canada, 1975.

Dunwoody, Sharon. "The Science Writing Inner Club: A Communication Link Between Science and the Lay Public." *Science, Technology, and Human Values* 5, no. 30 (1980):14–22.

————. "Newspaper Coverage of AAAS Annual Meetings: An Analysis of the 1977 and 1979 Years." Typescript, 1982.

————. "Communicating Risk Information: What Role Do the Media Play." Paper presented at the annual meeting of the American Association for the Advancement of Science, New York, 1984.

————, and Michael Ryan. "Scientific Barriers to the Popularization of Science via the Mass Media." *Journal of Communication* 35 (1985):26–42.

Dunwoody, Sharon, and B. T. Scott. "Scientists as Mass Media Sources." *Journalism Quarterly* 59 (1982):52–59.

Dunwoody, Sharon, and S. Holly Stocking. "Social Scientists and Journalists: Confronting the Stereotypes." In Eli Rubinstein and Jane Brown, eds. *The Media, Social Science, and Social Policy for Children: Different Paths to a Common Goal.* Norwood, NJ: Ablex, 1985.

Endreny, Phyllis. "News Values and Science Values: The Editor's Role in Shaping News about the Social Sciences." Unpublished doctoral dissertation, Columbia University, 1985.

Epstein, Edward J. *News from Nowhere.* New York: Random House, 1973.

Fishman, Mark. *Manufacturing the News.* Austin: University of Texas Press, 1980.

Fleiss, Joseph L. *Statistical Methods for Rates and Proportions,* 2nd ed. New York: Wiley, 1981.

Freimuth, Vicki S.; Rachel H. Greenberg; Jean DeWitt; and Rose Mary Romano. "Covering Cancer: Newspapers and the Public Interest." *Journal of Communication* 34 (1984):62–73.

Friedman, Sharon M.; Sharon Dunwoody; and Carol L. Rogers, eds. *Scientists and Journalists: Reporting Science as News.* New York: Free Press, 1986.

Gallagher, James J., and Joseph Sanders. "The Social Scientist, the Media and Public Policy." *UCLA Educator* 23 (1981):20–27.

Gallup, George. *Taking Education's Pulse: the 13th Annual Gallup Poll of the Public's Attitudes Toward the Schools.* Reston, VA: National Association of Secondary School Principals, 1981.

————. *The Gallup Poll: Public Opinion 1982.* Wilmington: Scholarly Resources, Inc., 1983.

Gamson, William. *What's News: A Game Simulation of TV News.* New York: Free Press, 1984.

Gans, Herbert J. *Deciding What's News.* New York: Pantheon Books, 1979.

Garfield, Eugene. *Essays of an Information Scientist,* vol. 3. Philadelphia: ISI Press, 1977–78.

Gieber, Walter. "Across the Desk: A Study of Sixteen Telegraph Editors." *Journalism Quarterly* 33, no. 3 (1956):423–32.

Golding, Peter, and Philip Elliott. *Making the News.* London: Longman Group, 1979.

Gollin, A. E. "Exploring the Liaison Between Polling and the Press." *Public Opinion Quarterly* 44, no. 4 (1980):445–61.

Goodell, Rae. *The Visible Scientists.* Boston: Little, Brown, 1977.

Goodfield, June. *Reflections on Science and the Media.* Washington, DC: American Association for the Advancement of Science, 1981.

Graber, Doris A. *Mass Media and American Politics.* Washington, DC: Congressional Quarterly Press, 1980.

Grant, Gerald, and Christine Murray. "James Coleman and the Coleman Reports." In E. A. Rubinstein and J. D. Brown, eds. *The Media, Social Science, and Social Policy for Children.* Norwood, NJ: Ablex, 1985.

Harris, Louis, and Associates. *Hospital Care in America.* Nashville: Hospital Affiliates International, Inc., 1978.

Haskins, Ron. "From the Social Policy Perspective: Comment and Critique." In E. A. Rubinstein and J. D. Brown, eds. *The Media, Social Science, and Social Policy for Children.* Norwood, NJ: Ablex, 1985.

Heren, Louis. *The Power of the Press?* London: Orbis, 1985.

Herrnstein, R. J. "IQ Testing and the Media." *Atlantic Monthly,* August 1982, pp. 68–74.

Herzog, Arthur. "Faking It." *Saturday Review of Society,* April 1973, pp. 36–37.

Hess, Stephen. *The Washington Reporters.* Washington, DC: Brookings Institution, 1981.

Hobbs, Renee. "Press Coverage of the 1982 NIMH Report on Television and Behavior." Paper presented at the annual meeting of the American Association of Public Opinion Research. Buck Hill Falls, PA, May 1983.

Hunt, Morton. *Profiles of Social Research.* New York: Russell Sage Foundation, 1985.

Janowitz, Morris. *The Professional Soldier: A Social and Political Portrait.* Glencoe, IL: Free Press, 1960.

———. *Political Conflict: Essays in Political Sociology.* Chicago: Quadrangle, 1970.

Johnson, Kenneth. "Dimensions of Judgment of Science News Stories." *Journalism Quarterly* 40 (1963):315–22.

Johnstone, J. W. C.; E. J. Slawski; and W. W. Bowman. *The News People.* Urbana: University of Illinois Press, 1976.

Jones, Lyle V.; Gardner Lindzey; and Potter E. Coggeshall. *An Assessment of Research Doctorate Programs in the United States: Social and Behavioral Sciences.* Washington, DC: National Academy Press, 1982.

Joslyn, Richard; Mark H. Ross; and Michael M. Weinstein. "Election Night News Coverage: The Limitations of Story Telling." *PS* 17, no. 3 (1984):564–70.

Kaplan, Norman. "The Norms of Citation Behavior: Prolegomena to the Footnote." *American Documentation* 16 (1965):179–84.

Kingdon, John W. *Agendas, Alternatives, and Public Policies.* Boston: Little, Brown, 1984.

Klapper, Joseph T., and Charles Y. Glock. "Trial by Newspaper." *Scientific American,* February 1949, pp. 16–21.

Knorr-Cetina, Karen D. *The Manufacture of Knowledge.* Oxford: Pergamon Press, 1981.

Krieghbaum, Hillier. *Science, the News, and the Public.* New York: New York University Press, 1958.

———. *Science and the Mass Media.* New York: New York University Press, 1967.

Landis, J. R., and G. G. Koch. "The Measurement of Observer Agreement for Categorical Data." *Biometrics* 33 (1977):159–74.

Lang, Kurt, and Gladys E. Lang. "The Unique Perspective of Television and Its Effect." *American Sociological Review* 18 (1953):3–12.

———. *Politics and Television.* Chicago: Quadrangle, 1970.

Lapham, Lewis H. "Gilding the News." *Harper's,* July 1981, pp. 31–39.

Lazarsfeld, Paul F., and Wagner Thielens, Jr. *The Academic Mind.* New York: Free Press, 1958.

Lichter, S. Robert, and Stanley Rothman. "Media and Business Elites." *Public Opinion* 4 (1981):42–46.

Likely, Audrey, and David Kalson. *Physics Goes Public.* New York: American Institute of Physics, 1981.

Lindsey, Duncan. *The Scientific Publication System in Social Science.* San Francisco: Jossey-Bass, 1978.

Linsky, Martin. *Impact: How the Press Affects Federal Policymaking.* New York: Norton, 1986.

Lippmann, Walter. *Public Opinion.* New York: Macmillan, 1947 [1922].

Lipset, S. M., and E. C. Ladd, Jr. "The Politics of American Sociologists." *American Journal of Sociology* 78 (1972):67–104.

Logan, Robert A. "Commentary: Rationales for Investigative and Explanatory Trends in Science Reporting." *Newspaper Research Journal* 7, no. 1 (Fall 1985):53–58.

MacDonald, Dick. *Reporting on Polls: Some Helpful Hints.* Toronto: Canadian Daily Newspaper Publishers Association, 1978.

Mannheim, Karl. *Ideology and Utopia.* New York: International Library of Psychology, Philosophy and Scientific Method, 1936.

McCall, Robert B. "Science and the Press: Like Oil and Water?" Unpublished manuscript, Father Flanagan's Boys' Home, Boys Town, Nebraska, 1985.

———, and Holly Stocking. "Between Scientists and Public: Communicating Psychological Research Through the Mass Media." *American Psychologist* 37, no. 9 (1983):985–95.

McTavish, Donald G., et al. *The Systematic Assessment and Prediction of Research Methodology.* Minneapolis: Minnesota Systems Research, 1975.

Merton, Robert K. *Social Theory and Social Structure,* 2nd ed. New York: Free Press, 1968.

———. "Priorities in Scientific Discovery." In *The Sociology of Science.* Chicago: University of Chicago Press, 1973 [1957].

———, and Paul K. Hatt. "Election Polling Forecasts and Public Images of Social Science." *Public Opinion Quarterly* 13, no. 2 (1949):185–222.

Meyer, Philip. "Social Science: A New Beat?" *Nieman Reports,* June 1967, pp. 3–6.

Morrison, D. F. *Multivariate Statistical Methods,* 2nd ed. New York: McGraw-Hill, 1976.

Nathe, Louise. "Changes in Science Reporting in Three Newspapers, 1963–73." In

Norman Metzger, ed. *Science in the Newspaper*. Washington, DC: American Association for the Advancement of Science, 1974.

Nelkin, Dorothy. "Why Is Science Writing So Uncritical of Science?" *SIPIscope* 12, no. 1 (1984):1–4.

———. *Science in the Streets*. New York: Twentieth-Century Fund, 1985.

Noelle-Neumann, Elisabeth. "The Public Opinion Research Correspondent." *Public Opinion Quarterly* 44 (1987):585–97.

New York Times. "Washington Talk: For the Love of Congress." By William E. Farrell and Marjorie Hunter, June 29, 1984, p. A16.

Nunn, Clyde Z. "Readership and Coverage of Science and Technology in Newspapers." *Journalism Quarterly* 56 (1979):27–30.

Olean, Mona Maria. *Communicating with the Public—via the Media—about Psychology*. Washington, DC: Psychological Association, 1977.

O'Leary, Virginia. "Giving Psychology Away." Paper presented at the meeting of the Eastern Sociological Society, Baltimore, Maryland, March 4, 1983.

Orlans, Harold. *Contracting for Knowledge*. San Francisco: Jossey-Bass, 1973.

Paletz, D. L., and R. M. Entman. *Media Power Politics*. New York: Free Press, 1981.

Paletz, D. L.; J. Y. Short; H. Baker; B. C. Campbell; R. J. Cooper; and R. M. Oeslander. "Polls in the Media: Content, Credibility, and Consequences." *Public Opinion Quarterly* 44, no. 4 (1980):495–513.

Polsby, Nelson W. "Hawks, Doves, and the Press." *Trans-Action* 4, no. 5 (1967):35–41.

Presser, Stanley. "The Use of Survey Data in Basic Research in the Social Sciences." In Charles F. Turner and Elizabeth Martin, eds. *The Survey Measurement of Subjective Phenomena*. New York: Russell Sage Foundation, 1985.

Prewitt, Kenneth, and David L. Sills. "Federal Funding for the Social Sciences: Threats and Responses." [Social Science Research Council] *Items* 36, no. 3 (1981):33–47.

Pulford, D. L. "Follow-up Study of Science News Accuracy." *Journalism Quarterly* 53 (1976):119–21.

Rhoades, Lawrence J. *A History of the American Sociological Association 1905–80*. Washington, DC: American Sociological Association, 1981.

Rich, Jonathan T. "A Measure of Comprehensiveness in News Magazine Science Coverage." *Journalism Quarterly* 58 (1981):248–53.

Rivers, William L. *The Opinion-Makers*. Boston: Beacon Press, 1965.

Robinson, Marshall. "Private Foundations and Social Science Research." *Society* 21 (1984):76–80.

Rokeach, Milton. "The Role of Values in Public Opinion Research." *Public Opinion Quarterly* 32 (1968):547–59.

Roper, Burns W. "Polls and the Media: For Good or Ill." Talk to the National Council on Public Polls, Washington, DC, November 11, 1983.

Rosenthal, Robert, and Ralph L. Rosnow. *The Volunteer Subject*. New York: Wiley, 1975.

Roshco, Bernard. *Newsmaking,* Chicago: University of Chicago Press, 1975.

Rosten, Leo. *The Washington Correspondents*. New York: Harcourt, Brace, 1937.

Rothman, Stanley, and Robert Lichter. "Media and Business Elites: Two Classes in Conflict?" *Public Interest,* Fall 1982, pp. 117–25.

Rovere, Richard H. *Senator Joe McCarthy.* New York: Harper & Row, 1959.

Rubin, Zick. "My Love-Hate Relationship with the Media." *Psychology Today* 13, no. 9 (1980):7, 12–13.

Rubinstein, Eli A., and Jane D. Brown, eds. *The Media, Social Science, and Social Policy for Children.* Norwood, NJ: Ablex, 1985.

Russell Sage Foundation. *Annual Report 1968–69.*

Ryan, Michael. "Attitudes of Scientists and Journalists Toward Media Coverage of Science News." *Journalism Quarterly* 56 (1979):18–26, 53.

Schlesinger, Philip. *Putting "Reality" Together.* London: Constable Press, 1978.

Schudson, Michael. *Discovering the News: A Social History of American Newspapers.* New York: Basic Books, 1978.

Schuman, Howard, and Graham Kalton. "Survey Methods." In Gardner Lindzey and Elliot Aronson, eds. *Handbook of Social Psychology,* 3rd ed. Reading, MA: Addison-Wesley, 1985.

Schuman, Howard; Eleanor Singer; Rebecca Donovan; and Claire Selltiz. "Discriminatory Behavior in New York Restaurants: 1950 and 1981." *Social Indicators Research* 13 (1983):69–83.

Scott, W. A. "Interreferee Agreement on Some Characteristics of Manuscripts Submitted to the *Journal of Personality and Social Psychology.*" *American Psychologist* 29, no. 9 (1974):689–702.

Shepherd, R. Gordon. "Science News of Controversy: The Case of Marijuana." *Journalism Monographs* 62 (1979):1–36.

———. "Selectivity of Sources: Reporting the Marijuana Controversy." *Journal of Communication* 3 (1981):129–37.

———, and Erich Goode. "Scientists in the Popular Press." *New Scientist* 76 (November 24, 1977):482–84.

Sigal, Leon V. *Reporters and Officials: The Organization and Politics of Newsmaking.* Lexington, MA: Heath, 1973.

Smith, Vernon, and George Gallup. *What People Think About Their Schools: Gallup's Findings.* Bloomington, IN: Phi Delta Kappa Educational Foundation, 1977.

Snider, Paul B. "'Mr. Gates' Revisited: A 1966 Version of the 1949 Case Study." *Journalism Quarterly* 44, no. 3 (1967):419–27.

Srole, Leo, et al. *Mental Health in the Metropolis.* New York: McGraw-Hill, 1962.

Stocking, S. Holly, and Sharon L. Dunwoody. "Social Science in the Mass Media: Images and Evidence." In Joan Sieber, ed. *The Ethics of Social Research: Fieldwork, Regulation and Publication.* New York: Springer-Verlag, 1982.

Sudman, Seymour. "The Network Polls: A Critical Review." *Public Opinion Quarterly* 47 (1983):490–96.

Sussman, Lynne. "Press Coverage of the 1982 Profile of American Youth Study: The Intersection of Journalism, Social Science Research, and the Pentagon." Paper presented at the meeting of the American Association of Public Opinion Research, Buck Hill Falls, PA, 1983.

Tankard, J. W., Jr., and Michael Ryan. "News Source Perceptions of Accuracy of Science Coverage." *Journalism Quarterly* 51, no. 2 (1974):219–25, 334.

Tankard, J. W., Jr., and S. W. Showalter. "Press Coverage of the 1972 Report on Television and Social Behavior." *Journalism Quarterly* 54 (1977):293–98.

Tichenor, P. J.; C. N. Olien; A. Harrison; and G. Donohue. "Mass Communication Systems and Communication Accuracy in Science News Reporting." *Journalism Quarterly* 47 (1970):673–83.

Tuchman, Gaye. "The Exception Proves the Rule: The Study of Routine News Practices." In P. Hirsch, P. V. Miller, and F. G. Line, eds. *Methodological Strategies for Communications Research,* vol. 6. Beverly Hills, CA: Sage, 1978a.

———. *Making News.* New York: Macmillan, 1978b.

Tunstall, Jeremy. *Journalists at Work: Specialist Correspondents: Their News Organizations, News Sources, and Competitor-Colleagues.* London: Constable, 1971.

Turner, Charles F., and Elissa Krauss. "Fallible Indicators of the Subjective State of the Nation." *American Psychologist* 33 (1978):456–70.

Turner, Charles F., and Elizabeth Martin, eds. *Surveying Subjective Phenomena.* New York: Russell Sage Foundation, 1985.

Wade, Serena, and Wilbur Schramm. "The Mass Media as Sources of Public Affairs, Science, and Health Knowledge." *Public Opinion Quarterly* 33 (1969):197–209.

Waldman, Steven. "The King of Quotes: Why the Press Is Addicted to Norman Ornstein." *Washington Monthly,* December 1986, pp. 33–40.

Walum, L. R. "Sociology and the Mass Media: Some Major Problems and Modest Proposals." *American Sociologist* 10 (1975):28–32.

Ward, A. W.; B. W. Hall; and C. F. Schram. "Evaluation of Published Educational Research—National Survey." *American Educational Research Journal* 12 (1975):109–28.

Weaver, David H., and G. Cleveland Wilhoit. *The American Journalist: A Portrait of U.S. News People and Their Work.* Bloomington: Indiana University Press, 1986.

Weaver, Paul. "The Politics of a News Story." In H. M. Clor, ed. *The Mass Media and Modern Democracy.* Chicago: Rand McNally, 1974.

Weber, Max. "Politics as a Vocation." In H. H. Gerth and C. W. Mills, eds. *From Max Weber.* London: Routledge & Kegan Paul, 1948 [1919].

Weigel, R. H., and J. J. Pappas. "Social Science and the Press: A Case Study and Its Implications." *American Psychologist* 36, no. 5 (1981):480–87.

Weiss, Carol H. "Validity of Welfare Mothers' Interview Responses." *Public Opinion Quarterly* 32, no. 4 (1968–69):622–33.

———. "What America's Leaders Read." *Public Opinion Quarterly* 37, no. 1 (1974):1–22.

———. "Research for Policy's Sake: The Enlightenment Function of Social Science Research." *Policy Analysis* 3 (1977):531–45.

———. "Improving the Linkage Between Social Research and Public Policy." In L. E. Lynn, Jr., ed. *Knowledge and Policy: The Uncertain Connection.* Washington, DC: National Academy of Sciences, 1978.

———. "Policy Evaluation as Societal Learning." In E. Yuchtman-Yaar and S. Spiro, eds. *Evaluating the Welfare State.* New York: Academic Press, 1983.

———. "U.S. Congressional Committees as Problematic Users of Analysis." In Martin Bulmer, ed. *Social Science Research and Government.* Cambridge: Cambridge University Press, 1987.

———, with Michael J. Bucuvalas. *Social Science Research and Decision-Making.* New York: Columbia University Press, 1980.

Wesker, Arnold. *Journey into Journalism.* London: Writers and Readers, 1977.

Wheeler, Michael. "Reining in Horserace Journalism." *Public Opinion* 3 (1980):41–45.

White, David M. "The 'Gatekeeper': A Case Study in the Selection of News." *Journalism Quarterly* 27, no. 4 (1950):383–90.

Wilhoit, G. Cleveland, and David H. Weaver. *Newsroom Guide to Polls and Surveys.* Washington, DC: American Newspaper Publishers Association, 1980.

Wilson, E. Bright, Jr. *An Introduction to Scientific Research.* New York: McGraw-Hill, 1952.

Winsten, Jay. "Science and the Media: The Boundaries of Truth." *Health Affairs* 3 (Spring 1985):5–23.

Yu, F. T. C. *Behavioral Sciences and the Mass Media.* Hartford, CT: Russell Sage Foundation, 1968.

Ziman, John. *Public Knowledge.* London: Cambridge University Press, 1968.

———. "Seeing Through Our Seers." *Listener,* June 24, 1976, p. 794.

Zuckerman, Harriet, and Robert K. Merton. "Patterns of Evaluation in Science: Institutionalization, Structure, and Functions of the Referee System." *Minerva* 9 (1971):66–100.

Index

ABC, 9, 14, 178, 182, 245–246
Academic Mind (Lazarsfeld and Thielens), 238
accuracy, 2, 4–5, 22, 32, 63, 75, 76, 76*n*, 78, 129, 159, 227; factors associated with, 76, 79, 80, 89; social scientists' view on, 64–66, 67–68, 70
action, 10–11, 159
Adler, Renata, 133
"Adolescent Despair, Suicide, and Violent Death" symposium, 104, 110
Adoni, Hanna, 179*n*
adversary process, 250
advocacy groups, 121
advocacy research, 250
aggression, 40
aging, 103
"Aging from Birth to Death" symposium, 101
agriculture beat, 56
alcoholism, 213
Allen, Ethan, 134
Almond, Gabriel, 238
alternative perspectives, 37–41
Altheide, D. L., 167
Alwin, Duane, 240
American Anthropologist, 126
American Association for the Advancement of Science (AAAS), 16, 94–116, 127, 128, 147, 166, 234, 241; *Abstracts of Papers*, 94; meeting *Program*, 94
American Association for Public Opinion Research, 259
American Association of University Women, 121
American Couples (Blumstein and Schwartz), 120, 125
American Criminological Society, 31

American Economic Association (AEA), 165
American Economic Review, 126
American Institute of Physics, 166
American Journal of Sociology, 242
American Meat Institute, 201
American Political Science Association (APSA), 165
American Political Science Review, 126
American Psychological Association (APA), 30, 164–165
American Psychologist, 126
American Society of Newspaper Editors, 69
American Sociological Association, 125, 166, 258; Press Relations Committee, 166–167
American Sociological Review, 126
"Analysis of News Coverage for the 148th Annual Meeting of the AAAS" (Bishop), 99*n*
"Analyzing Data: or Telling Stories?" 253
ancillary stories, 80, 81, 85, 178, 179, 183, 188–189, 212–213, 223, 241, 244–245
Ann Arbor News, 109
anthropologists, 25
anthropology, 14, 16, 110, 116, 262
Anthropology Newsletter, 121
anti-Vietnam war rally, 12
Archives of General Psychiatry, 121
area studies, 14, 262
arms control, 228
army, 141, 204
assignment: of reporters, 42, 79; of stories, 42–43, 75, 79
Associated Press (AP), 31, 95, 99, 100, 102, 117, 118, 119, 122, 124*n*, 133, 134, 182, 199, 242
Atkin, Charles K., 12